British Slaves and Barbary Corsairs, 1580–1750

British Slaves and Barbary Corsairs, 1580–1750

BERNARD CAPP

OXFORD

UNIVERSITY PRESS

OXFORD
UNIVERSITY PRESS

Great Clarendon Street, Oxford, OX2 6DP,
United Kingdom

Oxford University Press is a department of the University of Oxford.
It furthers the University's objective of excellence in research, scholarship,
and education by publishing worldwide. Oxford is a registered trade mark of
Oxford University Press in the UK and in certain other countries

First Edition published in 2022

Impression: 1

Published in the United States of America by Oxford University Press
198 Madison Avenue, New York, NY 10016, United States of America

British Library Cataloguing in Publication Data
Data available

Library of Congress Control Number: 2021951453

ISBN 978–0–19–285737–8

DOI: 10.1093/oso/9780192857378.001.0001

Printed and bound in Great Britain by
Clays Ltd, Elcograf S.p.A.

Preface

This book explores the story of the thousands of British and Irish men and women captured and enslaved in the lands then known as Barbary (the modern states of Algeria, Libya, Tunisia, and Morocco), the efforts of their friends and families to ransom them, and the attempts of successive governments to liberate them and curb the corsairs. These issues were of huge concern to contemporaries, especially in the early Stuart period, yet they have gone unmentioned in most surveys of early modern British history. I have therefore assumed no prior knowledge on the part of readers. Britons are the central focus in this book, but they were only one strand in a much wider and much older story of Mediterranean slavery. The Christians of southern Europe and the Moors of the Islamic Maghreb had for generations been both perpetrators and victims of a tradition of enslavement rooted in religious conflict and an appetite for plunder. In recent years some scholars have preferred to speak of 'captives' rather than 'slaves', pointing out correctly that Mediterranean bondage differed in many respects from the brutality of black slavery in the American plantations and the Caribbean. But slavery has taken a multitude of forms over the centuries, and 'captives' feels an inadequate term for people who had been sold in the marketplace, who often spoke of themselves as slaves, and who might also be subjected to brutal treatment. It would, I believe, be disrespectful to deny them retrospectively their own sense of identity. Most contemporaries used 'slave' and 'captive' interchangeably, and I have followed their example. I recognize that some readers will take a different view.

I would like to thank OUP's editors, Karen Raith and Cathryn Steele, for their help, and OUP's three anonymous readers for their comments, advice, and suggestions. I would also like to thank friends and Warwick colleagues for encouragement or references, or both: Angela McShane, Jasmine Kilburn-Toppin, Naomi Pullin, Peter Marshall, Iman Sheeha, Edith Roberts, and Rob Daniel. I would also like to acknowledge the work of Nabil Matar. Although we differ on many points of interpretation, his pioneering contributions in this field have been immense.

Spelling has been modernized throughout in quotations, but not for titles. In references, the place of publication is London except where otherwise indicated.

In old English currency, 12 pence (12d) made a shilling, and 20 shillings (20s) a pound. Many different currencies used in Barbary were mentioned by contemporaries, who offered varying figures for their equivalent value in English pounds. A ducat was usually valued at about 10s, and a dollar or 'piece of eight' at about 4s 6d to 5s. A doubloon or double was roughly 1s to 1s 4d. These should be taken, however, as only very rough approximations.

An important and very relevant new study, Eleanor Hubbard, *Englishmen at Sea: Labor and the Nation at the Dawn of Empire, 1570–1630* (New Haven, 2021), appeared after my book was already in the press.

September 2021

Contents

Abbreviations

APC	*Acts of the Privy Council*
Castries	Henri de Castries et al., eds., *Les Sources inédites . . . d'Angleterre* (Paris, 1918–36)
CJ	*Journals of the House of Commons*
Coxere, *Adventures*	*Adventures by Sea of Edward Coxere*, ed. E. H. W. Meyerstein (Oxford, 1945)
CSPD	*Calendar of State Papers, Domestic*
CSPVen	*Calendar of State Papers, Venetian*
D'Aranda, *History*	Emanuel D'Aranda, *The History of Algiers and it's Slavery* (1666)
Elliot, *Modest Vindication*	Adam Elliot, *A Modest Vindication of Titus Oates* (1682)
Gee, *Narrative*	Joshua Gee, *Narrative of Joshua Gee of Boston, Mass.*, ed. Alfred C. Bates (1943)
Harris, *Trinity House*	G. G. Harris, *Trinity House of Deptford Transactions, 1609–35* (1983)
Hasleton	Richard Hasleton, *Strange and Wonderfvll Things. Happened to Richard Hasleton* (1595)
Hebb, *Piracy*	D. D. Hebb, *Piracy and the English Government 1616–1642* (Aldershot, 1994)
HMC	Historical Manuscripts Commission
LJ	*Journals of the House of Lords*
Okeley	William Okeley, *Eben-ezer: or, a small Monument of Great Mercy* (1675)
Pepys, *Catalogue*	J. R. Tanner, ed., *A Descriptive Catalogue of the Naval MSS in the Pepysian Library* (1903–23)
Phelps	Thomas Phelps, *A true account of the captivity of Thomas Phelps, at Machaness in Barbary* (1685)
Pitts	Joseph Pitts, *A Faithful Account of the Religion and Manners of the Mohametans* (1731)
Rawlins	John Rawlins, *The Famovs and Wonderfvll Recoverie of a Ship of Bristoll* (1622)
Thurloe	T. Birch, ed., *A Collection of the State Papers of John Thurloe* (1742).
T. S., *Adventures*	*The Adventures of (Mr. T. S.) an English Merchant* (1670)
Vitkus, *Piracy*	Daniel J. Vitkus, ed., *Piracy, Slavery, and Redemption* (New York, 2001).

Prologue

In 1622 John Rawlins published a vivid account of his escape from slavery, entitled *The Famovs and Wonderfvll Recoverie of a Ship of Bristoll, called the Exchange, from the Turkish Pirates of Argier*. The emotive narrative throws light on many of the issues surrounding the Barbary corsairs, their victims, and the concerns of the English public. As such, it provides a helpful prologue to the issues this book explores.

On 18 November 1621 the crew of the 40-ton *Nicholas* of Plymouth spied five ships bearing down as they neared the Straits of Gibraltar. Rawlins and his little company of nine men and a boy attempted to reach the safety of the nearest port, but were quickly overhauled. When a Barbary *reis* (corsair commander) ordered them to strike sail and submit to mercy they complied, accepting that resistance would be futile against such overwhelming odds. A prize crew took control of the *Nicholas*, while Rawlins and most of his men were taken aboard the corsairs' man-of-war, and carried into Algiers a few days later. There they heard alarming stories of handsome young captives forced into sexual slavery, and others made to 'turn Turk' (or convert to Islam) by horrendous tortures—reports that Rawlins recounted in graphic detail. He and his men were taken to be inspected by the pasha, the Ottoman governor of Algiers, who selected one of their number as his tribute, as was standard practice. The ship's boy and the owner's servant, separated from the rest, were soon forced to apostatize. The rest were hurried 'like dogs' to the market-place to be auctioned, where they suffered the humiliation of being poked and prodded by prospective buyers. Rawlins' lame hand made him a less attractive commodity, and he was the last to be sold, for only 150 doubloons, equivalent to perhaps £7 10s. His new owner, a renegade named Villa Reis, thought that Rawlins' experience and skill would make him useful, but his disability left him unable to help fit ships for sea, and Villa Reis soon decided to dispose of him. Rawlins was now told to raise a ransom of £15 from English merchants in Algiers, which would yield a profit of 100% on the purchase price, and warned that if he failed he would be sent 'up into the country [i.e. inland], where he should never see Christendom again'. In the event, he was not ransomed but sold to two renegade Englishmen, who had bought another prize, the *Exchange*, to fit out as a man-of-war, and needed a skilled pilot. They had already bought other English slaves to serve as gunners and mariners, and had hired several renegade seamen. Barbary corsairs relied heavily on European seamen when they ventured into Atlantic waters.

British Slaves and Barbary Corsairs, 1580–1750. Bernard Capp, Oxford University Press. © Bernard Capp 2022.
DOI: 10.1093/oso/9780192857378.003.0001

The *Exchange* sailed out on 7 January 1622, carrying sixty-three 'Turkish' and Moorish soldiers, far outnumbering the fifteen English, Dutch, and French slaves. Rawlins' narrative stresses his impatience at the 'insulting tyranny' of the 'Turks', among whom he counted the renegades, and the blows, beatings, and abuse the slaves endured. Resolving to win freedom or die in the attempt, he persuaded the other slaves, and some of the renegades, to join the mutiny he devised. Several new captives, taken by the *Exchange* at sea, were also drawn in. The rising was carefully planned and bloodily executed. The gunnery crew seized control of the lower deck, slaughtering the 'Turks' there, and the mutineers then shot and killed many of those who had fled to the poop. The survivors eventually submitted, begging for mercy. It was not forthcoming; Rawlins and his company hacked several to death with their axes, manacled others, and threw them overboard. He spared only the renegade Captain Ramtham, alias Henry Chandler, and five other 'English Turks', along with several others now willing to revert to their Christian faith. Once the bodies had been cleared, Rawlins gathered his company together for a brief service of thanksgiving, using what they could remember of the traditional shipboard service. They sailed into Plymouth on 13 February, and the narrative ends with the 'English Turks' in prison, facing trial.

The mutineers' watchword, 'For God and King James and St George for England', captured the pamphlet's religious and patriotic spirit. It was dedicated to the marquis of Buckingham, Lord Admiral and royal favourite, but with none of the conventional obsequious flattery. Instead, with barely veiled criticism, Rawlins expressed hope that his pamphlet would persuade the marquis, as 'chief commander of our sea affairs', to remember the thousands of poor seamen who 'weigh up the anchors, toil in the night, endure the storms [and] sweat at the helm'.[1] Implicit was a further message. If a handful of enslaved mariners could perform such wonders, surely the crown, with all the resources at its disposal, could do far more to help those still languishing in Barbary.

Rawlins' pamphlet was a tale of courage and ingenuity in desperate circumstances, of success against huge odds. The narrative oscillates between the first and third person, and he clearly had help in polishing the text, as the final paragraph acknowledged. Offering reflections on divine providence, this urged readers to 'make use' of the narrative by learning to show patience in adversity and gratitude for divine deliverance:

Shall I fear death or some petty trial when God is to be honoured, my country to be served, my king to be obeyed, religion to be defended, the commonwealth

---

[1] *Rawlins*, sig. A2-v; cf. Nabil Matar, 'English Accounts of Captivity in North Africa and the Middle East: 1577-1624', *Renaissance Quarterly*, 56 (2001), 563-5.

supported, honour and renown obtained, and in the end, the crown of immortality purchased?[2]

Rawlins had experienced only a few weeks of captivity in Algiers, and his text reflected the conventional stereotypes of Barbary. It depicts 'Turks' and Moors as cruel barbarians and sodomites, and mocks their religion with a contemptuous passage on the rituals performed by the 'witch', 'conjuror', or 'soothsayer' carried on board to guide the corsairs' decisions. Yet if Rawlins was asserting the superiority of brave Englishmen and their Christian faith, he and his readers knew the wider context was far less comfortable. The text itself reminded readers that hundreds of Englishmen were still suffering in Algiers. Many, it claimed, had been tortured into 'turning Turk', and greed had persuaded others to convert voluntarily. The fact that English renegades had bought the *Exchange* to prey on fellow Christians, including their own countrymen, presented the English themselves in a far from flattering light. Rawlins also mentioned in passing the failed English assault on Algiers earlier in 1621, commenting that the corsairs were now taking their revenge. English slaves in Algiers had advised his company to view their plight as a punishment from God to 'cleanse the dross' from their faith. All this was far removed from the confident voice of British imperialism in later centuries. Rather, the narrative offered readers a rare picture of success against a dismal background of England's apparent impotence. Rawlins or his co-writer hoped it would comfort the weak and strengthen the faint-hearted. For several generations that message would remain relevant for thousands of others.

We have about two dozen accounts by former English slaves in North Africa, half of which remained unpublished until the twentieth century.[3] Most authors had endured slavery far longer than Rawlins, some of them for decades. Several had escaped, while others had been ransomed or eventually freed by their owners. Those who had chosen or were persuaded to publish their stories had a wide variety of motives. Thomas Saunders, the first to appear (in 1587), presented his account as a powerful demonstration of divine providence, a message that was repeated still more emphatically by the puritan William Okeley several decades later.[4] Edward Webbe, a gunner, was hoping for employment by the crown, while Richard Hasleton, writing during Elizabeth's war with Spain, used his sufferings in Barbary and at the hands of the Spanish Inquisition to assert the truth of the Protestant faith, the superstitious ignorance of the 'infidels', and the still greater

[2] *Rawlins*, sig. E2-3v.

[3] Most are conveniently listed in Daniel Vitkus, ed., *Piracy, Slavery, and Redemption* (New York, 2001), 371–6. The genre is discussed in G. A. Starr, 'Escape from Barbary: A Seventeenth-Century Genre', *Huntington Library Quarterly*, 29/1 (1965), 35–52, and Matar, 'English Accounts'. There were also several fictional accounts, as in Richard Head's *The English Rogue* (1665) and Defoe's *Robinson Crusoe* (1719).

[4] *Okeley, passim*; Thomas Saunders, *A true discription and breefe discourse, of a most lamentable voiage* (1587).

cruelty of the false Catholic Church.[5] Several authors hoped, like Rawlins, to inspire or shame the state into more decisive action, and urged the public to redeem slaves through charitable donations. Adam Elliot, who escaped from Morocco in 1670, published his narrative only twelve years later, after becoming entangled in the furore over the Popish Plot. The Plot's inventor, Titus Oates, had accused him bizarrely of being both a Catholic priest and a Muslim apostate, which prompted Elliot to set out his story in print and sue for defamation.[6] In 1640 Francis Knight devoted half his text to a pioneering description of the government and society of Algiers, and sixty years later Joseph Pitts followed his example. Pitts and Thomas Pellow also used their accounts to explain and extenuate the fact that they had 'turned Turk' during their captivity.[7]

Print, of course, was not the only form of publication. Other accounts, not intended for the press, were written to entertain, inform, and edify the authors' families, friends, and descendants.[8] Every captive returning home would have been eager to tell his tale and plied with questions by friends and strangers alike. Elliot, for example, had already told his story many times over the years. An enemy jibed that he had repeated it 'over and over again' in hackney carriages, alehouses, coffee houses, and taverns. And one man, who had heard Elliot retell it several times during the course of a long coach journey to Chester, said he was so impressed that he had repeated it at least a hundred times to his own acquaintances.[9] One brief account has come down to us indirectly through a London preacher, and another through a German traveller who had heard it at second hand.[10]

These narratives furnish us with vivid accounts of capture and of life in slavery. As historical sources they are, of course, far from objective. The authors' experiences gave them an obvious incentive to depict their captors in terms of a cruel, infidel, and depraved stereotype, and such images are easy to find in most texts. Some scholars have indeed interpreted the whole 'slave-account' genre within the framework of Orientalism, imperialism, and even capitalism, with narrators contrasting their superior Western, Christian, civilized world with a cruel,

---

[5] Edward Webbe, *The Rare and Most Wonderfull Things which Edward Webbe an Englishman borne, hath seene* (1590), sig. D4; *Hasleton*, sig. Biii^{r-v}, C^v- C iii^v.

[6] Elliot, *Modest Vindication*, sig. B-v, 20–46.

[7] Francis Knight, *A Relation of Seaven Yeares Slaverie* (1640); *Pitts*, 180–204; Thomas Pellow, *The History of the Long Captivity and Adventures of Thomas Pellow* (1751; first published 1740), 14–16; Giles Milton, *White Gold* (2005), 80–2.

[8] Stephen T. Riley, ed., 'Abraham Browne's Captivity by the Barbary Pirates, 1655', *Colonial Society of Massachusetts*, 52 (1979), 31; Coxere, *Adventures by Sea*.

[9] Elliot, *Modest Vindication*, 37, 46; Bartholomew Lane, *A Modest Vindication of the Hermit of the Sounding Island* (1683), 7.

[10] William Gouge, *A Recovery from Apostasy* (1639); Adam Olearius, *The Voyages and Travells of the Ambassadors sent by Frederick, Duke of Holstein, to the Great Duke of Muscovy and the King of Persia* [in 1633–39] (1669), ii.227–8.

tyrannical, and barbaric East.[11] Most accounts, however, cannot be reduced to such simplified patterns. Within the standard narrative arc of capture, life in bondage, and return home, they are remarkably heterogeneous in both form and content. Several authors took pains, moreover, to explain that while some owners had been brutal, others had proved kind and humane, a few even offering 'love and friendship'.[12] And the writers who chose to include valuable descriptions of the society and culture of Barbary itself identified elements to respect as well as criticize.[13]

Several of the narratives were published on the initiative of others, who in some cases had clearly helped shape or polish them. Rawlins appears in the third person in his text, while the title-page of Hasleton's narrative explains that it was 'penned as he delivered it from his mouth', rather than written down by him. The writing was among a 'store of papers' belonging to William Barley, perhaps the penman, and it was Barley who decided to put it into print. The publisher also helped shape the work, inserting numerous old woodcuts that belonged more to the genre of chivalric romance than Protestant piety. It was probably also the publisher's decision to publish the text in two editions, given different titles.[14]

Almost by definition, the narratives also laid bare the weakness of the English in the face of a powerful Muslim enemy, especially when they addressed the sensitive issue of Christians abandoning their religion to 'turn Turk'. The age of imperial domination still lay far ahead. Authors sought rather to provide readers with comfort and reassurance, stressing how God had given them the strength to endure, and how by faith and courage they had survived or escaped their oppressors. Whatever ordeals the captives had suffered, readers could remain confident that their God was the true God. That message was reiterated in a closely related genre—David-and-Goliath accounts of heroic English mariners repelling attacks by far more powerful Barbary men-of-war.[15]

To supplement the narratives we have numerous letters and petitions from slaves and their families, stressing the misery of their plight and begging the crown for help. Far less balanced than the best narratives, they nonetheless provide valuable evidence on contemporary perceptions of Barbary and of the captives' psychological as well as physical challenges. We also have reports from English consuls and merchants in Barbary, key intermediaries in the negotiation of

---

[11] E.g. Joe Snader, 'The Oriental Captivity Narrative and Early English Fiction', *Eighteenth-Century Fiction*, 9/3 (1997), 267–98; Joe Snader, *Caught between Worlds. British Captivity Narratives in Fact and Fiction* (Kentucky, 2000); Mario Klarer and Daniel Vitkus, 'Unkind Dealings', in M. Klarer, ed., *Piracy and Captivity in the Mediterranean 1550–1810* (2018), 65, 69–61.

[12] *Okeley*, 41.   [13] Notably Pitts and Pellow.

[14] *Strange and Wonderful Things Happened to Richard Hasleton*, and *A Discourse of the Miserable Captivitie of an Englishman, named Richard Hasleton*, both published in 1595 for William Bradley.

[15] On the theme of providential reassurance see Jonathan Burton, 'English Anxiety and the Muslim Power of Conversion: Five Perspectives on "Turning Turk" in Early Modern Texts', *Journal for Early Modern Cultural Studies*, 2 (2002), 35–67. On heroic defences see Chapter 2.

ransoms, from other diplomats, and from naval commanders. And we have a few depositions from former slaves. For the great majority of captives, alas, only a bare name survives, and often not even that. Many died in captivity, worn down by drudgery and harsh treatment, or swept away by plague. Throughout history, of course, the lives of slaves across the globe have left little trace in the record. We will never have sufficient material to construct a comprehensive and wholly accurate picture of life as a slave in Barbary. We are fortunate to have as much as we do. And while most narrators focused primarily on their sufferings and eventual escape or redemption, their incidental comments allow us to glimpse something of the flavour of their everyday lives in captivity.[16]

After Chapter 1, which sets out the Mediterranean context, the book explores the experiences of captives throughout their ordeal. Chapter 2 addresses the trauma of capture and sale in the slave market. Chapter 3 investigates life in captivity, and the factors that could make it horrendous for some and bearable for others. Chapter 4 examines issues of identity, both religious and national. What led some captives to apostatize and accept Islam, and what did 'conversion' mean? Were religious and national identities firm or fluid? How far did their Christian faith provide others with the strength to cope with both their miserable situation and their fear that God must be punishing them for their sins? Chapter 5 turns to the theme of escape, whether by flight or mutiny, and its many perils. Chapters 6 and 7 explore the issues of ransoming and redeeming captives. How were funds raised, how were ransoms negotiated, and what of the great mass of ordinary seamen, whose families could never hope to raise a ransom? What roles were played by private individuals, the Church, and the state in raising ransom funds and organizing redemptions? Chapter 8 turns to the growing role of the state, under heavy pressure to protect commerce and liberate its subjects. The early Stuarts had very little leverage in the Mediterranean, either military or diplomatic, while the Ottoman Empire's own ability to impose its will on its North African regencies was shrinking. The chapter traces the combination of naval pressure, diplomacy, and money that eventually brought the corsair threat to (almost) an end.

British slaves were only one group among many in the Mediterranean world. Slavery was a longstanding phenomenon throughout the region, and European corsairs carried Muslim captives to sell in the slave markets of Iberia and Italy. The Conclusion places the British story within this wider context, and also considers its cultural impact.

---

[16] This approach is employed effectively in Daniel Hershenzon, *The Captive Sea: Slavery, Communication, and Commerce in Early Modern Spain and the Mediterranean* (Philadelphia, 2019).

1

Introduction

In February 1613 Londoners gazed in wonder at a spectacular mock-battle on the Thames, staged to celebrate the marriage of James I's daughter. The king and his entourage also watched from Whitehall as a fleet of Barbary galleys captured several rich Venetian and Spanish merchantmen. An English naval force, streamers bravely flying, then arrived on the scene, gave battle, and predictably triumphed. The sailors boarded and overpowered the galleys, blew up a 'castle' that had been erected on the bank to represent Algiers, and liberated the merchantmen. A veteran commander, Sir Robert Mansell, then conducted the captured 'Turkish admiral' and several 'bashas' to be presented to the king. Pamphlet accounts declared that the pageant, designed to proclaim England's naval might, had delighted the royal party and the thousands of spectators 'of all sorts'. No expense had been spared. Almost forty vessels had been 'trimmed, furnished and painted' to represent the ships, with 500 watermen pressed to man them and 1,000 musketeers drawn from London's trained bands to fight the battles and storm the castle. One news-writer, unimpressed by the extravagant display, commented that it had cost an estimated £9,000, which, he might have added, could have redeemed 250 slaves at Algiers.[1]

This was not the first such spectacle. Three years earlier the Lord Mayor and aldermen had mounted their own drama on the Thames, to mark the return of the Prince of Wales to the capital. Featuring two English merchantmen engaging a 'Turkish pirate', it was also carefully choreographed, with 'divers men appearing on either side to be slain and hurled over into the sea' before the English prevailed. In June 1613 Bristol's corporation marked the visit of James' Queen, Anne of Denmark, by staging a similar encounter between two 'Turkish' galleys and a Bristol merchantman. The corsairs repeatedly boarded their prey in a hard-fought action, only to be repelled and finally driven away. An estimated 30,000 spectators watched the action.[2]

---

[1] *The Marriage of the two great Princes, Fredericke, Count Palatine, &c, and the Lady Elizabeth* (1613), sig. A4-Bv; a second impression had a slightly different title; John Taylor, *Heavens blessing, and earths ioy* (1613), sig. A3v-4v; John Chamberlain, *The Letters of John Chamberlain*, ed. Norman Egbert McClure (Philadelphia, 1939), i.416, 418, 421, 423.

[2] *Londons Love to the Royal Prince Henrie, Meeting him on the River Thames* (1610), 24–5; *A Relation of the royall magnificent, and sumptuous entertainement giuen to...Queene Anne, at... Bristoll* (1613), sig. C3v-D2; Samuel C. Chew, *The Crescent and the Rose* (New York, 1965), 459–62; Nabil Matar, *Turks, Moors and Englishmen in the Age of Discovery* (New York, 1999), 144–50.

British Slaves and Barbary Corsairs, 1580–1750. Bernard Capp, Oxford University Press. © Bernard Capp 2022.
DOI: 10.1093/oso/9780192857378.003.0002

Barbary had entered public consciousness in England in the last decades of the sixteenth century. It followed the expansion of English, Dutch, and other northern European traders into the Mediterranean, a development known as the 'Northern Invasion'. In the English case, this had been triggered in part by the papal excommunication of Elizabeth in 1570, which had gradually reduced commercial access to ports in Catholic Europe. Trade with the Levant, protected and regulated by an agreement with the Ottoman sultan, soon became highly lucrative, but merchant ships proved vulnerable to corsairs operating from Barbary.[3]

The mock-battles on the Thames thus reflected Barbary's importance as an issue of pressing public interest and concern. Though corsairs and captives rarely feature in modern histories of seventeenth-century England, they had a high profile for contemporaries. The propagandist displays, however, were mere fantasies. A stream of appeals from merchants, magistrates, captives, and distressed families better reflected the reality: that James' navy was incapable of curbing the corsairs or liberating their captives. Public pressure for action peaked in the 1610s, 1620s, and 1630s, leading one scholar to argue that Charles I's failure to address the problem helped bring about the collapse of his personal rule and trigger the civil war.[4]

For most people in early Stuart Britain, 'slavery' brought to mind the plight of their compatriots in Barbary, not the black Africans being shipped to the New World in increasing numbers from the mid-century. This book focuses on the English men and women enslaved, along with much smaller numbers of Irish, Scots, American colonists, and a few Welsh. Linda Colley has estimated the overall total as in the order of 20,000, though we will never have anything approaching precise figures. Until the mid-century it is probable that more died in captivity than ever returned home.[5] Slaves from the British Isles formed only a tiny proportion of the European total, estimated at more than a million and drawn from every part of the continent. A further estimated two million black slaves from sub-Saharan Africa were also sold or sent as tributes to Barbary in the seventeenth and eighteenth centuries, with no possibility of ever being redeemed.[6] Slavery had long been endemic throughout the Mediterranean region, and the Barbary corsairs had their European counterparts, Venetian, Florentine, and the

---

[3] Fernand Braudel, *The Mediterranean and the Mediterranean World in the Age of Philip II* (1973), i.606-42; Colin Heywood, 'The English in the Mediterranean, 1600-1630: A Post-Braudelian Perspective on the "Northern Invasion"', in Maria Fusaro, Colin Heywood, and Mohammed-Salah Omri, eds., *Trade and Cultural Exchange in the Early Modern Mediterranean* (2010), 23-44; A. C. Wood, *A History of the Levant Company* (1964).

[4] Nabil Matar, '"Imperialism", Captivity and the Civil Wars', in his *Britain and Barbary 1589-1689* (Gainesville, FL, 2005), 38-75.

[5] Linda Colley, *Captives. Britain, Empire and the World, 1600-1850* (2002), 44, 52, 56.

[6] Robert C. Davis, *Christian Slaves, Muslim Masters* (Basingstoke, 2003), 3-27, esp. 21; Fatiha Loualich, 'Emancipated Female Slaves in Algiers; marriage, property and social advancement in the seventeenth and eighteenth centuries', in Stephanie Cronin, ed., *Subalterns and Social Protest: History from Below in the Middle East and North Africa* (2008), 202.

Maltese Knights of St John. Malta has been dubbed the 'capital of Christian piracy'. There were many Muslim slaves in Spain, Portugal, Italy, and southern France, and those forced to toil in Christian galleys endured lives that differed little from those of their Barbary equivalents. Some unfortunates had experience of both. Other slaves had been captured on the land frontiers of the Ottoman and Habsburg empires.[7]

This book sets out to explore the lives that British slaves endured in captivity. Did their owners aim to extract ransoms from their families, or view them as a free labour-force, or both? What chance did they have of being redeemed, how was ransom money raised, how were redemptions arranged? Was escape a realistic possibility? How often were slaves coerced or induced to apostatize, and what did such 'conversions' mean? And how far was the state willing to intervene, whether by facilitating redemptions or mobilizing force against the corsairs?

Christian European slavery in Barbary differed significantly from the far more brutal African slavery in the Americas. It was predominantly male, overwhelmingly so in the case of the British, and with the sexes generally kept apart, no community of slave families developed to transmit their servile status down the generations. Moreover, European slaves had at least the possibility of one day being ransomed and freed. Writing in 1957 Sir Godfrey Fisher insisted that these differences were fundamental. 'A Christian slave was, in fact, a prisoner of war,' he argued, 'and regarded as a victim of temporary misfortune. His servile condition involved no "contempt of human dignity".' Fisher's verdict, still influential today, is deeply misleading. Barbary captives were sold into slavery in the market-place in public auctions that deliberately stripped away all human dignity, as victims testified. Thereafter they became their owners' private property, to be exploited, beaten, or resold at will. Many remained enslaved for years, sometimes decades, and many died in bondage. They would have been astonished by Fisher's claim that escape 'was by no means difficult'.[8]

The origin of the Barbary corsairs lay in the centuries-old conflict between Christian and Muslim powers. In the sixteenth century the main confrontation was between the Habsburg Empire and the Ottomans, whose conquests stretched from Egypt to the gates of Vienna. Their rivalry in the Mediterranean reached its apogee in the great battle of Lepanto in 1571. Though Spain triumphed on that occasion, the Ottomans continued to tighten their grip in the eastern Mediterranean, capturing Crete in 1669. The central and western Mediterranean

---

[7] David Eltis and Stanley L. Engerman, eds., *The Cambridge World History of Slavery. 3: 1420–1804* (Cambridge, 2011); Daniel Hershenzon, 'Towards a Connected History of Bondage in the Mediterranean: Recent Trends in the Field', *History Compass*, 15.8 (August 2017), 1–13; *idem., The Captive Sea: Slavery, Communication, and Commerce in Early Modern Spain and the Mediterranean* (Philadelphia, 2019). Géza Dávid and Pál Fodor, eds., *Ransom Slavery along the Ottoman Borders* (Leiden, 2007); Peter Earle, *Corsairs of Malta and Barbary* (1970), 97 and *passim*.

[8] Sir Godfrey Fisher, *Barbary Legend. War, Trade and Piracy in North Africa 1415–1830* (Oxford, 1957), 102–3.

remained spheres of constant rivalry, with Muslim forces now led from Algiers, Tunis, and Tripoli, the so-called Barbary Regencies, and from Morocco.[9] Spain abandoned its earlier crusading appetite, and instead of 'Holy War' there were now what have been labelled two 'Faithless Empires', with Christian and Muslim corsairs alike driven primarily by profit.[10] Francis Bacon, who called in vain for a Holy War against the mighty Ottoman Empire, dismissed Algiers as no more than a pirate base.[11]

The Barbary lands

Barbary was a term widely used to describe the Maghreb, North Africa west of Egypt and as far as Morocco, which had an Atlantic as well as Mediterranean coast.[12] In the early sixteenth century the whole region, except Morocco, came under the sway of the Ottoman Empire. A band of corsairs, led by the brothers Aroudj and Kheir-ed-din, established a base and fledging state in Algiers, and under threat from a Spanish force, Kheir-ed-din (better known as Barbarossa) offered to place it under the authority of the Ottoman sultan, in return for a force of janissary troops and permission to recruit more. The sultan also supplied arms, and granted Kheir-ed-dun the title of beglerbeg, governor of all North Africa. A succession of beglerbegs appointed from Constantinople ruled until 1587, when the sultan decided to appoint separate rulers (pashas) for Algiers, Tunis, and Tripoli, each to govern for only three years. This move, designed to preserve his authority, had the opposite effect. The pashas had paid large bribes to secure their posts, and once installed devoted most of their efforts to recouping their outlay. Three years proved too short to gain a proper grasp of the complex politics of Barbary, let alone establish control. Power gradually slipped away from the pasha to the janissary corps, exercised through the divan (or duana), the assembly of their leading officers, under their Aga (commander). By 1600 the janissaries of Algiers numbered more than 20,000, mostly peasants recruited from Anatolia and the Levant. In effect an army of occupation, they jealously guarded their position, treating indigenous Moors and Arabs with contempt. After 1659 the pasha lost what little was left of his authority. While the post was no longer limited to three

---

[9] The classic survey remains Braudel, *Mediterranean*, ii.904–1237.

[10] On 'Holy War' see Matar, *Turks, Moors and Englishmen*, 139–67; Barbara Fuchs, 'Faithless Empires: Pirates, Renegadoes, and the English Nation', *English Literary History*, 67 (2000).

[11] Francis Bacon, *Certaine Miscellany Works of the Right Honourable Francis Lo. Verulam* (1629), 126–7, and 93–134 *passim*.

[12] For modern overviews see Houari Touati, 'Ottoman Maghrib', and Stephen Cory, 'Sharifan Rule in Morocco (tenth/twelfth-sixteenth/eighteenth centuries', in M. Fierro, ed., *The New Cambridge History of Islam*, ii, chaps. 16, 18 (Cambridge, 2011). For a survey of government, society, and corsairs in Algiers, see Paul Auchterlonie, ed., *Encountering Islam. Joseph Pitts: an English Slave in 17th-Century Algiers and Mecca* (2012), 7–48.

years, henceforth he had to be content with a fixed salary, and lost his claim to a share of the corsairs' booty.[13]

The janissaries' main concern was always their pay, which remained modest. Much of the wealth of Algiers came from the prizes captured by the corsairs, and the janissaries were naturally eager for the right to participate. From 1568 they were allowed to take part in the *corso* (corsair expeditions) and share in the booty. Violent unrest broke out among the janissaries whenever their pay was not forthcoming. The army commander and divan, ruling from 1659, faced repeated opposition from rival factions and disgruntled soldiers. Every Aga in the 1660s was assassinated or overthrown and executed, and European observers dismissed the regency's system of government as little more than anarchy. Another upheaval, in 1671, saw the officers overthrown and power seized by the *reis*, or corsair commanders. They persuaded a respected, retired *reis*, Hadj Mohammed, to assume power. Hadj Mohammed laid down strict conditions: he was to have supreme and permanent power, with the new title of dey, and the power of the divan was drastically reduced. In practice he shared power with his son-in-law, Babba Hassan, and key advisors, and held power for a decade. A successor, another veteran corsair, was toppled by the janissaries in 1689, who installed one of their own number. But the structure created in 1671 survived, and while politics remained volatile and violent, there was no return to the earlier anarchy. Contemporaries recognized that the authority of the Ottoman sultan had become merely notional, with deys now able, for example, to make war or peace as they chose. Yet it suited both parties to preserve the notion of 'regency'. It was the sultan who gave permission for Algiers to recruit new janissaries, every three or four years, and in return he could call upon the naval forces of Algiers (and Tunis and Tripoli), even if they now demanded to be paid for sending their ships and men to serve in Ottoman campaigns.

The corsairs and their ships

The corsairs were—and still are—often described as pirates. The label is misleading, for they operated with authority from the regencies' rulers, who had a stake in their expeditions, and a strict code of conduct regulated their actions and the division of spoils. They were more like privateers, though that label is also problematic. Queen Elizabeth licensed privateers, but she also commanded a royal navy. There was no such distinction in Barbary. The *reis* were significant figures, and in Algiers they had their own organization, the *taiffe*. The spoils of war (merchandise, slaves, and ships) were shared out between rulers, *armadors*

---

[13] This paragraph and the next are based mainly on John B. Wolf, *The Barbary Coast. Algeria under the Turks, 1500 to 1830* (New York, 1979), chaps. 1–6, and sources there cited.

(rich Moors who financed the *corso*), officers, and men, according to precise rules carefully observed.[14]

In the sixteenth century the corsairs used war-galleys propelled by slaves. The largest vessels might have twenty-five banks of oars, with five men to an oar, totalling 250 oarsmen. They carried a fighting force of up to 140 soldiers, with their own commander (Aga) and armed with scimitars, muskets, and bows and arrows. Most were janissaries, sometimes supplemented by Moors. Galleys generally carried provisions for only six to eight weeks, minimizing weight in the interests of speed, and could overhaul almost any merchant ship they sighted. The *reis* would then order it to surrender, and if it refused, the soldiers would swarm aboard and overwhelm its crew. Few merchantmen could resist such a force, and most did not try. The galley-slaves had no fighting role and remained chained to their benches throughout an action.

From the early 1600s the corsairs started to roam the Atlantic, venturing through the Straits or operating from bases at Mamora and Salé on Morocco's Atlantic coast. They were soon ranging as far as the English Channel and North Sea. Oared galleys proved ill-suited to northern waters and the corsairs increasingly adopted sailing vessels, carrying more and heavier guns. This reduced the need for oarsmen, and one writer estimated in 1676 that of 18,000 European slaves in Algiers only 900 were labouring as galley-slaves.[15] Tactics changed far less; the corsairs still relied on speed to overhaul their target, and on the soldiers to intimidate it into surrender or board and overwhelm it. The regencies could deploy an impressive force at sea, though numbers fluctuated. In 1581, thirty-six galiots and brigantines were operating out of Algiers, alongside many smaller vessels. In 1618 a Venetian correspondent estimated its naval resources at 100 ships of all sorts, with 600 pieces of ordnance and 6,000 fighting men.[16] A list from c.1669 detailed twenty-five ships, most carrying more than thirty guns, with five galleys and six more ships on the stocks.[17] Europe's maritime powers could set out more powerful warships, but this was always an asymmetric conflict. Corsairs were raiders preying on merchant shipping, and had no desire to join battle with European fleets, well aware that in any encounter they were likely to come off worse. European navies were nonetheless slow to establish an indisputable superiority. In the later seventeenth century the corsair fleets included powerful men-of-war carrying forty or fifty guns, making them formidable adversaries. Hard-fought encounters in the late 1660s and 1670s saw four English naval

---

[14] For this paragraph and the next see Wolf, *Barbary Coast*, chap. 7; Earle, *Corsairs*, chaps. 3–4; Alan G. Jamieson, *Lords of the Sea. A History of the Barbary Corsairs* (2012).

[15] George Philips, *The present state of Tangier...to which is added the present state of Algiers* (1676), 92.

[16] Wolf, *Barbary Coast*, 136–8; *CSPVen. 1617–19*, 272.   [17] TNA, SP 71/1, f.472.

commanders killed in action, while another was court-martialled and executed for not daring to give battle.[18]

The corsairs themselves were a heterogeneous breed. The *reis* were largely drawn from the Greek islands, Balkans, and Egypt, all under Ottoman control, alongside Andalusians and European renegades, among them many Italians. The Moriscos, expelled from Spain from 1609, became an increasingly important element, especially in Morocco.[19] Dutch and English renegades also played a key role in the first decades of the century. Many of the English had fought against Spain during Elizabeth's long war, finding a friendly base in Tunis or Algiers, and then thrown in their lot with the corsairs, often eventually 'turning Turk'. John Ward, the Fleming Simon Danser, Peter Easton, and their associates were the leading figures in this world in the early seventeenth century. They played a major role in extending corsair operations beyond the Straits and out into the Atlantic, and in what accompanied that development: the shift from oared galleys to more heavily-armed sailing ships, and with renegade Europeans and slaves serving as pilots, gunners, boatswains, and carpenters.[20]

Ward operated ships with English and European crews and Barbary soldiers. He and his companions disposed of most of their plunder in Tunis, selling at cheap rates to Cara Uthman, Aga of the janissaries and its effective ruler. Much of the rest was sold in Italy by European merchants at the free port of Livorno (Leghorn), or carried there in the corsairs' own ships, now masquerading as merchantmen. The corsairs thus had the effect of redirecting as well as disrupting trade, facilitating commercial ties between southern Europe and the Maghreb. The wealth that Ward and his friends brought into Tunis was quickly dissipated. A French traveller remarked in 1606 that their 'profuse liberality' made them popular with the janissaries, and though they would run drunk through the streets 'every kind of debauchery and unchecked licence is permitted to them'. Another traveller commented scornfully that 'all they got, they basely consumed it amongst Jews, Turks, Moors, and whores'. The fact that most remained notionally Christian was also overlooked, at least initially.[21]

North Africa lacked many of the resources and skills essential to build and set out men-of-war. Algiers, Tunis, and Tripoli had to import timber for masts, cordage, cannon, and gunpowder from northern Europe. In theory, European states could have starved Barbary of most of the materials on which the corsairs'

[18] Pepys, *Catalogue*, i.357, 369, 373, 391, 429; *CSPVen. 1669–70*, 253; *CSPD 1670*, 325, 395; Nabil Matar, *British Captives from the Mediterranean to the Atlantic, 1563–1760* (Leiden, 2014), 172–89.
[19] Mercedes Garcia-Arenal, 'The Moriscos in Morocco. From Granadan Emigration to the Hornacheros of Salé', in M. Garcia-Arenal and G. Wiegers, eds., *The Expulsion of the Moriscos from Spain* (Leiden, 2014), 286–328.
[20] C. M. Senior, *A Nation of Pirates. English Piracy in its Heyday* (Newton Abbot, 1976).
[21] *ODNB*, John Ward; Greg Bak, *Barbary Pirate. The Life and Crimes of John Ward* (Stroud, 2006); *Newes from Sea of two notorious Pyrats Ward the Englishman and Danseker the Dutchman* (1609); Earle, *Corsairs*, 50; Castries et al., *Sources Inédites*, ii.272–3.

business depended. Early Stuart proclamations prohibited the export of munitions to Barbary, but the lure of profit outweighed such decrees. Sir John Pennington, commanding in the Downs in 1635, intercepted several ships carrying gunpowder to Barbary, and grumbled that it was 'a great shame that Christians should furnish these heathenish pirates against themselves'.[22] For states, too, self-interest prevailed over any sense of Christian solidarity. When Barbary rulers negotiated with Europeans they generally insisted on marine supplies, while Moroccan rulers demanded that ransoms be paid in kind, mostly in gunpowder and armaments.

Barbary society

Most Europeans used simple terms to describe the peoples of the Maghreb, labelling them 'Turks', 'Moors', or more disparagingly 'barbarians'. Merchants and diplomats recognized a far more complex reality. Only a brief outline is necessary here, with the Algerian regency serving as the model. Military and political power lay in the hands of the 'Turks', the janissaries, and their commanders.[23] Estimates of their numbers in the seventeenth century ranged from 12,000 to 22,000, divided between several garrison towns. Many were originally peasants from Anatolia, with others recruited from the Levant and Egypt. The generic label 'Turk' served to differentiate them from the native Moors of North Africa, known as the *baldi*. These included the 'Tagarines' or Moriscos banished from Andalusia in the early seventeenth century, and their descendants. Though numbering only about 800 families by the 1670s, they were the principal figures among the *armadors* who set out corsair ships and traded in slaves. Most of the urban Moors engaged in crafts and trade. There were perennial tensions between the communities. Essentially an army of occupation, the janissaries adamantly refused to open their ranks to Moors. Some married local Moorish women, and their offspring, the *coulougli*, constituted a problematic group, for many naturally wished to follow their fathers. Only a limited number were allowed to enrol, and they were barred from reaching the higher ranks. Frustration triggered a massive rebellion in 1633, in which thousands perished. For almost twenty years thereafter they were barred altogether, and restrictions always remained on how far they could rise.

The Kabilye and other tribes of the Atlas Mountains and inland areas were only loosely controlled by the regency's rulers, and often broke out in rebellion. To collect taxes, or more accurately 'exact tributes' from the Kabilyes, the janissaries

---

[22] Wolf, *Barbary Coast*, 142; James F. Larkin and Paul L. Hughes, eds., *Stuart Royal Proclamations* (Oxford, 1973–83), i.203–6, ii.574–5; *CSPD 1635*, 570.

[23] Wolf, *Barbary Coast*, chap. 6; for a contemporary English account see Philips, *The present state of Tangier [and] Algiers*, reproducing the account by the English consul Samuel Martin (TNA SP 71/2, fos. 62-72v). Cf. Francis Baker's similar account of Tunis in 1675 in TNA SP 71/26, fos. 233–7.

conducted massive sweeps each year that frequently encountered bloody resistance. Barbary society also included substantial Jewish communities. Algiers alone
had an estimated 13,000 Jewish families in the 1670s. While most were modest
craftsmen, a group of financiers and merchants controlled much of the commerce
between Barbary, other parts of the Ottoman Empire, and Europe. They were key
figures in channelling plundered cargoes back to European consumers, and in
arranging the redemption of slaves. Yet commentators agreed that Jews throughout Barbary were abused and treated with contempt. They lived apart, forbidden
to carry knives or own horses, and their children had to endure being beaten by
gangs of Moorish boys without any hope of redress. One observer described their
condition as 'no other than a better sort of slavery'.[24] Lastly, European renegades
formed a significant element among both the corsairs and janissaries, and small
numbers of merchants resided in the major towns. There were also, of course, the
thousands of slaves, both Christians from every part of Europe and sub-Saharan
Africans, many supplied as tribute.

English observers sketching outlines of Barbary society emphasized the friction
between its constituent parts. Francis Knight observed that 'the Turk' kept the
Moors 'as vassals in great subjection, yet in substance is but a slave to them', for
most of the wealth and land was held by Moors and Tagarines, who financed the
corsairs.[25] In 1663 Robert Browne, consul at Algiers, advised that a new peace with
England was unlikely to last. The 'soberer sort' in the divan supported it, he
explained, but the janissaries would not give up their appetite for plunder at sea,
and those nominally in control let themselves 'be swayed by the commonality'.
Government, he claimed, was 'in the hands of the scum of the people, ignorant
and inconstant', and 'overawed by the soldiers, in whom the itch of robbery
prevails'. Philip Rycaut agreed, explaining that no peace could endure long
because 'the people are the dregs of the Turks, pirates and renegades, without
religion, faith or honour'.[26] Both men shared the widespread conviction that any
peace would last only as long as a powerful naval force was on hand to act as
deterrent.

The outline above also serves broadly for the regencies of Tunis and
Tripoli. Morocco, sometimes known as Western Barbary, displayed significant
differences.[27] It successfully preserved its independence against Ottoman pressure, so there were no janissaries. Its rulers styled themselves kings or emperors,
but for many years Morocco was torn apart by civil wars. The main corsair base

[24] Lancelot Addison, *The Present State of the Jews (more particularly relating to those in Barbary)*
(1675), 7–10.
[25] Francis Knight, *A Relation of Seaven Yeares Slaverie* (1640), 32.
[26] HMC, 71, *Finch MSS*, i.281–2.
[27] For surveys see Jamil Abun-Nasr, *A History of the Maghrib in the Islamic Period* (Cambridge,
1987), chap. 5; Stephen Cory, 'Sharifan Rule in Morocco (tenth-twelfth/sixteenth-eighteenth
centuries)', in M. Fierro, ed., *The New Cambridge History of Islam* (Cambridge, 2011), ii, chap. 16;
P. G. Rogers, *A History of Anglo-Moroccan Relations to 1900* (1977).

was initially Mamora, until captured by Spain in 1614, and then Salé, a town transformed in the early 1600s by an influx of Moriscos expelled from Spain. One group, the Hornacheros, had remained faithful to Islam and had retained their weapons and much of their wealth. Driven by hatred of Spaniards and all Christians, they quickly took control of corsair operations. Dominating the new town, on one side of the Bou Regreg river, they looked down on the other Andalusian incomers. Both groups were resented by Salé's original inhabitants, in the old town on the other side of the river, while all three resented the crumbling Moroccan government. In 1627 Salé broke away to become, in effect, an autonomous republic. A sand-bar at the river's mouth made access impossible for large ships, which for the corsairs proved both an advantage and a liability. Their men-of-war needed to have a shallow draught, and could not match the armaments carried by the largest ships of Algiers or Tunis. But European warships could not cross the bar to attack Salé, and found it impossible to overhaul its swift men-of-war. In the mid-1620s it was Salé that posed the greatest threat to British merchant shipping in the Atlantic, the Channel, and beyond. And while British naval power had ended the corsair threat from the regencies by the close of the seventeenth century, Salé and Morocco remained a menace well into the eighteenth.

Slaves and the slave-economy

We will never how many Europeans were enslaved in Barbary between the sixteenth and eighteenth centuries. Contemporary observers offered estimates for particular places and times, and we have some figures for British slaves redeemed, mostly from the mid- and late-seventeenth century. But we know that many slaves, probably the majority before the mid-seventeenth century, died in captivity. The harsh conditions accounted for thousands. Many more were swept away by virulent outbreaks of plague, even more lethal with large numbers confined in filthy and crowded conditions. A petition to Parliament stated that of 600 British captives at Algiers taken since the outbreak of war in August 1677, only 250 remained by the end of 1680. Most of the rest had died, it claimed, allegedly from their 'barbarous usage', though plague had probably accounted for most.[28] It was endemic in the Maghreb. One English slave, writing from Algiers early in 1682, begged to be redeemed before summer arrived, explaining nervously that the previous summer had seen 1,800 Christians swept away by pestilence.[29]

---

[28] *To the Right Honourable the Commons of England in Parliament assembled. The humble petition of disconsolate fathers and wives* (1681).

[29] HMC, 32, *Fitzherbert MSS*, 11.

The American historian Robert C. Davis has analysed the surviving sources and calculates that in the period 1580–1680, when corsair activity was at its peak, roughly 35,000 European slaves were held in Barbary at any given time. That figure is close to the estimate of the best contemporary commentator, the French priest Pierre Dan. Of this total, Davis suggests, around 27,000 were in Algiers and its dependencies, 6,000 in Tunis, and 2,000 in Tripoli and other smaller centres. The slave population was constantly changing. Roughly 17% of slaves may have died each year, he also suggests, with another 3–4% ransomed. Renegades, converting to Islam in the hope of better treatment or freedom, may have accounted for another 4%. If the total attrition rate was in the order of 25% each year, and the average population remained stable at 35,000, some 8,500 new slaves would have been needed annually to sustain the numbers. That would produce a total of 850,000 during the century 1580–1680, a total that could rise to more than a million when we take into account those captured before and after those dates.[30] Moreover, Davis did not include Morocco in his calculations. Salé corsairs were recognized as the greatest predators, certainly of British shipping, in the 1620s and 1630s, and again from the 1680s. Some contemporaries claimed that several thousand European slaves laboured at Moulay Ismail's capital at Meknes in the later seventeenth century and early eighteenth, with similar rates of attrition.[31] That would lift the overall total higher still. Though Davis' figures may be too high, as Nabil Matar believes, no one doubts the numbers were huge.[32]

British captives thus constituted only a small fraction of the overall total of enslaved Europeans. The great majority were Spanish, Portuguese, French, and Italian. For England, several lists survive of ships and seamen captured and carried into Algiers between 1627 and 1640. Piecing together the evidence, David Hebb arrived at an estimate of 184 ships lost and 3,228 captives in these years. Trinity House figures relating to Salé in the mid-1620s add another 2,400–2,800. There are no reliable figures for Tunis, Tripoli, and Tetuan for these years, but Hebb suggests an overall total of 400 British ships and 8,000 captives seized between 1616 and 1642.[33] Algiers re-emerged as a major threat after the Restoration, with more than 153 ships carrying more than 1,850 men captured in the war of 1677–82 alone. A petition in 1681 reported 971 Britons still enslaved there, with many hundreds more swept away by plague.[34] Salé remained a threat well into the following century. Linda Colley suggested an overall total in the order of at least 20,000, while my own calculations would indicate a total of 15,000–20,000.[35] We

---

[30] Davis, *Christian Slaves*, 15 and 3–26 *passim*; Pierre Dan, *Histoire de Barbarie et de ses Corsairs* (Paris, 1649), 318–19.

[31] Giles Milton, *White Gold* (2005), 99.   [32] Matar, *British Captives*, 9–17, 32–41 and *passim*.

[33] Hebb, *Piracy*, 137–40.

[34] *A List of Ships taken since July 1677 from his Majesties subjects, by the corsairs of Algiers* (1682); *To...Parliament. The humble petition of disconsolate fathers and wives.*

[35] Colley, *Captives*, 56. Matar views this figure as a considerable over-estimate.

should also remember that many mariners perished without ever setting foot in Barbary: killed trying to resist, drowned attempting to escape, or slaughtered and thrown overboard.

The surviving lists show that while some prizes had been carrying rich cargoes, most were small vessels with crews averaging 8–12. Most of the ships had come from London or the south and south-west, and were trading to Spain or the Mediterranean, with Newfoundland fishing boats especially vulnerable. Lord Carew lamented in 1616 that the corsairs were inflicting 'incredible damage' to the economy, and that all trade with the Levant could soon be rendered impossible. That year, one bold corsair ventured into the Thames, and Carew feared the corsairs would begin raiding ashore, as they often did in Spain and Italy.[36] Hebb calculates that the value of the ships and goods captured throughout 1622–40 approached £900,000. Had all the estimated 8,000 slaves been ransomed, at an average figure of £45 per head, that charge would have added another £360,000.[37] The crown's ordinary annual revenue by the early 1630s was a little more than £600,000, which indicates the scale of the financial and economic burden. That burden, of course, fell on the people, not the Treasury. While the crown lost customs revenues, ordinary families lost the wages on which they depended, and local communities had to provide relief for the women and children rendered destitute. Moreover, in the 1620s and 1630s, as we will see, local communities in the south-west were sometimes paralysed by the corsair threat, leaving mariners unemployed. Most ordinary families had no prospect of ever raising a ransom, and England had no equivalent to the religious orders that organized large-scale charitable collections in France and Spain. Until the later seventeenth century, the majority of slaves probably died in captivity. Most of the slaves were ordinary seamen, with much smaller numbers of merchants, emigrants, and other passengers. But anyone venturing to sea became a potential victim, and notable captives included the earl of Inchiquin, Seth Sothell, governor of Carolina, and Queen Henrietta Maria's dwarf Jeffrey Hudson.[38]

Slavery in Barbary is sometimes described as a system of 'ransom slavery'. The corsairs hunted for booty as well as slaves, however, and in the sixteenth and early seventeenth centuries this was probably their primary objective. Hebb's figures suggest that the value of the ships and cargoes they seized was considerably higher than the ransom value of the slaves. Later in the century, Thomas Baker, consul at

[36] John Maclean, ed., *Letters of George Lord Carew to Sir Thomas Roe, 1615–1617*, Camden Society, Old Series, 76 (1860), 51, 61, 125. Carew gave details of numerous ships captured by the 'circumcised pirates'.

[37] Hebb, *Piracy*, 141–3; Nabil Matar, 'British Captives in Salé (1721)', in Stefan Hanss and Juliane Schiel, eds., *Mediterranean Slavery Revisited (500–1800)*, (Zurich, 2014), 515–30; C. R. Pennell, ed., *Piracy and Diplomacy in Seventeenth-Century North Africa. The Journal of Thomas Baker, English Consul in Tripoli 1677–1685* (Cranbury, NJ, 1989), 189–90.

[38] For Inchiquin and Sothell see Chapters 7 and 8, below; for Hudson see *ODNB* and James Wright, *The History and Antiquities of the County of Rutland* (1684), 105.

Tripoli, kept a tally of the ships, goods, and seamen captured by its corsairs each year, and their respective value. In the twelve months to April 1685, he noted, they had brought in sixteen ships. He valued the seventy-nine seamen enslaved at $300 apiece, or $23,700 in total. The ships and goods he valued at $81,800, more than three times higher.[39] Tripoli was a minor corsair centre, however, and slaves increasingly became the main prize in the major centres of Algiers, Tunis, and Salé. With rich merchantmen generally now well-armed and often protected by convoys, most corsairs could only hope to capture smaller prey, with relatively low-value cargoes. After seizing crew-members, they would quite often spurn the cargoes and sink the vessels. When two famous corsairs captured nine vessels on a cruise in 1679, they sent only three back to Algiers, burning and sinking the others.[40] The slaves' value, moreover, was not limited to the potential ransoms; they were bought for their labour, too, whether skilled or unskilled. A few kept accounts for their owners, who might have no wish to lose their valuable services. Joseph Pitts, for example, captured in his early or mid-teens, soon learned to read and write Turkish and keep accounts, and feared that if he progressed any further he might be transferred into the service of the dey and lose any possibility of ever being freed.[41] The galleys of the sixteenth century required large numbers of oarsmen, while in the next century slaves and former slaves provided most of the expertise needed to operate sailing ships, with skilled carpenters and gunners especially valued. Slaves played a crucial role in the dockyards too, constructing and fitting out men-of-war, and in casting ordnance. Other slaves provided a free labour supply in quarries and on building sites, or worked as craftsmen in a wide range of occupations. Even the galley-slaves also served in a range of other capacities, for the galleys did not operate in the winter months. And in Morocco, as we will see, the sultan Moulay Ismail viewed slaves as a valuable labour force for his vast new palace-fortress complex.

English perspectives on the Orient

From the reign of Elizabeth, the English became fascinated by the exotic world of Islam. It is important to recall that around 1600 the Muslim 'Orient' was still perceived, correctly, as powerful and expansionist, not weak and backward. The English, like other western Europeans, viewed the Ottoman Empire with ambivalent feelings of admiration, fear, contempt, and revulsion. They dismissed its religion as false and superstitious, its rulers as cruel tyrants, its legal system and

---

[39] Hebb, *Piracy*, 142; Pennell, ed., *Piracy and Diplomacy*, 189–90.

[40] William Okeley, *Eben-ezer ... with a Further Narrative of James Deane and others* (1684), 89–90; cf. *Phelps*, 200; *Pitts*, 4–5.

[41] Thomas Sweet, *Deare Friends: it is now about six yeares* (1647); *Pitts*, 226.

social order as strange and barbaric. At the same time, they were awed by its power and wealth, its sophisticated administrative system, and its military might. Henry Blount explained that he had travelled to the Levant in 1634 to see if the Turks were 'absolutely barbarous, as we are given to understand, or rather another kind of civility, different from ours, but no less pretending'. He found much to admire, marvelling at the 'incredible civility' of Turkish mariners, and assured Ottoman officials that their sultan was generally acknowledged as 'the greatest monarch in the world'.[42] Half a century earlier, in 1576, the French philosopher Jean Bodin had declared the Ottoman Empire far more sophisticated and powerful than its Spanish rival.[43] English ambassadors travelled to Constantinople as supplicants, their mission to preserve trading concessions. The Ottomans felt no need to send ambassadors to London. A few English voices might call for a Holy War against this mighty, infidel empire, but the crown had neither the means nor appetite for such a hopeless venture. Its only outcome would have been the ruin of the highly profitable trade with the Levant.[44]

Attitudes to Barbary were more mixed. Morocco was viewed with respect, as a valuable trading partner and, especially in the Elizabethan period, a potential ally. Elizabeth and her contemporary, sultan Ahmad al-Mansur (d.1603) had a common enemy in Spain, and recognized their shared interests. The Moroccan ambassador sent to England in 1600 brought a proposal for a joint attack on Spain, and outlined the sultan's audacious plan to drive the Spanish out of America and establish permanent Muslim colonies in their place.[45] The idea of an alliance would periodically resurface in the seventeenth century. Moroccan ambassadors were welcomed with lavish ceremony, with ethnic and religious issues downplayed or ignored. A semi-official account of an embassy in 1637, which included an engraved portrait of the ambassador, explained that he was Portuguese by birth and that the young ruler was also 'a white man, of... a majestical aspect'. Several later rulers had black mothers and dark skins, but the crown continued to recognize their status and authority. Morocco had been a powerful state in the late sixteenth century, and despite civil wars there was a general recognition that it might rise again, as indeed it did a century later. The poet Edmund Waller reviled Salé's corsairs as a 'crude/ And savage race', the 'pest of mankind', but he spoke with respect of the Moroccan Emperor.[46]

Yet there was also a strong popular current of hostility and suspicion, which found expression on the stage. From the later sixteenth century, playwrights and

[42] Henry Blount, *A Voyage into the Levant* (1636), 2, 15, 75 and *passim*.

[43] Noel Malcolm, 'Positive Views of Islam and of Ottoman Rule in the Sixteenth Century: the Case of Jean Bodin', in Anna Contadini and Claire Norton, eds., *The Renaissance and the Ottoman World* (Farnham, 2013), 212.

[44] Matar, *Turks, Moors and Englishmen*, 139–67.

[45] Jerry Brotton, *The Sultan and the Queen* (New York, 2016), 257–64, 271.

[46] *The Arrival and Intertainements of the Embassador, Alkaid Jaurar Ben Abdella* (1637), 5, 19 and *passim*; Edmund Waller, *Poems* (1645), 67–8.

their audiences were both fascinated and repelled by the Orient, including Barbary. In *The Merchant of Venice*, the dignified Prince of Morocco is presented as an eligible suitor for Portia, but she is secretly very relieved to see his suit fail. More often, Moorish characters were depicted in stereotypical terms as cunning, cruel, and treacherous. In *Titus Andronicus*, Shakespeare presents the scheming Moor Aaron as the embodiment of evil.[47] The 'noble Moor' Othello, a Christian commander in the service of Venice, dazzles Desdemona and her father with stories of his brave exploits, but his innate 'Turkish' traits of lust, jealousy, and cruelty soon emerge to overwhelm this adopted identity.[48]

In the case of Algiers and Tunis, contemporaries were far readier to dismiss their rulers and people as savage barbarians, and curse the piratical corsairs. Yet even here, contempt was often accompanied by grudging respect. In 1600 Algiers was larger and with far stronger defences than London. European rulers accepted that conquest was out of the question, and for several generations found it impossible to curb the corsair threat. And while many contemporaries were content to dismiss the Moors as cruel barbarians, former slaves such as Joseph Pitts explained that they had found things to admire as well as condemn in Algerian society.

---

[47] Jerry Brotton, *This Orient Isle. Elizabethan England and the Islamic World* (2016) 191–7, 202–4.
[48] Brotton, *This Orient Isle*, 281–97.

2

From Capture to Slave Market

In July 1639 the *Mary* of London, outward bound for Providence Island in the West Indies, sighted three ships a dozen miles to leeward. Its master, Mr Boarder, decided to wait and speak to them, a decision hastily reversed when they were identified as Barbary corsairs. The *Mary* and its companions now desperately sought to escape, but by dusk the corsairs had overhauled them. The *Mary*'s company of sixty included many passengers, mainly emigrants, and though it carried only six guns they resolved to fight. During the night their courage ebbed away and they made another attempt to escape, but at dawn the *Mary* was boarded and overrun, with six killed and many wounded. Looking back on this miserable episode William Okeley, one of the passengers, delivered a scathing verdict. Had they taken flight on first sighting the corsairs, they might have escaped. Had they submitted quietly, no lives would have been lost. And having decided to fight, had they fought 'like men of courage', they might, perhaps, have prevailed.[1] Such fatal irresolution was not uncommon. The following year another master, already warned of corsairs lurking in the mouth of the Channel, showed little concern when two ships were sighted far off. Instead of making sail to escape, he remarked complacently that 'it was not the custom of the English to run away at sea', and waited for them to draw nearer. Only when they were close did they raise the colours of Algiers, whereupon he surrendered without any attempt to resist.[2]

Fight, flight, or surrender?

In the face of danger, humans instinctively decide to fight or flee. In this situation, however, neither flight nor fight might be a realistic option. Barbary's men-of-war were built for speed, and few merchant vessels could outrun them. The company of the *Sarah galley*, sailing for Barbados, tried for twenty-four hours to shake off their pursuer, throwing their water-casks and boat overboard to lighten the ship, to no avail. Finally overhauled, they submitted quietly to an assailant with a

---

[1] *Okeley*, 2–4. On the themes of this chapter see also Robert C. Davis, *Christian Slaves, Muslim Masters* (Basingstoke, 2003), chap. 2.
[2] D'Aranda, *History*, 2–5. Only one of the ship's four guns was in working order, making resistance futile.

British Slaves and Barbary Corsairs, 1580–1750. Bernard Capp, Oxford University Press. © Bernard Capp 2022.
DOI: 10.1093/oso/9780192857378.003.0003

heavily armed crew almost ten times larger.[3] It took great courage or rash bravado to defy a well-armed man-of-war with a far larger crew.

Many ships did not realize their danger until it was already too late to escape. It was impossible to determine whether a distant sail was likely to prove friend or foe, and while some masters sought to avoid contact, most recognized that this might deprive them of valuable information about possible dangers ahead. Even when a ship drew near, its identity might remain in doubt. Identifying it as English- or Dutch-built offered little reassurance, for many of Barbary's men-of-war were ships that had been captured and refitted for their new role. And while a ship's colours were supposed to signal its identity, many sailed under false colours. Nathaniel Knott, a veteran mariner, explained in 1634 that it was impossible to identify a Barbary man-of-war by its appearance; only its behaviour would provide reliable clues.[4] Uncertainty could linger even when a ship had been identified as a Barbary man-of-war, for England might have war with Algiers and peace with Tunis, or vice versa, a situation the corsairs regularly exploited. Striking sail and allowing boarders to search for strangers' (i.e. foreigners') goods carried risks, but so did flight, which might suggest its own colours were false or that it was carrying illicit cargo. One former slave described watching anxiously as two ships drew near off the Spanish coast in 1648: 'we were all between hope and fear, as in such cases is usual', he recalled, with sailors disputing whether they were French, Flemings, or corsairs. Drawing closer the ships ran up French colours, but old hands remained suspicious and urged the master to try to reach safety in port. Their advice was ignored by 'our giddy headed skipper', as the narrator dubbed him. At the last moment the ships ran up Barbary colours and poured fifty broadsides into their quarry, overwhelming it, and killing or wounding more than eighty of the 100 passengers and crew.[5]

Such deceptions were among the corsairs' regular tactics. The crew of the *Friendship*, chased for a day and a night in 1657, feared the worst when their pursuer put out a 'Turkish' flag and ran out its guns. It was obviously a Barbary corsair, but from where? They dared not open fire in case it was from Algiers, currently at peace with England. Their pursuers came within hailing distance before identifying themselves as Tunisian and unleashing a devastating broadside and volley of small shot. The *Friendship* fought back, but with only ten guns and ten fit crewmen had no chance of repelling an enemy carrying thirty-five guns and 300 men.[6] The corsairs also employed more subtle deceptions. Salé's corsairs

---

[3] TNA SP 71/16, f.235. The *Sarah*'s crew of sixteen are listed in Nabil Matar, 'British Captives in Salé (1721): a Case Study', in Stefan Hanss and Juliane Schiel, eds., *Mediterranean Slavery Revisited (500–1800)* (Zurich, 2014), 524.

[4] Knott, 'Advice of a Sea-man touching the Expedition', TNA, SP 16/279, fos. 244v-45.

[5] T. S., *Adventures*, 6–11. Naval warships and the corsairs themselves were often unsure about the identity of ships they sighted.

[6] Coxere, *Adventures*, 54.

sometimes pretended to be from Algiers, at peace with England, demand to inspect the master's pass, and then, with the ships lying alongside, overrun their victim. The *William and Mary* of Bristol fell for this subterfuge in 1681. No sooner had the corsairs' lieutenant pronounced its pass legitimate than his men swarmed aboard and seized control. The crew had no chance against 300 Moors.[7] A corsair who came aboard the *Success* swore on oath that he was from Algiers and intended no harm, before revealing his true identity and carrying its master and men to slavery in Salé.[8]

The corsairs employed a wide range of tactics.[9] A master would often allow an inspection, as required by articles of peace with the Barbary regencies, trusting that his pass would protect his ship, cargo, and crew. But the corsairs might then claim his crew were not really British, or perhaps beat them into 'confessing' that their merchandize was foreign-owned, and then take the vessel into Algiers. Richard Haddock of the *Supply*, a former Cromwellian commander, was forced to carry his ship into Algiers in December 1663, and was grilled for hours by the divan. Although he could prove that its lading was English, the corsair *reis* bribed the divan to rule otherwise and declare the entire cargo prize.[10] In the case of the *Blessing*, seized the same month, its master was beaten into 'confessing' that he was really Jewish, and his captors then proposed to sell him to a Jewish slave-owner.[11] Another master was killed by corsairs who then claimed that he and the ship were Spanish, and had both ship and cargo declared prize.[12] Although intimidation and violence were explicitly forbidden in successive treaties, enforcement was a different matter. European consuls in Barbary always expected corsairs to break agreements whenever they could do so with impunity. John Ward criticized one master who had trusted in the protection promised by the treaty, and had allowed his vessel to be searched and carried into Algiers in 1672. It had been strong enough to fight off its attackers, he thought, and should have done so.[13]

Many of the larger merchant ships sailing to the Levant were strongly built, well-armed, and able to repel or deter attacks. One mariner described in 1650 how his company had watched nervously as two Barbary men-of-war approached off the coast of Sardinia: 'they looked on us but they did not like us', he wrote with relief. They had sailed away, and 'we were very joyful'. Anne, Lady Fanshawe, described a similar incident that year. When a powerful galley bore down on the Dutch ship taking her and her husband to Spain, they expected to be captured and enslaved, but when she ventured on deck, dressed as a man, she found that 'the 2 vessels were engaged in parley and so well satisfied with speech and sight of each

[7] Francis Brooks, *Barbarian Cruelty* (1693), 2–7.   [8] *Phelps*, 1–4.
[9] For an account by a former corsair see G. E. Manwaring and W. G. Perrin, eds., *The Life and Works of Sir Henry Mainwaring*, Navy Records Society, 54, 56, (1920–2), ii.23–5.
[10] TNA SP 71/1, fos. 246, 250. Haddock did at least recover his ship.   [11] TNA SP 71/1, f.252.
[12] TNA SP 71/1, f.310.   [13] TNA SP 71/2, f.16.

other's forces that the Turks' man-of-war tacked about and we continued our course.' The Dutch ship was carrying 200 men, sixty guns, and a rich cargo, and the master and crew, fortified with brandy, had been determined to fight.[14] By the later seventeenth century, moreover, many British ships in the Straits sailed in convoys protected by naval escorts.[15] Most corsairs therefore pursued weaker and solitary targets, with small crews and few guns. Facing almost impossible odds, their masters usually surrendered without resistance, to save lives. A list of thirty English prizes brought into Algiers in 1669–70 recorded 348 new captives, so, if we take into account the mariners killed on board the vessels that had fought back, the average crew numbered about twelve. The thirty-nine English ships carried into Salé between 1715 and 1721 had an average crew of only nine.[16] There is a flavour of resignation in the narrative of John Rawlins, master of a small bark with a crew of eight men and a boy. When they encountered five Algerian men-of-war near Gibraltar in 1621, the *reis* commanded him 'to strike his sails and submit to his mercy, which, not to be gainsaid nor prevented, was quickly done'.[17] Many others yielded in a similar spirit of resignation. The *Speedwell*, carrying fish from Newfoundland, had only four fit crewmen when it was overhauled in 1678 and its master submitted quietly, remarking that they would 'probably fare the worse if we continue our flight'.[18] Even much larger ships sometimes yielded without a fight. In 1622, a large Hamburger surrendered tamely to a small Salé man-of-war they had initially thought a harmless fishing-boat. The corsairs had approached warily, circling several times, 'daunted with the vastness of the prize', and fearing a trap. William Atkins and his companions, English passengers on the Hamburger, wanted to resist, and were dismayed to see its crew 'woefully whining and wringing their hands'. When the corsairs finally ventured aboard and met with no resistance, they could hardly believe their good fortune. Atkins recalled how they had 'skipped and danced and clipped and hugged and kissed one another', from relief as well as joy.[19]

Mariners often hoped that if they submitted without resistance the corsairs might be content to seize their cargo, and spare the ship and crew. That was indeed an informal convention, among pirates and corsairs alike, if booty was their main concern. In 1621, the diplomat Sir Thomas Roe found fourteen English ships at Malaga that had been 'taken, rifled and dismissed, because they made no resistance'. By contrast, he added, 'Such as have fought, they have fired and burnt,

---

[14] BL MS Sloane 3494, f.1; John Loftis, ed., *The Memoirs of Anne, Lady Halkett and Ann, Lady Fanshawe* (Oxford, 1979), 127–8.

[15] Sari R. Hornstein, *The Restoration Navy and English Foreign Trade, 1674–1688.* (Aldershot, 1991), 53–96.

[16] TNA SP 71/1, fos. 422-3v; Matir, 'British Captives', 523–8.   [17] *Rawlins*, sig. A4v.

[18] *Pitts*, 2–3.

[19] Martin Murphy, ed., 'William Atkins, A Relation of the Journey from St Omers to Seville, 1622', in *Camden Miscellany*, 32 (1994), 231–3.

men and all, taking none to mercy'.[20] The corsairs might judge it a sensible trade-off to free sailors who had submitted without a fight, which would leave their own man-of-war able to continue undamaged and with a full complement. When five men-of-war attacked the *Dolphin* in 1617, the corsairs promised that if it submitted they would treat the crew well and seize only part of its cargo.[21] Many sailors facing the prospect of imminent death or enslavement would be tempted by such an offer, and a master eager to fight might discover his crew unwilling to throw away their lives. Samuel Harres described in 1610 that when his ship encountered two Tripoli men-of-war, the master 'demanded of us what we were willing to do. The most part of us would have fought', he went on, 'but some would not, for fear we should be made slaves; so the master commanded to strike our sails'.[22] In desperate situations such collective decision-making was not uncommon. On this occasion, mercy had not been forthcoming. An informal convention was far from a guarantee, with promises often disregarded, and it declined over time. James Frizzell, consul in Algiers, reported with disgust in 1630 that when British ships were seized, the men were enslaved 'fight or no fight'—that is, regardless of whether or not they had resisted.[23] Even so, Parliament believed that many crews yielded tamely and unnecessarily, and in some cases with a degree of complicity. In 1664 a new statute made it an offence to surrender to corsairs without resisting, if the vessel was of at least 200 tons and carried sixteen guns. A master proved to have done so would be barred from ever commanding another ship, while his men would forfeit their wages and face up to six months' imprisonment.[24]

As larger ships became more heavily armed, corsairs increasingly targeted smaller vessels with less valuable cargoes, and seamen themselves became the main prize. In some circumstances, however, the corsairs might still spare men if their own ship was overcrowded or short of victuals and water. The corsairs who captured the *George Bonaventure* in November 1621 set a dozen of its company ashore 'to try their fortunes in an unknown country'.[25] In other cases, they had insufficient competent seamen to install a prize-crew to carry a vessel home. The corsairs who seized the *Faulcon* off the Portuguese coast plundered its cargo, tackle, and rigging, and then abandoned it to its fate. The crippled vessel was soon driven ashore, but the crew had at least escaped with their lives and their freedom.[26]

---

[20] Henry Blount, *A Voyage into the Levant* (1636), 74; *The Negotiations of Sir Thomas Roe* (1740), 4; C. M. Senior, *A Nation of Pirates. English Piracy in its Heyday* (Newton Abbot, 1976), 22–4.

[21] *A Fight at Sea, Famously fought by the Dolphin of London* (1617), sig. Bv.

[22] Daniel J. Vitkus, ed., *Piracy, Slavery, and Redemption* (New York, 2001), 347.

[23] *Newes from Sea of two notorious Pyrats* (1609), sig. D3-4; TNA SP 71/1, f.97; cf. Blount, *Voyage*, 74.

[24] 'An Act to prevent the delivering up of Merchants ships', in J. Raithby, ed., *Statutes of the Realm*, v, *1628–80* (1819), 521–2.

[25] *Rawlins*, sig. A4v.   [26] Harris, *Trinity House*, 54.

Attempts to escape by guile rarely succeeded. The 40-ton *Success*, pursued off the coast of Portugal in October 1684, carried only a single gun, so resistance was not an option. Instead, the master, Thomas Phelps, sought to escape by cunning. When the corsairs' boat came alongside, his sailors give three shouts as if they were about to open fire. Surprised and alarmed, the boat-crew backed off, whereupon Phelps clapped on all sails and made away. The corsairs overhauled him again, and sent their boat a second time. And a second time, Phelps sailed away while the boat was crossing. There was no third escape; the corsairs threatened to sink the *Success* if Phelps refused to yield.[27] The *Marigold*, overhauled in 1620, owed its lucky escape simply to chance. It had two lions on board, gifts from Algiers to James I, and the corsairs realized that taking it prize in such circumstances would invite trouble.[28]

Sailors knew that resistance, especially against the odds, would almost certainly carry a heavy price. When the *Experiment* was overhauled by a Tetuan man-of-war in 1720, its master assembled his crew of sixteen and urged them to fight against a far more powerful assailant. They did so, firing a broadside and killing thirteen Moors before being forced to submit. Furious at their futile defiance, the corsairs threatened to have the master executed as soon as they returned to port. Though his life was in fact spared, the crew were all punished by being bastinadoed.[29] Resistance was a more realistic option for vessels with a larger crew and more guns. Ships built for the Levant trade were strong, well-manned, and well-armed, and often proved ready to defend themselves. Some crews were prepared to fight even against impossible odds, opting for death and glory. When the *Three Half Moons* was surrounded by eight Ottoman galleys near the Straits of Gibraltar in 1563, a force that may have numbered more than 1,000, officers urged the thirty-eight crewmen 'to show their manhood' and prove that 'God was their God and not their enemy's'. Brandishing his sword and shield, the master breathed defiance. The mariners sounded their drums and trumpets, fired guns, and rained arrows on the enemy with lethal effect, though against such odds there could be only one outcome.[30] Similarly, Edward Webbe recalled how he and shipmates had resisted fifty Ottoman galleys in the eastern Mediterranean in the mid-1570s. Only ten of the sixty mariners survived.[31]

Many masters had little if any experience of combat, and they could badly misjudge the situation. When the *Mary Marten* was intercepted by two Algerian galleys in July 1580, its gunner was allowed to exhaust most of the ship's powder

---

[27] *Phelps*, 1–4.

[28] Francis Cartwright, *The Life, Confession, and Heartie Repentance of Francis Cartwright, Gentleman* (1621), sig. C2v.

[29] *A Description of the Nature of Slavery among the Moors* (1721), 2–4.

[30] 'The Worthy Enterprise of John Fox', in Richard Hakluyt, *The Principal Navigations* (1599–1600), Part II, 131–2.

[31] Edward Webbe, *The Rare and most wonderfull things which Edw. Webbe an Englishman borne, hath seene* (1590), sig. B-v.

and shot before the enemy was even within range. When the galleys came alongside, pouring great shot and musket-fire into their ship, the crew fought on bravely until they were overwhelmed and the ship was sinking. Most drowned, along with numerous corsairs who had swarmed aboard, intent on plunder.[32] Instances of such brave but futile resistance occur throughout the period. In December 1622 the *Jacob* of Bristol fought on until it foundered, with only two survivors, while the ill-named *Delight* went down with all hands after a desperate fight against three Barbary men-of-war.[33] William Agle, captured in 1632, told his wife in a tearful letter that his men had fought for many hours, yielding only when their ship was ablaze.[34] Another crew held off two Algerian men-of-war for several hours in 1648, killing 300 of their assailants and yielding only after four-fifths of their own number had been killed or wounded.[35] In another striking case, a company fought off a Salé man-of-war, killing thirty of its crew, until they ran out of powder. Challenged by the victorious *reis* why he had persisted in such a futile action, the master allegedly retorted that 'he would have killed all the rest, and him too, if he had had powder; with that the pirate cut him down with his cutlass, and ripped him open, and said, there was an end of a dog, and threw his murdered body into the sea'.[36]

Several incidents make it clear that some mariners, albeit a minority, preferred to die rather than endure slavery, and behaved with literally suicidal defiance. In 1674 the masters of two ships captured by a Salé man-of-war blew up their own armouries, killing most of the sixty Moors of the prize-crews, as well as most of their own men. In revenge, the Moors killed several of the English survivors, leaving only four men and two boys to be carried to Algiers and sold.[37] The defiance of the *Little James* in 1632 ended in similar carnage. Although forced to surrender, it was blown up by one of its own company, taking with it a rich cargo, twenty-three English seamen, and the prize-crew of sixteen.[38] Joshua Gee, a slave serving on an Algerian man-of-war, described another huge explosion on board a French prize they had just taken, with only three of its sailors surviving. It later emerged that the crew had blown up their ship in an attempt to destroy both vessels, 'on purpose that we might perish rather than they would be slaves'.[39] Such episodes underline the horror with which contemporaries viewed enslavement in Barbary.

Resistance, however, was by no means always futile. A well-armed ship with a determined commander and crew might eventually repel boarders and drive away

---

[32] *Hasleton*, sig. A4-v.   [33] Harris, *Trinity House*, 54, 56; *Negotiations of Roe*, 4.
[34] TNA SP 71/1, f.117.   [35] T. S., *Adventures*, 2–5.   [36] Brooks, *Barbarian Cruelty*, 24–6.
[37] TNA SP 71/2, f.35. They were ransomed by the consul, Samuel Martin, without being sent to market.
[38] TNA SP 71/1, f.115. The saboteur, one Betsome, had formerly been a renegade in Algiers.
[39] Joshua Gee, *Narrative of Joshua Gee of Boston, Mass., when he was captive in Algeria of the Barbary pirates, 1680–1687*, ed. Albert C. Bates (Hartford, Conn., 1945), 24; Brooks, *Barbarian Cruelty*, pp. xviii–xix; Peter Earle, *Corsairs of Malta and Barbary* (1970), 62.

assailants. Several such episodes were celebrated in print, with authors urging all mariners to place their trust in God and show similar courage. In 1615 two small ships, together carrying only fifty-six men and boys, drove away six Tunisian war-galleys with 1,800 men, inflicting heavy casualties.[40] Similarly, when the *Dolphin*, homeward-bound from Zante in 1617, was attacked by five Barbary men-of-war, its master, Edward Nichols, refused to surrender. According to a published account, he had urged his men to fight for their honour as Englishmen, crying 'let us prefer a noble death before slavish life'. Aware that in such circumstances sailors did not automatically obey orders, he also promised to cover the medical care and maintenance of those wounded or incapacitated. The largest of the assailants carried twenty-five to thirty-five guns each, with the force comprising in all roughly 1,500 men. Despite being boarded and set on fire, the *Dolphin* fought on, and the attackers eventually withdrew when it appeared about to sink. The success came at a heavy price, with eleven of the thirty-eight crewmen killed or dying of their wounds, and several others badly injured. Two pamphlet accounts described the action. *A Fight at Sea*—a jingoistic text—boasted that the encounter 'showed the noble worth and brave resolution of our English nation'. The company had preferred to die rather than yield, it declared, 'as it is still the nature and constitution of all Englishmen'. A more sober account appeared the same year, dedicated by the master to Prince Charles, and including verses by John Taylor the water-poet. Both texts revealed that three of the corsair commanders were notorious English renegades, Walsingham, Kelley, and Sampson, which cast a very different light on the 'noble worth' of all Englishmen.[41] Taylor reported later that Prince Charles had visited the ship on its return to England, to commend its brave crew.[42]

Well attuned to popular taste, John Taylor published accounts of several similar episodes. One told how the *George and Elizabeth* had been attacked by nine large men-of-war neat Tetuan in 1635. Although their Admiral carried forty guns, and the *George and Elizabeth* was outnumbered 60:1 in manpower and 10:1 in ordnance, it had fought back; and despite being boarded six times, beat off its assailants.[43] Another account recorded an attack in 1640 on the *Elizabeth* of Plymouth, homeward bound from Virginia, by three Barbary men-of-war in the mouth of the Channel. Only five of its ten guns could be used, but the master, 'a man of an excellent and invincible spirit', resolved 'with Christian courage to fight it out so long as his life lasted'. Battle raged for around eight hours. The *Elizabeth* was boarded three times, the round-house and mainsail were fired, and the

---

[40] Henry Robarts, *A True Relation of a most notable and worthy Fight* (1616); cf. *CSPVen.*, 1632–6, 128.

[41] *A Fight at Sea … by the Dolphin*, title-page, sig. A3v, Bv; John Taylor, *The Dolphins Danger: and Deliuerance* (1617).

[42] John Taylor, *A Brave Memorable and Dangerovs Sea-fight* (1636), 15.

[43] Taylor, *Brave … Sea-fight*, 1–10.

master, mate, pilot, and quartermaster were killed. But each time the boarders were repelled, and Taylor represents the crew as undaunted. When the hogs carried on board were also killed, the mariners raised the carcases to show the Muslim corsairs, 'in a merry or jeering way, to invite them to come aboard of their ship to eat some pork'. He boasted that the baffled corsairs had eventually 'slunk away making their moans to Mahomet'. Taylor's account, though heavily propagandist, drew on a lengthy examination of the gunner by the mayor of Plymouth, taken two days after the action and forwarded to the Privy Council. Taylor had evidently been given access, and printed it as an appendix, giving his pamphlet a semi-official character. The funerals of the master and mate at Plymouth were accompanied by sermons, no doubt also full of patriotic and religious sentiment.[44] The public and the seafaring community were both hungry for morale-boosting news.

Printed accounts of such episodes disappeared in the second half of the century, with attention now focused instead on the exploits of brave naval commanders. Similar acts of heroic defiance continued, however, throughout the period. The *Lisbon Merchant*, attacked in 1670, fought on with success even after the death of its master. In another encounter that year, mariners killed sixty corsairs in fierce hand-to-hand fighting, though their own ship was so badly damaged that it later sank.[45] Another master, who had repelled an attack by Canary, the Admiral of Algiers, was awarded a medal and gold chain by James II.[46] Corsairs wanted easy pickings, not bitterly fought actions against well-armed merchantmen. If a large and powerful vessel refused to surrender, they might withdraw rather than risk serious damage and heavy casualties. Salé's men-of-war, smaller and lighter than the best of Algiers, could not withstand heavy broadsides, and were likely to retreat if faced with determined resistance. Thomas Phelps, a shipmaster and former captive, claimed that 'no Salé man will fight a ship of ten guns', and urged mariners always to resist if there was any chance of success.[47]

Not all the British slaves in Barbary had been captured at sea. Some had been seized while in port, like the company of the *Jesus* at Tripoli in 1584, or the crews of four English ships at Larache and Salé in 1607. Forced to unload their ordnance, they were made to serve Muley Sheck, king of Fez, as gunners in the civil war then raging. The liberty they were promised meant little. Forty-five of the seventy-two, including two of the captains, were killed in battle, and their bodies were left to be eaten by dogs.[48]

---

[44] John Taylor, *A Valorous and Perillous Sea-fight, Fought with three Turkish Ships* (1640).

[45] *CSPD 1670*, 186, 374; cf. *CSPD 1675–6*, 506; *CSPD 1678*, 56; *CSPD 1686–7*, 144; Gee, *Narrative*, 17–18.

[46] *Calendar of Treasury Books, 1685–9*, 308. Thomas Grantham's exploit had been in 1678, when he was master of the *Concord*.

[47] Phelps, 5.   [48] *The Fierce and cruel Battaile fought by the three Kings in Barbarie* (1607), 1–9.

From the 1620s to the 1640s there were also captives of a very different kind. When corsairs ventured into northern waters they sometimes landed raiding parties ashore in Cornwall, Devon, and southern Ireland, and seized men, women, and children in their homes, even in their beds. In the summer of 1625, thirty men-of-war ranged around the Cornish coast and the Bristol Channel, seizing small vessels and raiding ashore. An attack on a church at Mount's Bay saw sixty captives carried away.[49] Women—who attracted higher ransoms than ordinary seamen—were often the main targets.[50] The most notorious episode was a night-time raid in 1631 on Baltimore, in southern Ireland, by Algerian corsairs led by a Dutch renegade. The raiders carried away eighty-nine women and children and twenty men, mostly English settlers and their servants.[51] A few years later about fifty victims were seized in a raid on neighbouring Dungarvon.[52] Corsairs raiding along the Cornish coast near Fowey in 1645 were reported to have seized 240 men, women, and children, among them several gentlewomen.[53] Raids of this kind were common throughout the Mediterranean, and captives seized on the coast of Italy, or by Christian corsairs operating in the Aegean and Levant, might often be ransomed by relatives within a few days and released.[54] There is no record of any such swift redemption for the British and Irish victims. The Baltimore women were to face years of captivity in Barbary, and few ever returned home.

After the Restoration, the slave population came to include another new category. The British occupation of Tangier (1662–84), which had been ceded by Portugal, saw frequent clashes between the garrison and Moroccan forces, and soldiers taken captive might be enslaved, along with deserters. Some fifty-three were captured and enslaved during the two-month siege in spring 1680, including the commander of the Henrietta fort. The following year the number stood at about seventy.[55] And long after Tangier had been abandoned, seamen ship-wrecked off the coast of Morocco were also likely to be seized and enslaved if they survived and struggled ashore.[56]

---

[49] *CSPD 1625–6*, 86, 89;.*CSPVen. 1625–6*, 30, 157.

[50] *CSPD 1636–7*, 140–1; TNA SP 16/332, f.46.

[51] Des Ekin, *The Stolen Village. Baltimore and the Barbary Pirates* (Dublin, 2006).

[52] Mark Empey, ed., 'The Diary of Sir James Ware, 1623-66', *Analecta Hibernica*, 45 (2014), 101; *CSPVen. 1636–9*, 73.

[53] Nabil Matar, *Britain and Barbary, 1589–1689* (Gainesville, FL, 2005), 94; *CSPVen, 1643–5*, 209.

[54] Davis, *Christian Slaves, Muslim Masters*, 33–45; W. Hacke, *A Collection of Original Voyages* (1699), Part IV, 8–11.

[55] *An Exact Journal of the Siege of Tangier* (1680), 13; Linda Colley, *Captives. Britain, Empire and the World, 1600-1850* (2002), 23–41, esp. 37–40; P. G. Rogers, *A History of Anglo-Moroccan Relations to 1900* (1977), 55.

[56] Rogers, *History*, 92, 107–9, 113–14.

The first taste of captivity

Joseph Pitts began his narrative by recalling how one day in 1678 a man-of-war had borne down on his fishing boat, the *Speedwell,* off the coast of Spain. With only four of the company fit, resistance would have been futile. Pitts, a youngster in his mid-teens, watched in terror as a party of 'monstrous, ravenous creatures' clambered on board. 'O master!', he cried, 'I am afraid they will kill us and eat us'. The master explained that they faced a very different fate, but the corsairs' next actions offered little comfort. 'The very first words they spoke,' Pitts recalled, 'and the first thing they did, was beating us with ropes, saying, "Into boat, you English dogs!"'[57]

The corsairs had immediately set out to break the spirit of their new captives, as was their custom. One aim was to make them reveal any valuables hidden aboard or about their persons, and discover if any belonged to wealthy families. Pitts recalled how he and his shipmates had been 'tumbled' ignominiously into the corsairs' boat, and that once aboard their man-of-war, 'diligent search was made about us for money'. They were then clapped in irons in the hold, where they remained for several weeks, unable to stand and with only 'a small quantity of black biscuit and a pint of water a day'. As intended, this treatment left them weak, psychologically cowed, and 'almost weary of our lives'.[58] Pitts' experience was shared by countless others. Another captive recalled how the corsairs had smashed open and plundered the sailors' sea-chests, and new captives were commonly stripped and kept in irons in the hold.[59] Edward Coxere described being dropped into it head-first.[60] Richard Hasleton, after being stripped, was carried before the *reis*, who suspected he was a merchant, not a common seaman. When he refused to admit this, he recalled, the corsair 'gave me fifteen strokes with a cudgel' and had him thrown in the hold. The master of the *John* fared worse; the *reis* had him tied to the mainmast, along with a passenger, and whipped until they revealed whatever valuables might be concealed on board.[61] Abraham Browne, an American merchant captured in 1655, described how the corsairs had fallen on the captives 'more like ravenous beasts than men...stripping of us all stark naked', even the wounded.[62] Capture was always a traumatic experience.

Officers, merchants, and passengers sometimes attempted to conceal their identities and pass themselves off as ordinary seamen, in the hope of avoiding a steep ransom demand. Men usually proud of their status might now be willing to throw their fine clothes into the sea before the prize-crew arrived, and beg the

---

[57] *Pitts,* 3–4.   [58] *Pitts,* 4–6; cf. Gee, *Narrative,* 15–16.
[59] T. S., *Adventures,* 13–14; *Phelps,* 4, 6.   [60] Coxere, *Adventures,* 55.
[61] *Hasleton,* sig. A4v; Adam Elliot, *A Modest Vindication of Titus Oates* (1682), 3.
[62] Stephen T. Riley, ed., 'Abraham Browne's Captivity by the Barbary Pirates, 1655', *Colonial Society of Massachusetts,* 52 (1979), 37–8; Giles Milton, *White Gold* (2004), 59, 61.

company not to divulge their true identity.[63] Edward Coxere recalled asking the ship's master not to reveal his position as mate, or the fact that they were brothers-in-law, so the corsairs 'might have the less esteem of me to set the less ransom on me'. He was dismayed when the master did reveal these facts, claiming that they would have been impossible to conceal.[64] Abraham Browne also concealed his identity, and was helped by older slaves on board the man-of-war, who advised him and his companions on 'what to say and do'. Sadly, one of the new captives, a Dutch carpenter, eventually betrayed him.[65] T.S., a wealthy young merchant known only by his initials, also devised a new identity before the corsairs arrived on board. Unlike Coxere, he could not pass as an ordinary sailor, for his speech, hands, and clothes would instantly give him away, so he asked the mariners to say he was only a servant, and that the cargo belonged to his master. The new captives were closely examined, and English renegades on the man-of-war doubted his story. When the corsairs returned to Algiers, T.S. now claimed to be a cook, hoping to escape being sent to the galleys or put to hard labour. This ruse proved more successful, though not for long; working in the pasha's kitchen, his culinary disasters earned him a beating and expulsion.[66] Robert Adams, a youthful captive at Salé, also 'pleaded poverty' until a ship's boy, perhaps currying favour, revealed that his father was very rich, whereupon his owners promptly demanded a huge ransom.[67] Adam Elliot, a young Cambridge graduate, had a similar experience. He too could never have passed for an ordinary seaman, but he was dismayed when one of the ship's boys reported that he was related to Lord Henry Howard, a close kinsman of the duke of Norfolk. He was bought by a Moor who naturally now anticipated a large ransom. Elliot initially denied the boy's story, earning himself a savage beating, but then took the gamble of playing along with this false identity, in the hope of finding some way to exploit it—as he eventually did.[68]

Such attempts at subterfuge occurred wherever slaves were held for ransom, for ransoms were set according to status. John Smith reported similar practices in the slave markets of the Caucasus: 'the better they find you, the worse they will use you...therefore many great persons have endured much misery to conceal themselves, because their ransoms are so intolerable'.[69] Well aware of such practices, owners did their best to foil them, sometimes setting another slave as a spy to trick a new captive into revealing his real identity.[70] But deceptions might sometimes succeed. When Ellis Veryard, a physician and traveller, was captured by a Tripoli man-of-war, he wrapped his money in pitch, pushed it to the front of his old shoes, and pretended to be the servant of a French passenger, who

[63] Davis, *Christian Slaves*, 51–2; Earle, *Corsairs*, 60; Gillian L Weiss, *Captives and Corsairs. France and Slavery in the Early Modern Mediterranean* (Stanford, CA, 2011), 18.
[64] Coxere, *Adventures*, 57.   [65] Riley, ed., 'Abraham Browne's Captivity', 39, 41.
[66] T. S., *Adventures*, 14.   [67] Vitkus, *Piracy*, 349.   [68] Elliot, *Modest Vindication*, 7–9.
[69] John Smith, *The True Travels, Adventures, and Observations of Captaine Iohn Smith* (1630), 30.
[70] Laurent D'Arvieux, *Memoires du Chavalier D'Arvieux* (Paris, 1735), iv.7.

connived in the story. France and Tripoli enjoyed good relations at the time, and they were both soon freed. This was Veryard's second stroke of luck. Earlier on his travels he had been captured by Algerian corsairs, only to be liberated within days when other captives staged a successful mutiny.[71] Emanuel D'Aranda and his friends—Flemish military officers captured on board an English ship in 1640— also concealed their true identities, giving false names. Their deception was never exposed.[72] The story of Elizabeth Marsh, captured in 1756, offers perhaps the boldest example of successful deception. She agreed to pretend to be the sister and then the wife of a fellow passenger, in the hope that this would afford some protection and help her avoid the seraglio. She was closely questioned by the acting sultan, Sidi Muhammed, who appears to have doubted her story and tried to entice her to enter the seraglio voluntarily. Luckily for her, he did not force the issue. Marsh and her companions, though captives, were never enslaved, and were held to provide Sidi Muhammed with leverage in a dispute with the British government. Released after a few months, without the payment of any ransoms, they were far more fortunate than most.[73]

The harsh treatment meted out to new captives had a second and equally important objective: to deter any thought of resistance before they were landed in Barbary. Desperate and with little to lose, many dreamed of rising against their captors. Keeping them shackled and half-starved served to render them powerless, physically weakened, and often broken in spirit. Adam Elliot and his companions languished for forty days in a stinking and ever more crowded hold. He recalled some shipmates weeping in despair, and gloating captors spitting in their faces to humiliate and demoralize them further. They were occasionally allowed on deck, briefly, to breathe fresh air and wash, and on one occasion they were put to the oars in pursuit of a prize. But once it was overhauled they were returned to the hold under guard to ensure there was no opportunity for resistance.[74] William Atkins and his companions—Catholic seminary students captured on their way to Spain in 1622—endured similar conditions, lying 'in the keel of the boat upon stones wherewith it was ballasted'.[75] The corsairs were right to take seriously the possibility of resistance. Over the course of a cruise, captives might come to equal the number of soldiers on board a small man-of-war. In such circumstances, as we will see, resistance became ever more tempting.[76]

Slave narratives often reveal the psychological as well as physical trauma of capture. Browne and his companions had been stripped naked, flogged, and

---

[71] Ellis Veryard, *An Account of Divers Choice Remarks, as well Geographical as Historical* (1701), 236, 285–6. These events had occurred in the 1680s.

[72] D'Aranda, *History*, 8–9, 20.

[73] Mrs Crisp, *The Female Captive* (1769); Linda Colley, *The Ordeal of Elizabeth Marsh* (New York, 2008), chap. 2.

[74] Elliot, *Modest Vindication*, 3–5.   [75] Murphy, ed., *William Atkins*, 234.

[76] See Chapter 5.

thrown into the hold, and he admitted later that he had been 'overwhelmed with sorrow' and longed to die.[77] Atkins and James Wadsworth, a fellow captive, both describe how on two successive nights a corsair 'inflamed with raging lust' had come down, blown out the light, and attempted to sodomize 'two of the youngest and fairest amongst us'. The youngsters had resisted, but they and their companions dared not report the assault, knowing they would not be believed and fearing they would simply receive another beating.[78] Few captives recalled any trace of pity from their captors. In one rare exception, an English renegade told a new captive, as he stripped him of his money, 'Have patience, brother, this is the chance of war; today for you, and tomorrow for me'. Possibly he too had once been captured and enslaved, and he would certainly know that a corsair's own life was always fraught with danger.[79] T.S. claimed that after a bloody fight lasting several hours his captors had praised the courage of the vanquished. If true, that was a very unusual response, for resistance usually brought harsh retribution. The ship was a very rich prize, and the corsairs' delight possibly explains their good humour. While they remained at sea, the captives received the same simple fare as their captors, and T.S. conceded that 'we were as civilly treated as we could expect from Turks'. Civility was relative, of course. He and his companions had been stripped of their clothes, which, he added sardonically, 'some lusty rogues did us the kindness to wear for our sakes before our eyes'. The dead and badly wounded had been stripped and thrown overboard 'to feed the sharks'. And any trace of civility vanished once they were brought ashore in Algiers.[80]

The slave market

Corsairs generally returned to their home port after cruising for six to eight weeks. Within a day or two the new captives would then be driven in chains to the house of the pasha (or later the dey), who had the right to claim one in eight for himself, without payment. Emanuel D'Aranda remembered the pasha of Algiers presiding over the ritual on a seat draped with blue satin, clad in a gown of red silk and holding a fan-shaped plume of ostrich feathers, a symbol of authority.[81] T.S., in a similar account, described the 'king' clad in green, with a diamond set into his huge turban, seated under a canopy while his attendants and the captains remained standing. The pasha had scrutinized the slaves closely, making a jest about each to amuse the company. As his personal tribute he chose the ship's master, likely to furnish a good ransom, a 'pretty German boy' whose good looks

[77] Riley, ed., 'Abraham Browne's Captivity', 37–8.
[78] Murphy, ed., *William Atkins*, 235–8; James Wadsworth, *The English Spanish Pilgrime* (1629), 37–8.
[79] D'Aranda, *History*, 5.   [80] T. S., *Adventures*, 12–14.
[81] D'Aranda, *History*, 7. Some accounts said one in ten.

compensated for his humble origin, and T.S. himself, young, handsome, and plainly no common sailor. Several officials had come on board the man-of-war before they were taken ashore, including a friendly Cornish renegade, who offered to spare them the ordeal of the slave market. If they gave him details of their families and estates, he promised, he would buy them himself. They initially agreed, only to draw back when they realized he was a slave-trader simply attempting to forestall the market. So T.S. and his companions were led through the streets, shackled in heavy chains, and found their fierce resistance at sea now held against them. Many corsairs had been killed in the action, and their angry relations hurled abuse and threats. T.S. claimed that one had attacked a captive with a knife, hacked off part of his cheek, and eaten it—though this may well be one of the points where his editor had embellished the narrative.[82] Richard Head, in a wholly fictional account, has the protagonist tell how he and his companions had been led in chains through the streets of Salé, and 'as as we passed along, we had our heads washed with women's rose-water [urine], thrown down upon us from balconies, with other filth, in derision and contempt of the name of Christian'.[83] While that detail might also be a colourful invention to demonstrate the barbarism of the Moors, most accounts describe abuse and contempt.

Those captives not claimed by the ruler were taken to the *battistan,* or slave market, on the next market-day, to be paraded by specialist dealers, inspected, and auctioned. At Salé, Abraham Browne and his companions had been kept for a week in the notorious dungeons *(matamores)*, brought up each day to be inspected and assessed by prospective buyers. Older slaves, held at night in the same dungeon, told them about the leading slave-owners and their reputations, though of course they could make no use of this information. They were, at least, well fed during this brief interval, to make them appear healthy on market day and fetch a better price.[84] There was much hard bargaining and, like slave auctions in the Americas, the market furthered the process of breaking and dehumanizing the captives. Many narrators employed animal imagery to underline how the proceedings had stripped them of all human dignity. Adam Elliot recalled how he and his companions had been driven into Salé 'like a drove of sheep', amidst the 'horrid barbarous shouts' of hundreds of 'idle rascally people and roguish boys'. Another author incorporated the experience into his title, part of which told readers that the captives had been 'brought and sold like Beasts at Publick Market'.[85]

William Okeley, sold at Algiers in 1639, provides the fullest English description of such an event. He and his companions were also 'driven like beasts' to the market, and found only a little comfort in the reflection 'that it was not to the

---

[82] T. S., *Adventures,* 15–28.   [83] Richard Head, *The English Rogue* (1666), Part 3, 78.
[84] Riley, ed., 'Abraham Browne's Captivity', 39–40.
[85] Elliot, *Modest Vindication,* 6; *A Description of the Nature of Slavery.*

slaughterhouse to be butchered'. Prospective buyers, 'loath to buy a pig in a poke', had then tried to gauge their age by examining their teeth. A 'good, strong entire set of grinders will advance the price considerably', Okeley explained, for their future diet would be coarse fare, and only those with sound teeth would be able to eat and remain strong enough to work. Their limbs were then examined for 'anything analogical to spavin or ringbone'—bone diseases affecting horses. Okeley was employing animal references again to underline their degrading treatment. Their hands were studied too. Calloused and brawny hands would indicate a man used to heavy labour, but 'delicate and tender' hands were still more prized, for they suggested a 'gentleman or merchant, and then the hopes of a good price of redemption makes him saleable'. Once the slaves were sold they were 'trotted' back to the pasha's house, where he had the right to buy any of them for himself at the market price.[86]

Other narrators used similar imagery, in accounts of the Constantinople as well as Maghreb markets.[87] Thus John Rawlins recalled how soldiers at Algiers had 'hurried us, like dogs, into the market, where, as men sell hackneys in England, we were tossed up and down to see who would give most for us'. Prospective buyers prodded them, tested their arms and muscles, inspected the asking prices written on their chests, and haggled over the deal.[88] Joseph Pitts remembered the market thronged with idle onlookers as well as buyers, while the vendors hawked their wares: 'Behold what a strong man this is! What limbs he has! He is fit for any work. And see what a pretty boy this is! No doubt his parents are very rich and able to redeem him with a great ransom'.[89] Another mariner recalled being among 130 new captives exposed for sale like cattle or horses at Meknes, in Morocco, in 1720; 'stripped naked as we were born, we were to stand, with every part of our bodies open' to be viewed and handled in arms, legs, backs, and even 'our very privities'.[90] James Deane, sold at Algiers, described how he and his companions had been 'led about the market, one by one, by a negro', who cried up their fine qualities: 'Here is a brave Captain, a mate, a merchant &c, one has bid so much, who bids more?'[91] Abraham Browne was still suffering from wounds inflicted when his ship was captured, and was not expected to fetch more than £15—only half the usual price of an ordinary seaman. A shipmate revealed that Browne was in fact a merchant, whereupon his value immediately soared to £75. Browne, a canny man, described later how he had tried to stop it rising still further: 'I made my self worse than I was for some time, as they led me I pretended I could not go

---

[86] Okeley, 8–11.

[87] For Constantinople see Sir William Foster, ed., The Travels of John Sanderson in the Levant, 1584–1602, Hakluyt Society, Second Series, 67 (1931), 78; Henry Marsh, A New Survey of the Turkish Empire and Government (1663), 54.

[88] Rawlins, sig. B2-v; cf. TNA SP 71/1, f.150.   [89] Pitts, 8–9.

[90] A Description of the Nature of Slavery, 5–6.

[91] Wiliam Okeley, Eben-ezer...with a Further Narrative of James Deane and others (1684), 92–3.

and did often sit down'. Without this performance of apparent decrepitude, he claimed, his market price would have reached £150, pushing the probable ransom figure still higher.[92]

Ship's boys, many in their mid-teens or younger, were often separated after being brought ashore. Some were claimed by the ruler, or gifted by him to favoured officials. Those sold at market fetched higher prices than ordinary seamen. The two boys sold alongside Browne and his companions fetched £40 each.[93] Youngsters were seen as more malleable than adults, and were prized as servants. In some cases their valuation also had, or was suspected to have, a sexual dimension. When some new captives were paraded before the sultan Moulay Ismail at Meknes in 1720, he chose to keep two 'very handsome lads', both aged about 17, for himself. Their shipmates assumed it was to serve his 'own brutish lusts'. Whatever the truth, they were permanently lost to their companions, and never ransomed.[94]

Women not claimed by the ruler were sold in a slightly different fashion, though no surviving account refers specifically to Britons. The traveller George Sandys reported that at Constantinople, attractive young women were displayed in their finest attire. Once a price was agreed, they would be taken to a private room for the buyer to conduct a bodily examination before the deal was concluded. At Cairo, Pitts reported, women and girls were veiled, but in private buyers could view their faces, inspect their teeth, feel their breasts, and sometimes, he was informed, even check they were virgins. The market at Algiers appears to have provided at least a modicum of privacy for the women being sold.[95]

The public auction was not, however, the end of the sale process. Contemporaries often referred to the 'first sale' and the 'first market price'. This was the sum that would be paid to the corsair captors, and the *armadors* who had funded their expedition. The final sale took place a day or two later in a different location, the pasha's palace or courtyard. The pasha (or the dey) had the option to buy any more of the slaves at the same price they had fetched at the auction. The remainder then became the subjects of a second round of bargaining, and were often sold for a price considerably higher than in the first round. The difference was paid, in cash, to the city's treasury.[96]

We turn next to explore the conditions of a life in slavery.

---

[92] Riley, ed., 'Abraham Browne's Captivity', 41.

[93] Riley, ed., 'Abraham Browne's Captivity', 41.

[94] *Description of the Nature of Slavery*, 5–6. The young men, James Richards and Henry Negus, are absent from the list of shipmates on the *Expedition*: ibid., 19.

[95] George Sandys, *A Relation of a Iourney begun An. Dom. 1610* (1632), 69–70; Pitts, 106; Earle, *Corsairs*, 78.

[96] Philémon de la Motte, 'A Voyage to Barbary for the Redemption of Captives', in *Several Voyages to Barbary* (1736), 42–4; Joseph Morgan, *A Compleat History of the Piratical States of Barbary* (1750), 222; Davis, *Christian Slaves, Muslim Masters*, 64–5.

3

The Experience of Slavery

John Rawlins found slavery 'insufferable and more than flesh and blood can endure'. Even death would be preferable, he declared, for suffering endless abuse and indignities was to be 'continually a-dying'. Francis Brooks gave his account of enslavement in Morocco the emotive title *Barbarian Cruelty*—a title also adopted several decades later by another writer.[1] But John Braithwaite, an official writing in 1729, insisted that even in Moulay Ismail's Morocco, conditions had been 'not near so bad as was represented'. Several scholars have argued that negative accounts merely reflected and reinforced traditional stereotypes. In reality, they tell us, slaves were generally well treated, and one has dismissed accounts of abuse as 'hysteria', not 'history'. Sir Godfrey Fisher suggested, like Braithwaite before him, that Christians may have been 'actually better off as slaves than as free men in their own land'.[2] This chapter revisits and seeks to make sense of these wildly contradictory assessments. How far can we recover the shape of captives' lives?

The diversity of slave conditions

The accounts left by former slaves demonstrate that there was in fact no 'typical' experience of captivity in Barbary.[3] They reveal, instead, a pattern of diversity and mutability that reflected the interplay of several key variables, social and economic status foremost among them. Captives identified as officers, merchants, or passengers might fare reasonably well if they were willing to co-operate over ransom demands. Ordinary seamen, whose families could never hope to redeem them, fared significantly worse.[4]

Shipmasters, merchants, and wealthy passengers were regarded as valuable assets, and were often separated from the ordinary seamen. Three masters brought to Salé in 1684 were held in the governor's house for ten days, grinding corn for

---

[1] *Rawlins*, sig. B4-v; Brooks, *Barbarian Cruelty* (1693); Thomas Troughton, *Barbarian Cruelty; or an Accurate and Impartial Narrative* (1751).

[2] John Braithwaite, *The History of the Revolutions in the Empire of Morocco* (1729), 352–3; Nabil Matar, 'Introduction', in Daniel J. Vitkus, ed., *Piracy, Slavery, and Redemption* (New York, 2001), 20; Peter Earle, *Corsairs of Malta and Barbary* (1970), 80–2; Sir Godfrey Fisher, *Barbary Legend. War, Trade and Piracy in North Africa 1415-1830* (Oxford, 1957), 103.

[3] Robert C. Davis, *Christian Slaves, Muslim Masters* (Basingstoke, 2003), chaps. 3–4, provides the best overview of life and labour in Barbary.

[4] See Chapter 2.

British Slaves and Barbary Corsairs, 1580–1750. Bernard Capp, Oxford University Press. © Bernard Capp 2022.
DOI: 10.1093/oso/9780192857378.003.0004

his family, until word arrived on what the sultan wished to be done with them.[5] Masters sold at market might enjoy quite favourable conditions if they were ready to accept a substantial ransom figure. Thomas Highway, enslaved at Tunis in 1657, still had access to money, presumably borrowed from resident merchants, and was able to buy decent food and wine.[6] The merchant Abraham Browne, bought by 'the best master to captives in the place', was very willing to discuss ransom terms and performed only light work while negotiations proceeded.[7] Adam Elliot had more mixed fortunes. The Jewish merchant who bought him in Morocco in 1670 had been told that he came from a wealthy family, and when Elliot insisted that he was in fact poor, he was savagely beaten and left almost for dead. But when he changed his story and claimed that he did, indeed, have wealthy connections able to pay a large ransom, his circumstances changed again. A few months later we find him drinking wine with his owner, singing songs from the London shows to entertain his owner's friends, and serenaded by them with Moorish songs.[8]

If shipmasters and merchants refused to cooperate, however, they were likely to suffer far harsher treatment than the ordinary seamen. William Agle, a master captured in 1633, initially refused to accept a ransom demand that was twice what his owner had paid for him. He reported morosely that the other survivors had decent owners who supplied their basic needs, 'only myself am driven to beg for my bread, because I was master, for here are 20 masters more which are in my case besides myself. God help us all'. After being starved for three days his resistance collapsed, and he penned a sorrowful letter asking his wife to contact merchants and friends who could arrange his redemption.[9] Robert Adams found himself in a similar situation at Salé in 1625, after the ship's boy revealed that he was the son of its owner, who was very rich. Armed with this new information, Adams' owner now made him 'work at a mill like a horse' from morning till night, in heavy chains, beat him 'continually', and allowed him only bread and water. This brutal regime had its intended effect. Infested with vermin and so weak he could barely walk, Adams eventually agreed to a huge ransom demand of 730 ducats (around £275), and wrote home begging his parents to send it speedily. If it failed to arrive soon, he ended pitifully, 'I must arm myself to endure the most misery of any creature in the world'.[10]

Much of the evidence of extreme cruelty comes from such letters, sent home by captives thought to be from wealthy families and pleading for help. They had an

---

[5] *Phelps*, 7.   [6] Coxere, *Adventures*, 57.

[7] Stephen T. Riley, ed., 'Abraham Browne's Captivity by the Barbary Pirates, 1655', *Colonial Society of Massachusetts*, 52 (1979), 41.

[8] Adam Elliot, *A Modest Vindication of Titus Oates* (1682), 7–13.

[9] TNA SP 71/1, f.117-v; cf. Joseph Morgan, *A Compleat History of the Piratical States of Barbary* (1750), 224–5.

[10] Vitkus, *Piracy*, 349–50.

obvious incentive to exaggerate their sufferings, and may well have done so. It is probably better, however, to see their accounts as substantially true but as the experience of only a small and very specific category of captives. Robert Adams, who bewailed his endless beatings, acknowledged that most of the 1,500 Englishmen at Salé were 'something better used, for they misuse none but such as are able to pay their ransom'.[11] Owners knew that most ordinary sailors would never be able to raise a ransom, and bought them primarily as servants or labourers. It would make little sense to inflict beatings that might leave them physically incapacitated. We do not have letters from poorer captives, most of whom would have been barely literate. The letters we do have are probably broadly reliable, but they do not represent the experience of most captives.

Galley slaves and seamen

The popular image of Mediterranean slavery has always focused on the miserable plight of the galley slave. All the Mediterranean powers warring in the sixteenth century, Christian and Muslim alike, employed armed galleys and other oared vessels propelled by captives. The Barbary corsairs of the period found most of their oarsmen from the merchant ships they captured. It was and remains generally accepted that conditions were harsh and discipline fierce. Oarsmen who fell sick and died were thrown overboard without ceremony, and those who became too weak to row might suffer the same fate. Richard Hasleton recalled his wretched life as a galley slave in the 1580s, sick and weakened by endless toil and repeated beatings. 'I [was] constrained either to labour or else to lose my head', he wrote, 'I had no other choice.'[12] At the same time, the corsairs needed to ensure that most of their oarsmen remained sufficiently fit to function. While the weak and sick were disposable, it was in their own interests to keep the rest healthy enough to work.

British captives were among the tens of thousands forced to labour as galley slaves, sometimes for years, and a few accounts provide a glimpse of their experiences. Before going to sea, slaves had their heads shaved to the skull, and their beards and even eyebrows shaved too. It was a degrading ritual that proclaimed their shameful status and destroyed their masculinity, leaving their faces 'disfigured', as one put it.[13] The food provided by the *armadors*, who set out the ships, consisted of little more than bread ('very black, worse than horse-bread')

[11] Vitkus, *Piracy*, 350.

[12] *Hasleton*, sig. B; Francis Knight, *A Relation of Seaven Yeares Slaverie* (1640), 29.

[13] Knight, *Relation*, 29; Thomas Saunders, *A true Discription and breefe discourse, Of a most lamentable voiage made latelie to Tripolie in Barbarie* (1587), sig. B3; D'Aranda, *History*, 10; Davis, *Christian Slaves*, 59. Cf. Laurent D'Arvieux, *The Chevalier D'Arvieux's Travels in Arabia the Desart* (1718), 152.

and water. The clothing supplied was minimal too. Galley slaves wore drawers but their legs and feet were bare, and some had nothing to protect their upper bodies from the fierce sun or the cold. Francis Knight described oarsmen with the skin burnt from their back, and their bodies bruised and covered in blood and sweat. They had to eat and sleep with one leg chained to the bench where they rowed, and defecate through a hole close to it. Boatswains paced through the galley, hurling curses and lashing them with a bull's pizzle to punish any sign of slacking and spur them on. Knight said almost nothing about his experience of captivity ashore; his sufferings on land had paled into insignificance against his 'diabolical' experience as a galley slave.[14] Edward Coxere, working in the shipyard at Porto Farina in 1657, was told that their overseer had once 'cut off a slave's arm and beat the rest of the slaves with it to make them row the more'. If that sounds improbable, Coxere soon experienced the overseer's cruelty for himself: he and his companions were savagely beaten when their vessel ran aground in the harbour.[15] Galleys carried a large sail that also provided some propulsion, and the oarsmen were driven hardest when the wind failed or during a chase. On a large galley, the slaves could number 300 or more, often outnumbering the soldiers, and in any action most would be hoping for the Europeans to prevail and liberate them. The corsairs kept them shackled, taking no risks, and if the vessel was sunk in the action the oarsmen drowned. Galley slaves were allocated one share of the proceeds from the sale of captured booty, but two-thirds of this money was paid to their owners.[16]

English accounts do not go much beyond these bare details. Narrators chose not to linger on this miserable phase of their sufferings, for life as a galley slave was also tedious and repetitive. It was still a new experience, however, for young Samuel Harres when he wrote home from Tripoli in 1610. He had been put to the oars as soon as his ship was captured, presumably to replace a dead oarsman. 'I was chained to a bank', he wrote, 'and made to row naked and beaten, and then I took such a cold, which brought me to a bloody flux', or dysentery. Still sick, he was terrified of being sent to sea again.[17] A group of theology students captured in 1622 were similarly put to the oars, and when they failed to keep stroke they were beaten, bound, and thrown back into the hold.[18] But if life on a Barbary man-of-war was harsh, the plight of an Ottoman galley slave based at Constantinople was

---

[14] Edward Webbe, *The Rare and most wonderfull things which Edw. Webbe an Englishman borne, hath seene* (1590), sig. Bv-2; Saunders, *True Discription*, sig. B3v; D'Aranda, *History*, 10; Knight, *Relation*, sig. A3, pp. 9–10, 29; *A Narrative of the Adventures of Lewis Marott, pilot royal of the galleys of France* (1677), 61.

[15] Coxere, *Adventures*, 65. Knight and Pierre Dan also mention officers hacking off the heads or arms of galley-slaves: Knight, *Relation*, 29; Pierre Dan, *Histoire de Barbarie et de ses Corsairs* (Paris, 1649), 409–10.

[16] *Pitts*, 15; Earle, *Corsairs*, 74; Davis, *Christian Slaves*, 82.   [17] Vitkus, *Piracy*, 348.

[18] James Wadsworth, *The English Spanish Pilgrime* (1629), 38. One of his companions claimed the students were being deliberately uncooperative: Martin Murphy, ed., 'William Atkins, A Relation of the Journey from St Omers to Seville, 1622', in *Camden Miscellany*, 32 (1994), 239.

generally recognized as worse. Barbary slaves had at least some hope of being ransomed, or even escaping. Mariners serving on Ottoman galleys and ships were likely to be enslaved for life. One Florentine commander, overwhelmed by a combined Ottoman–Algerian force, was careful to surrender to the Algerian admiral, knowing that at Constantinople 'no money would prevail for his ransom'.[19] Edward Webbe, one of the very few ever to return home, had endured six years as a galley slave, and many more as a gunner with the Ottoman armies. Webbe's earlier life had been equally hard. As part of the retinue of the English ambassador in Moscow, he was among thousands captured and enslaved when the Cossacks overran and burned the city in 1571. He was finally freed in 1589, through the direct intercession of Queen Elizabeth. Like Voltaire's Candide, however, poor Webbe proved eternally unlucky. On his way home he was arrested in Italy as a suspected spy, tortured, and then forced to serve in the Spanish navy before eventually reaching England.[20] The ordeal of Thomas Gallilee had no such happy finale. The son of a London merchant, Gallilee had ploughed most of his estate into buying and lading the *Relief*, a ship of 300 tons carrying twenty-four guns, to trade to the Mediterranean. In 1651 he hired his ship and men to serve the Venetian Republic against the Ottomans, but a year later, near Constantinople, they encountered a huge fleet of twenty-seven Turkish galleys. Gallilee fought a long and desperate action against these overwhelming odds, but the ship was eventually taken and burned. Gallilee was picked up from the sea and made a galley slave. For many years his parents made desperate attempts to secure his release, winning support from Oliver Cromwell, Charles II, and the Venetian senate, all to no avail. When we last hear of him, in 1669, he was still a slave, and he almost certainly died in captivity.[21]

Life as a Barbary galley slave, however wretched, differed little from the conditions endured by Muslim and other captives on Spanish, Italian, Maltese, or French galleys.[22] Galley slavery was a Mediterranean phenomenon, and some English mariners had also experienced it at the hands of fellow Christians. One, a barber-surgeon named William Davies, later published an account of his 'most miserable captivity' in the galleys of the Grand Duke of Tuscany. Davies had been serving on a vessel trading around the Mediterranean, and painted a damning picture of the plight of Christian slaves in Algiers and Tunis. When his ship was captured by Florentine galleys, around 1602, he discovered that Christians could be equally cruel to one another. The new captives were stripped and clapped in

[19] *Pitts*, 234; *Narrative of Lewis Marott*, 18; cf. Cervantes, *Don Quixote* (Ware, 1993), i.328.

[20] Webbe, *Rare and most wonderfull things*, passim.

[21] *CSPD 1652–3*, 379; *CSPD 1654*, 94; *CSPD 1655*, 217–18, 327; *CSPD 1667–8*, 576; *CSPD 1668–9*, 607; Allin, *Journals*, i.21; *CSPVen. 1669–70*, 82–3, 112, 154, 168.

[22] Earle, *Corsairs*, chaps. 5–9; cf. John Bion, *An Account of the Torments the French Protestants Endure aboard Galleys* (1708); Ellis Veryard, *An Account of Divers Choice Remarks, as well Geographical as Historical* (1701), 252; F. N. L. Poynter, ed., *The Journal of James Yonge [1647–1721]* (1963), 69; E. S. de Beer, ed., *The Diary of John Evelyn* (6 vols., Oxford, 1955), ii.164–5.

irons, and many died before the galleys returned to Livorno, Florence's port, a month later. The survivors were chained, beaten, and set to heavy labour, carting sand, limestone, and bricks. Davies complained bitterly that they were treated like horses, cows, or sheep, echoing the language of Christian slaves in Barbary. After three years, he and the others still physically strong were made galley slaves, with even less bread and water, even more beatings, and with their heads and beards shaved. Chained, and clad only in linen breeches, they also had to serve their masters in attacks on Muslim shipping and on raids ashore. Davies endured this life for another six years. By then, he recalled, only thirteen of the original thirty-seven captives were still alive—a mortality rate of roughly two-thirds in the space of just under nine years. His account parallels closely the stories told by Europeans enslaved in Barbary. 'The misery of the galleys doth surpass any man's judgement or imagination,' he wrote, 'neither would any man think that such torture or torment were used in the world but only they that feel it'. It was not uncommon, he added, for slaves to commit suicide to escape their misery, or launch a desperate assault on their tormentors. But for such an act of defiance, the offender would have his nose and ears cut off, or suffer a hundred lashes on his back and belly with a rope or bull's pizzle. In brutality, the Florentines fully matched their 'barbarian' enemies.[23]

From the early 1600s the Barbary corsairs gradually turned away from galleys to vessels driven by sail. As they ranged into the Atlantic, and as far as the English Channel and Irish Sea, they found galleys ill-suited to heavy seas and harsher conditions. The shift to sail had important and beneficial consequences for the slaves. Instead of large numbers of oarsmen, the corsairs now required a much smaller body of skilled mariners, especially pilots, carpenters, and gunners. The janissaries and Moors serving on board were soldiers, not seamen, and the corsairs relied heavily on slaves and renegades to handle their ships. Moreover, the slaves could no longer be kept in chains, for they needed to move freely around the vessel. While discipline remained harsh, conditions were far better than in the galleys. In handling the ship, and especially in times of danger, corsairs and slaves recognized they were interdependent, and over time this might even generate an element of mutual respect. In the 1680s Joshua Gee served on several expeditions under his first owner, whom he calls by the less opprobrious name of 'master', and speaks of acts of kindness. He was allowed to go aboard prizes to supply himself with better clothes, and on one occasion, when he fell overboard and was thought drowned, there is a suggestion of affection in the master's cry that 'my little

---

[23] William Davies, A *Trve Relation of the Travailes... of William Davies* (1614), sig. Cv and *passim*. On Livorno and its galley slaves see Stephanie Nadalo, 'Negotiating Slavery in a Tolerant Frontier: Livorno's Turkish *Bagno* (1547-1747)', *Mediaevalia*, 32 (2011), 275–324; de Beer, *Diary of Evelyn*, ii.183–4.

carpenter is lost'.[24] Edward Coxere, a slave at Tunis in 1657, volunteered to serve at sea, confident that it would be better than the misery of his life ashore. He calculated, too, that he might find an opportunity to escape or be liberated by a European warship. He was dismayed when he was ordered to remain ashore, reflecting gloomily that he would now have little prospect of ever returning home.[25] Robinson Crusoe, enslaved at Salé in Defoe's novel, had similar hopes, and was similarly dismayed when his owner left him to perform 'drudgery' ashore.[26]

Slave life and labour ashore

The galleys did not operate during the winter months, and the other men-of-war greatly reduced their activities. Between cruises, the slaves belonging to the pasha, dey, or other great figures were kept in bagnios, locked overnight. These slave pens were originally large bath-houses, with narrow entrances and few windows. Edward Webbe describes being held with 2,000 chained slaves in such an establishment in Constantinople.[27] The Grand Bagnio at Algiers was equally capacious, and there were several other large bagnios there and at Tunis. Conditions were somewhat better than at Constantinople. A large courtyard was surrounded by stalls which served as taverns, with rope ladders providing access to the sleeping quarters above.[28] The best account available to English readers was by the Flemish captive Emanuel D'Aranda, whose memoirs were translated and published in 1666. Twenty-five years earlier he had shared a bagnio in Algiers with more than 500 other slaves from across Europe, speaking between them, he recalled, twenty-two languages. They were all owned by Ali Pichellin (or Pegelin, or Bitchnin), the leading corsair *reis* of his time, and during the day they were generally hired out to labour. In Algiers, as in other centres, carpenters and caulkers worked on ships in the harbour and dockyard. Unskilled men worked in quarries, on building sites, and on repairs to the harbour mole; they felled trees for timber and fuel, and made ropes; they sold water through the streets, dragged carts laden with sacks of grain, and ground corn.[29] Other slaves served the janissaries in their quarters, and accompanied them on campaign.[30] Thomas Saunders, enslaved at Tripoli in 1584–85, described a similar life of quarrying, carting, making mortar, and also

[24] Joshua Gee, *Narrative of Joshua Gee of Boston, Mass., when he was captive in Algeria of the Barbary pirates, 1680–1687*, ed. Albert C. Bates (Hartford, Conn., 1945), 18, 23.

[25] Coxere, *Adventures*, 57–8.

[26] Daniel Defoe, *The Life and Strange Surprizing Adventures of Robinson Crusoe* (1719), 20–1.

[27] Webbe, *Rare and most wonderfull things*, sig. C2v; Dan, *Histoire*, 411–12.

[28] Earle, *Corsairs*, 84.

[29] D'Aranda, *History*, 11–15, 25–6. Knight also described Pichellin, his fourth owner, as a harsh figure: *Relation*, 14.

[30] *Several Voyages to Barbary* (1736), 44.

fetching wood. This required the slaves to journey thirty miles inland to the forest, led by Moors and travelling overnight on camels. On one occasion, he recalled, he had been at the rear of the train and had fallen asleep on his camel. He woke to find himself alone, lost, and terrified of being murdered by fierce tribesmen.[31] James Deane, a slave in Algiers, recalled cleaning out stables, cowsheds, and slaughterhouses, working on the mole and prize-ships in the harbour, and in his owner's gardens and vineyards.[32] Owners who hired out a slave kept two-thirds of the wages he earned, and might expect to recoup 10–12% of their original outlay each year, as well as enjoying the benefit of the unpaid work he did for them.[33]

Richard Mitchael, also enslaved in Algiers, wrote to his wife in 1679 that 'it would make a heart of stone weep to see the barbarous and inhumane usage of Christians', hauling carts, like horses, shackled in heavy irons, and half-starved.[34] Some slaves clearly continued to experience the dehumanizing treatment they had endured in the marketplace. In Morocco, it was reported, 'country people' would buy a 'big lusty' captive 'for the yoke, for there their ploughs are drawn by slaves yoked by couples', whipped with a bull's pizzle to spur them on. The same practice was recorded in the Ottoman Empire.[35] At Porto Farina, where Edward Coxere laboured in the dockyard, there was no bagnio. Instead, he and up to eighty others were chained in pairs and locked overnight in a dungeon beneath the castle, a 'hot stinking hole'. There they 'lay without beds, like dogs on the ground', with 'two great tubs' serving as latrines. To use them, a slave had to wake his companion and shuffle over together. On one wretched occasion, he recalled, the upper floor collapsed and the slaves sleeping there, still in their chains, fell in a tangled heap.[36] At Salé, Wadsworth described being manacled each night in a huge dungeon near the market place with 800 others, lying on old straw and plagued by 'millions of lice and fleas'.[37] Conditions in the dungeons of Meknes, Fez, and other Moroccan towns were little better and at times considerably worse. Thomas Troughton and his companions were left to starve in a Tangier dungeon in 1746, told by the jeering alcaid to eat stones if they were hungry. They were driven to contemplate cannibalism. On another occasion, several years later, Moors threw dead cats and dogs into their dungeon to humiliate them further.[38]

Slaves housed in a bagnio were generally allowed a few hours, later in the day, to earn a pittance by whatever means they could devise. The boldest spirits pilfered food and goods from Jews and Moors, to sell or barter in the bagnio. Taverns in the bagnios did a brisk trade selling wine to janissaries and renegade soldiers as

[31] Saunders, *True Discription*, sig. C-v.

[32] William Okeley, *Eben-ezer... with a Further Narrative of James Deane* (1684), 93–4.

[33] Davis, *Christian Slaves*, 70–1; Morgan, *Compleat History*, 223.

[34] HMC 32, Fitzherbert MSS, 11; Dan, *Histoire*, 406.

[35] Murphy, *William Atkins*, 248; Henry Marsh, *A New Survey of the Turkish Empire and Government* (1663), 54.

[36] Coxere, *Adventures*, 59–61.   [37] Wadsworth, *English Spanish Pilgrime*, 40–1.

[38] Troughton, *Barbarian Cruelty*, 23, 194.

well as to fellow captives. They were run by slaves, who paid a proportion of the profits to their owners. D'Aranda heard of one born entrepreneur, a slave from Majorca, who had established taverns in three different bagnios, hiring other slaves to manage two of them. The business was so lucrative that he had turned down an opportunity to be ransomed and return home. There were other ways to make a reasonable living. D'Aranda knew of six captives 'practising surgery, treating both Moors and Turks. Another earned a living as a scribe, penning letters from illiterate captives to their families. Others fashioned simple toys to sell to the Moors' children, while an enterprising one-armed German had set up a ninepins establishment. By contrast, a poor Muscovite, aged 80, scraped a pittance cleaning latrines and begging alms. Looking back, D'Aranda reflected wryly that 'there can be no better University to teach men to shift for their livelihood, than one of the Baths at Algiers'. He too soon learned to shift for himself, bribing an overseer to avoid being put to heavy labour.[39]

Life in the bagnios had a far darker side, however, for slaves crammed together were desperately vulnerable to plague and other infectious diseases. A correspondent reported from Algiers in 1663 that only one galley had been able to go out that summer, 'by reason the slaves died'. A slave writing home in January 1679 reported that a virulent outbreak the previous year had swept away 1,800 Christians, adding that pestilence returned every summer.[40] It was the same at Tunis. An outbreak in 1676 devastated the bagnios as well as the city at large, and there was said to be no prospect of any galleys going out for the next year, for almost no galley slaves remained alive.[41]

Many slaves in Barbary belonged not to the ruling elite but to private owners or *patrons*, whether Turks, Moors, Jews, or European renegades. Their circumstances were generally less onerous than those housed in the bagnios. Many were allowed to live semi-independently, earning a livelihood by whatever means they could devise, and paying their owner a monthly fee of up to $3. For the *patron*, this removed the need to find them work each day, or to provide for them. If the slave failed to earn enough, he would go hungry, and if he failed to pay his monthly due, his owner could still beat or sell him. For the slaves, the arrangement provided some degree of autonomy, and freedom from the fear of daily beatings. William Okeley's first owner initially found him work in the shipyard and sent him to sea with the corsairs, but later told him to pay $2 a month, 'live ashore where I would and get it where I could'. Okeley initially found this a daunting prospect, for he had no trade, money, or stock, until a fellow slave came to his rescue. This man kept a little shop from which he drove a furtive trade in iron, brandy, tobacco, and other goods, and invited Okeley to become his partner, lending him some money to begin trading. Their business thrived. On one occasion, 'finding the world to

---

[39] D'Aranda, *History*, 13–21, 48, 153–8.
[40] TNA SP 71/1, f.239; HMC, 32, *Fitzherbert MSS*, 11.   [41] TNA SP 71/26, f.252.

come in upon us', they bought a butt of wine and set up a covert tavern. Success eventually corrupted the partner, who became an idle drunkard, but Okeley found a new partner in an emigrant named John Randal who had been captured on the same ship, along with his wife and child. Randal, a glover by trade, learned to make canvas clothes for seamen, and the pair worked together for several years. Okeley knew of other English slaves working as carpenters, linen-weavers, brick-layers, tailors, and surgeons. Some already had a trade they could practise, while others had been driven to learn one, often helped by one of their countrymen. They could socialize with their friends and, with luck, make an adequate living.[42] We hear of one enslaved English doctor who was allowed to live with a merchant at the consul's house, and practise his profession there. The merchant paid a monthly fee to the owner.[43]

The conditions of life as a privately owned slave in Barbary were shaped primarily by the character and circumstances of the owner, and varied enor-mously. That simple fact goes far to explain the wildly different assessments cited at the start of this chapter. Some owners treated their captives with decency and even affection. No slave was free from the risk of a beating, however, and almost every account included descriptions of floggings and other harsh punishments. One common form was the bastinado, in which the victim was pinned to the floor on his back, his legs were raised, and his feet were then beaten, leaving him crippled temporarily, and occasionally for life. Okeley's friend John Randal, falsely accused of planning to escape, was sentenced by his *patron*, 'a very termagant', to receive 300 blows on the soles of his feet, leaving him lame and unable to work.[44] We also find references to former slaves, begging alms in England, who had had their tongues cut out as a punishment.[45]

Throughout Barbary, slaves belonging to the dey, pasha, or another great figure generally fared worse than those privately owned. Francis Knight had two private owners, both decent men, before passing into the hands of Ali Pichellin, 'a great tyrant'. 'We were all exquisitely miserable that were his slaves', he recalled.[46] Housed in the bagnios, captives had no opportunity to build a personal relation-ship with their owner, and it was harder to send a message home. By contrast, a slave lucky to have a kindly private owner sometimes became in effect a trusted and valued family member, especially if raised in the household from childhood or adolescence As Daniel Hershenzon has remarked, a slave who had been turned into a mere 'commodity' in the market-place could be partly 'rehumanized' in his owner's household.[47] Very often he would be allowed to visit friends and fellow

---

[42] *Okeley*, 14–20, 33, 37. 45.   [43] *Pitts*, 229.   [44] *Okeley*, 35–7.

[45] HMC, 55, *Various Collections, vii, Dunwich*, 95–6; Des Ekin, *The Stolen Village. Baltimore and the Barbary Pirates* (Dublin, 2006), 254; Hebb, *Piracy*, 146; cf. *Rawlins*, sig. Bv-2.

[46] Knight, *Relation*, 9, 15.

[47] Daniel Hershenzon, *The Captive Sea. Slavery, Communication, and Commerce in Early Modern Spain and the Mediterranean* (Philadelphia, 2019), 23–4.

countrymen when his chores were finished. He might take his owner's little child with him, and 'if the child be a boy,' Joseph Pitts recalled, 'it rides on the slave's shoulders'. Affectionate ties might naturally develop between slave and child, which the slave would encourage, knowing he would be likely to 'fare much better for the children's sakes'.[48] Joseph Morgan, writing in the mid-eighteenth century, said that most owners in Algiers kept their slaves well dressed, which brought honour on the family. Some slaves were treated like their own children, and might enjoy considerable influence in the household.[49]

By Morgan's day there were no longer any British slaves in Algiers, but a century earlier Okeley had acknowledged that his own conditions there were by no means unbearable. He was even able to save some money, and recalled years later that he and his partner had become 'so habituated to bondage that we almost forgot liberty and grew stupid and senseless of our slavery'. 'Long bondage breaks the spirits', he reflected. His final owner, a kindly old man, treated him with respect and such kindness 'that it took off much of the edge of my desire . . . after liberty'. For slaves in his situation, there was time for leisure too. He mentions seeing a group of English slaves playing quoits, and alcohol was readily available. One slave had always been a drunkard, he commented tartly, and 'captivity had not made him sober'.[50] D'Aranda, enslaved in Algiers at the same time, also mentioned the leisure that slaves in the bagnios could enjoy once the day's labour was over. While many found escape in drink, he claimed that the bagnios could also be educational. Conversing every day with men from many different nations, he felt, had provided a breadth of knowledge impossible to equal in normal life. There was occasionally even some cultural activity; he remembered a group of Spanish slaves mounting an amateur performance of a play, 'the story of Belizarius', a Byzantine general, in the bagnio.[51]

Slave narratives generally tell us most about the first few days or weeks, from the trauma of capture to the humiliations of the auction. No account provides a detailed narrative of life as a galley slave, or of labour ashore. However wretched, their experiences quickly blurred into a dreary routine that former slaves had no wish to recall, and felt readers would find of little interest. Of his first months as a slave in Algiers, Okeley simply comments that it consisted of 'trudging on errands, bearing burdens', and 'other domestic services at command'. He describes his nervousness when he was ordered to earn his own livelihood, but once he had found a way, he adds only that it would be 'tedious to trouble the reader how I wore out three or four irksome years in this way of trading'.[52] It was more

[48] *Pitts,* 68; cf. D'Aranda, *History,* 48; Dan, *Histoire,* 406.   [49] Morgan, *Compleat History,* 224.
[50] *Okeley,* 21, 33–4, 40.
[51] D'Aranda, *History,* 158, 261. Belasarius (*d.*565) was a Byzantine general in the service of the Emperor Justinian. After reconquering much of North Africa he fell from favour, but was eventually restored. The performance was probably a version of the play by Antonio Mira de Amescua (1625).
[52] Ibid., 14, 20.

rewarding, both for him and his readers, to tell the dramatic story of his escape after five years of captivity.

We have only rare glimpses into captives' inner lives, and how they accommodated themselves to their situation.[53] Okeley, for example, describes how after the humiliation of the market-place, his new owner's father had taunted him with insults about his Christian faith. Okeley had responded with offensive gestures disparaging Mahomet, a recklessness that almost cost him his life. His furious owner lunged at him with a knife, and he escaped only because the owner's wife protested that a dead slave would be worthless.[54] 'My neck was not yet bowed nor my heart broken to the yoke of bondage'; Okeley soon learned the need for discretion and self-control. Reflecting on this incident, years later, he described his younger self as 'a martyr to my own folly'. He was to hear worse insults about Christ and Christians, but learned to keep his thoughts to himself, accepting that it was 'fair for slaves to enjoy the freedom of their own consciences without reviling another's religion, though erroneous'.[55]

Many letters and accounts confirm that slavery could reduce men to a condition of despair, and D'Aranda claimed that the English were less adaptable and emotionally resilient than other nations. They were 'not so shiftful', he wrote, 'and it seems also they have no great kindness one for another'. During the winter he spent in the bagnio, in 1640–41, he witnessed more than twenty Englishmen die of starvation. He also claimed that English slaves generally fetched at auction less than half the price of Spaniards or Italians. Considered less likely to survive, they appeared a riskier investment.[56] It remains doubtful, however, that these claims had much foundation. William Okeley received help and offered assistance to his countrymen, and mentioned others who had done the same.

The misery of slavery could drive some individuals to angry outbursts or desperate actions. Okeley had responded to insults against Christ with insulting gestures about Mahomet, while Adam Elliot hurled abuse at his cruel owner in broken Spanish. Both had discovered the folly of such behaviour when they were kicked and beaten with such ferocity that they felt ready to kill themselves.[57] Okeley described how a desperate Dutch youth had drawn a knife on his owner, and was then executed on the wheel by having 'his arms and legs broken in pieces with the great sledgehammer'. He never forgot the victim's terrible screams. A group in Morocco, similarly desperate, hatched a plan to poison their brutal overseer, though they did not implement it.[58]

Most slaves recognized that open resistance would be futile. Covert resistance was a far better option, though by its nature hard to document and impossible to

[53] On the inner lives of Muslim slaves see Steven A. Epstein, *Speaking of Slavery. Colour, Ethnicity, and Human Bondage in Italy* (Ithaca, 2001), 124–9.
[54] *Okeley*, 7–8, 12–14.   [55] *Okeley*, 14.   [56] D'Aranda, *History*, 157.
[57] *Okeley*, 12–13; Elliot, *Modest Vindication*, 7–8.
[58] *Okeley*, 33; *The Travels of the Sieur Mouette in the Kingdoms of Fez and Morocco* (1710), 24.

measure. It was certainly rife among the slaves housed in the bagnios, where it mainly took the form of pilfering during the daytime hours they spent outside. Many operated by bribing a guard, who would then conceal and fence the stolen goods. Bold galley slaves stole nails, pieces of iron, and on one occasion even an anchor from the galleys.[59] Edward Coxere, at Porto Farina, described how he too 'took up a resolution to steal what I could from my patron, to get a little money to refresh myself now and then'. He began modestly by stealing a parcel of nails from the ship he was working on, planning to sell them to a smith and buy drink with the proceeds. But he panicked when he heard that the slaves' sleeping quarters were about to be searched for missing goods, and hastily returned his little booty, undetected. He gave up all thought of pilfering after witnessing another slave being flogged for a similar offence. Coxere claimed that he had remained 'full of waggery', but we can only guess what form it had taken.[60]

Pilfering from a private owner was far harder, and might prove dangerously provocative. Meriton Latroon, the antihero of Head's *English Rogue,* was beaten repeatedly by his cruel Jewish owner and desperate to alleviate his situation. He devised an elaborate stratagem, staging a fake suicide attempt that he knew would be observed and prevented, in the hope that it would make his owner moderate his treatment rather than risk losing his investment. In the event, his ploy had an even better outcome: the Jew, wanting to take no risks, promptly sold him to another owner, who proved more merciful.[61] But this episode was, of course, no more than a literary flight of fancy.

Most slaves never lost their longing for freedom—a dream that helped sustain them. Okeley hid some of his earnings, clinging to the hope of eventual liberation. When he broached the possibility of escape to some friends, he recalled how they had found pleasure in the very idea: 'the name of liberty made music in our ears, and our wishing hearts danced to the tune of it'. Two of his companions had been enslaved for eleven and fifteen years, but were still ready to risk their lives for a chance of freedom, however desperate. Even those who enjoyed a degree of auton- omy knew it could be withdrawn at any moment, as Okeley discovered when one owner suspected him of planning to escape. His final owner, though a decent man, was old, and Okeley knew that if he died, the next might be very different.[62]

The experience of slavery: some case histories

Slavery in the regencies was for life, except for those ransomed. The regencies did not practise the system of 'indentured slavery', found in some Ottoman lands,

---

[59] Laurent D'Arvieux, *Memoires du Chevalier D'Arvieux* (Paris, 1735), iv.4; D'Aranda, *History,* 13–14, 153–4, 157.
[60] Coxere, *Adventures,* 63–5. [61] Head, *English Rogue* (1666), iii.79–80.
[62] *Okeley,* 39–44, 48.

where a slave would be liberated after working for his owner for a certain number of years. Private ownership did nonetheless take a variety of forms. One French slave in Salé had been purchased by a partnership of two Moors, a Jew, and the governor.[63] Slaves were also frequently resold or mortgaged in private transactions, so that over time an individual might belong to a succession of owners. The public auctions were for new captives; subsequent sales were arranged privately. At Salé an owner wishing to sell his property would drive him 'up and down the streets crying "Who buys a slave?"'. Joseph Pitts described being led through Algiers by the public crier for three days, to publish the fact that he was once more for sale.[64] James Carter and his shipmates, taken initially to Arcila, were sold five times over the course of a few months in 1619–20, and transferred to Tetuan. Thomas Sweet's owner used him to keep his trading accounts, and transferred legal ownership to a friend in Tunis in 1646, to thwart any move to redeem him.[65]

An individual slave might well experience both benign and brutal treatment, at the hands of different owners. Joshua Gee's first owner had treated him with some humanity, but his second inflicted savage beatings and on one occasion threatened to gouge out his eyes with a knife.[66] Joseph Pitts, who passed through three masters during his long years of captivity, described how the first, the sadistic Mustapha, would tie him up and flog him every few days, pausing only to rest his arm and smoke his pipe. When he ran short of funds, Mustapha sold him to an army officer named Ibrahim, and again Pitts recalled a miserable life, 'oftentimes so beaten by him that my blood ran down upon the ground'. He slept in a stable with other slaves, surviving on a coarse fare of bread and sour milk.[67] This period ended abruptly in 1683 when Ibrahim, now a wealthy man, schemed to make himself dey of Algiers but was instead beheaded when the plot failed. Pitts was sold again, this time to an elderly bachelor named Omar. His situation was now totally transformed; he kept house, prepared food, and washed clothes, the sort of work, he commented, that in England would be done by a maidservant. Life was very comfortable, as he later acknowledged; 'I must own I wanted nothing with him: meat, drink, clothes, and money, I had enough.' A year later he accompanied his master on pilgrimage to Mecca, and was eventually given his freedom after their return. He continued to live with Omar, enjoying free lodging, food, coffee, clothes, and washing. In short, he recalled, Omar 'loved me as if I had been his own child, which made me sincerely to love him'. Omar had become 'like a father to me', and had promised to leave him a considerable sum when he died.[68]

Pitts' story exemplifies both the huge diversity of slaves' lives and the volatility of their situation. In the letters they sent home, slaves invariably stressed its misery, but several accounts by former slaves acknowledged that their conditions

---

[63] *Travels of Mouette*, 8–9.   [64] Murphy, *William Atkins*, 248; *Pitts*, 218.
[65] Harris, *Trinity House*, 43; Vitkus, *Piracy*. 352.   [66] Gee, *Narrative*, 21–2, 29.
[67] *Pitts*, 47–8, 183–4, 192–6, 207.   [68] *Pitts*, 215–19, 228, 241.

had varied enormously. Francis Knight, captured in 1631 and enslaved for seven years, denounced 'Turks' as 'monsters more like than men', but conceded that for more than two years he had belonged to a renegade who was 'an honest moral man' and treated him decently.[69] William Okeley had a somewhat similar experience. His first owner, a cruel man, had to dispose of his slaves after falling on hard times. Okeley and another man were mortgaged jointly to two Moors, and became their property when the loan was not repaid. One, an artisan, was reputed 'a brutish, ill-humoured creature', whereas the other, 'a grave old gentleman', was said to be good-natured and moderate, 'as good nature and moderation go in Algiers'. They cast lots and, to his immense relief, Okeley fell to the gentleman. And, as he felt bound to acknowledge, he 'found not only pity and compassion but love and friendship from my new patron. Had I been his son', he added, he could not have found more tenderness. His owner had a farm in the country, and apparently planned to make Okeley his farm manager. He took him to markets to learn how they operated, and plied him with provisions 'that I might make merry with my fellow Christians'. Such kindness blunted Okeley's longing for freedom. He even worried whether it could be morally justifiable to deprive such an owner of his property by absconding. But freedom still beckoned. He reflected that if he was sent to manage the farm, he might live like a 'petty lord' but would lose all contact with other Englishmen, along with any possibility of redemption or escape. And if his elderly owner died, he would be sold again and perhaps once more at the mercy of a tyrant. These considerations were sufficient to overcome his scruples, and his thoughts turned back to escape.[70] The prospect of being taken inland filled all slaves with despair for, as one wrote home, 'if we go up to the country, you may never hear of us again'.[71]

Another captive, a young merchant known only as 'Mr. T. S.', had a still more chequered experience, though it is generally accepted that his account, published after his death, had been heavily embroidered by its editor. Claimed initially by the pasha of Algiers, T. S. was set to work in the kitchens, and then made keeper of the royal Bath. Suspected of being familiar with one of the pasha's wives, he was sent to be sold at market but was bought by one of her kinsmen and became, or so he claimed, her attendant and secret lover, fathering a child. He even offered to marry her if she would run away with him—a proposal she firmly rejected. This period he understandably recalled as 'the happy time of my slavery'. But when she died, possibly poisoned by a rival, he was sold to a Moorish landowner, and then successively to English and Italian renegades, all three cruel and violent. By contrast, his sixth owner, a military officer, liked his 'person and countenance' so much that he vowed never to part with him. He accompanied this new owner, Hally Hamez, on military campaigns for several years, and although Hamez had a

[69] Knight, *Relation*, 2–3.   [70] *Okeley*, 39–42.   [71] Vitkus, *Piracy*, 351.

fiery temper, there was also mutual trust and affection. Hamez honoured a promise to free him when they finally returned to Algiers, and even gave him money to pay for his journey home to England.[72]

Changes in a *patron*'s circumstances inevitably affected the lives of his slaves. The story of John Hart, a young man captured in 1668, offers another striking example. Initially gifted by the dey to the commander of the Arab irregulars, within a year Hart had been put in charge of his owner's treasury, a responsible position. Living in the remote and violent interior, he did not see another Christian for almost four years. When his master was killed in battle, Hart was passed to his successor, whose own life was also cut short when he fell out of favour and was strangled on the dey's orders. That rendered Hart now the dey's property, though not for long, for the dey was soon murdered by disgruntled janissaries. Hart was then bought by yet another soldier, a harsh man who took him on campaign to Crete and Smyrna, where he was eventually redeemed by English merchants.[73] Even without any change of ownership, changing circumstances might still transform a slave's situation. One slave, held in Meknes, experienced a dramatic deterioration when his master was made to surrender a beautiful young concubine to the sultan's seraglio, and vented his rage on all around him. The slave's easy life as a gardener came to an abrupt end. He was now subjected to ferocious discipline (a hundred lashes a day, he claimed), and set to heavy labour carting bricks, sand, and lime, sometimes yoked to a mule to intensify his humiliation.[74]

The lives of slaves in Morocco differed in some particulars from those of captives in the regencies. A much higher proportion belonged to the ruler, rather than private individuals, and worked in gangs organized according to nationality. Thomas Troughton, enslaved in Morocco for several years in the late 1740s, painted a picture of relentless hard labour and savage punishments. They were expected to feed themselves on an allowance of 2d a day, often subsisting on a broth made from horse-beans, with one man in each group of thirty responsible for finding and cooking their food. They were lodged overnight in underground dungeons, under close watch. Set to build or repair fortifications, they were forced to continue working regardless of weather or sickness. Even when suffering from dysentery they had to work on, 'to our great mortification'. Some kept up their spirits with loud singing at night, while a rare supply of food or a brief respite from work would trigger a brief outburst of celebration.[75] Earlier accounts had painted a similar picture, though conditions varied according to the character of different

---

[72] T. S., *Adventures*, 29–41, 55–62, 246 and *passim*. On T. S. see Gerald M. MacLean, *The Rise of Oriental Travel* (Basingstoke, 2004), chap. 15.

[73] TNA SP 29/385, f.244 (*CSPD 1675–6*, 424–5).

[74] *A Description of the Nature of Slavery among the Moors* (1721), 6–11.

[75] Troughton, *Barbarian Cruelty*, 31, 52, 84–5, 105–9, 121 and *passim*; *Travels of Mouette*, 23–4, 37–8, 44–6.

rulers. Abdala Malik (1627–31) relied heavily on his English slaves' expertise in gunnery and treated them relatively well, allowing them some freedom of movement, and sometimes gave them money. His father, by contrast, had kept his slaves shackled by the neck and legs, and his successor, his younger brother, treated them equally cruelly.[76] For many years, Moulay Ismail, sultan from 1672 to 1727, claimed all slaves as his personal property, and had them brought to his capital at Meknes to work on his vast building projects. Moulay Ismail terrified all who encountered him. Thomas Phelps, captured in 1684, was horrified when other slaves claimed to have seen the sultan 'butcher many thousands with his own hands'. Only two days later Phelps saw Ismail in a rage 'lance seven and twenty negroes one after another', and every day thereafter he witnessed or heard of other barbarous killings.[77] Thirty years later another English slave described seeing nine men crucified, and then decapitated the following morning when they were found to be still just alive.[78] Ismail's slaves endured lives of terrifying insecurity, hard labour, and brutal discipline. Thomas Goodman, writing home in 1716, lamented that each morning 'when we go out to work we don't know whether we shall come in alive or not, for they are very barbarous people'. Each day, the slaves were 'driven like sheep' to work on the sultan's palace and fortress complex, a project that continued for decades. They quarried limestone, carted materials, and worked on the walls, 'carrying prodigious loads of dirt and stones from morn till night', and pounding the mixture of earth, stones, and water with a heavy wooden 'stamper'.[79] John Willdon and his fellows dragged carts by ropes tied round their shoulders, 'all one as horses', and carried iron bars they could barely lift to their shoulders. It was brutally heavy work, and intentionally dehumanizing.[80] Slaves were beaten or bastinadoed for trivial offences, or merely at the whim of a black overseer or the sultan. Phelps raged that even the brutality he had witnessed in the Caribbean fell short of 'this monster of Africk, a composition of gore and dust, whom nothing can atone but human sacrifices'.[81] Francis Brooks, who endured ten years of slavery in Morocco, described numerous other instances of Moulay Ismail's savagery. On one occasion, he reported, when work had fallen behind schedule because many labourers were sick, Ismail had them dragged out, and slaughtered seven on the spot.[82]

Yet even Ismail recognized the value of slaves with particular skills. Writing to William III in 1699, he explained that he needed his British slaves for the

---

[76] John Harrison, *The Tragicall Life and Death of Mvley Abdala Melek the last King of Barbarie* (Delft, 1633), 1, 5–6, 13–14, 19.

[77] *Phelps*, 8.   [78] TNA SP 71/16, fos. 253–4.

[79] TNA SP 71/16, fos. 256-v; Giles Milton, *White Gold* (2004), 100–9.

[80] TNA SP 71/16, f.255.

[81] *Phelps*, 8–9; cf. TNA SP 71/16, f.255; Simon Ockley, *An Account of South-West Barbary* (1713), 92–6.

[82] Brooks, *Barbarian Cruelty*, 38–40.

construction of his new buildings, 'some of marble, having none that cut it but them, and they set up the pillars, which none but them understand'.[83] Men with other specialist skills were also valued and protected. When Henry Archer assaulted a *marabout*, or holy man, he was sentenced to have his tongue cut out and hand cut off, but his renown as a skilled watchmaker meant that he was spared.[84] Slaves with rare skills enjoyed a modicum of protection even in Ismail's Morocco. Contemporaries recognized that the sultan's own subjects fared little better, for he regarded them all as his slaves. Soldiers, officials, sons, and concubines knew they too could be put to death at any moment for some trivial reason or merely for his amusement. This was a society brutalized from top to bottom.[85]

Women in Barbary

The British slave population in Barbary consisted mainly of captured seamen. Most of the women had been passengers crossing between England and Ireland or across the Atlantic. In 1632 the churchwardens of Wandsworth gave 12d 'to a poor man with a pass from Ireland, that had his wife and children and all his goods taken by the Turks'. They had probably been travelling to join him there.[86] Other women had been seized in raids on coastal communities in south-west England or southern Ireland, especially the notorious attack on Baltimore. No British women escaped from captivity, and until the mid-eighteenth century none left any account of her experiences. Our evidence about their lives is accordingly sparse.[87] We have no contemporary estimates even of numbers, though lists of slaves redeemed offer a few pointers. A list of those freed at Salé by an expedition under William Rainborough in 1637 contains 302 names, only eleven of them women. Six were from England (London, Exeter, Bristol, and Dorchester), the others from southern Ireland (Youghal, Bantry, and Kinsale).[88] Edmund Cason, an agent sent by Parliament to Algiers in 1646, listed 256 slaves he had redeemed, among them nineteen women. He freed a further 262 the following year, including twenty-eight women, an overall average of about 9%.[89] In 1690 Robert Cole drew up a list of 392 slaves redeemed from Algiers, only four of whom were women;

---

[83] TNA SP 71/14, f.305.

[84] John Smith, *The True Travels, Adventures, and Observations of Captaine Iohn Smith* (1630), 35.

[85] *Phelps*, 8–9; *A Description of the Nature of Slavery*, 27–32.

[86] Cecil T. Davis, ed., *Wandsworth Churchwardens' Accounts from 1631 to 1639*, Surrey Archaeological Collections, 24 (1911), 114.

[87] For a survey see Nabil Matar, *Britain and Barbary, 1589–1689* (Gainesville, FL, 2005), 92–105.

[88] TNA SP 71/13, fos. 29–32.

[89] Edmund Cason, *A Relation of the whole proceedings concerning the Redemption of the Captives in Argier and Tunis* (1647), 17–24; *An Account of what captives hath been freed since the 14th of December Anno Dom. 1647* (1647).

three had been captured together aboard the *Kent* of London.[90] Only one woman was recorded among the 384 Britons enslaved in Salé between 1714 and 1721.[91]

Numbers and names do not take us far, and the sources are frustratingly thin. We know that when a woman was captured together with her husband and children, the whole family was sometimes bought by the same owner.[92] Richard Burke of Plymouth was redeemed in 1576 together with his wife and their four children, so this family had evidently survived as a unit.[93] John Randal had been captured with his wife Bridget and their child, and may have been able to live with them; he was certainly expected to support them both. He refused to join an escape plan because he was unwilling to leave them behind. Fortunately, all three survived to be redeemed by Cason in 1646.[94] Cason's first list includes several mothers and children, and several sisters, but no other married couples. In the case of Joan Broadbrook, one of the very few Baltimore captives ever to return home, there was no mention of her husband or children. They had presumably died, 'turned Turk', or been kept back by owners refusing to part with them.[95] The 1647 list, by contrast, included five married couples, two with children. There were also several women ransomed together in twos or threes, either sisters or mothers and daughters. Whether they had lived in Algiers separately or together, their family bonds had clearly survived.[96] The most intriguing shard of evidence comes in a letter from Cason in 1653, listing another group of captives he had freed. Among them were William Hunter, Rose Baven, and their child, 'with another child she had by a former man'. The phraseology appears to suggest that she was not married to her current partner, while the status of his predecessor is ambiguous. Had they been able to enjoy informal liaisons during their captivity?[97] It would appear that the most common practice was for families to be separated and sold to different owners. These English and Irish couples may have been fortunate in remaining together or at least in contact.[98] In Morocco, men were usually sent to labour in the capital, with women consigned to a harem or domestic service. One apparent rare exception is recorded at Salé in 1656, where the Aga adamantly refused to free 'two children which were born of English parents there'. Though

---

[90] TNA SP 71/3, fos. 182-4v. Only two women were among the 110 redeemed at Algiers by Consul Baker in 1692–94: TNA SP 71/3, fos. 302–4.

[91] Nabil Matar, 'British Captives in Salé (1721)', in Stefan Hanss and Juliane Schiel, eds., *Mediterranean Slavery Revisited (500–1800)*, (Zurich, 2014), 521–8.

[92] Henry Marsh, *A New Survey of the Turkish Empire and Government* (1663), 55–6.

[93] Betty Masters, *Tales of the Unexpected: the Corporation and Captives in Barbary*, Guildhall Historical Association (2005), 4.

[94] *Okeley*, 19–20, 44; Cason, *Relation*, 23.

[95] Cason, *Relation*, 19; Eken, *The Stolen Village*, 301, 355.

[96] *An Account of what Captives*. The list (p. 1) included one more woman from Baltimore, Katherine Cook, ransomed cheaply for $70.

[97] TNA SP 18/57, f.121. Rose's surname is barely legible.

[98] Ellen G. Friedman, *Spanish Captives in North Africa in the Early Modern Age* (Madison, WI, 1983), 57–8.

nothing is known of the circumstances, the issue was sufficient to scupper redemption negotiations.[99]

European women of high status might be well treated, prized for the large ransoms that would almost certainly be forthcoming, and held as captives rather than being sold into slavery. Elizabeth Gordon, described as daughter of the Scottish Viscount Kenmure, was even able to marry at Algiers in January 1645, and presumably lived with her new husband. Their infant daughter was baptized there later the same year.[100] Another of the very few elite British captives was an unnamed lady seized with her maid by Algerian corsairs in 1670 on their way to Venice, where her uncle was consul. They were carried to Tunis, where the English consul negotiated their redemption and took care of them until the ransom money arrived. A naval warship then conveyed them to Livorno and safety.[101] By contrast, women from ordinary families were generally sold into domestic servants, while the young and attractive would be despatched to the ruler's seraglio, or acquired by a high official. A few of these fared well. At least two went on to achieve high status as one of the ruler's wives, with both wielding considerable influence. One was married to the elderly dey of Algiers, Hadj Mohammed, and was said to dominate him. The English consul described her in 1676 as 'a cunning covetous English woman that will sell her soul for a bribe'. It had proved very expensive, he added, 'to be kept in her favour, which I have never a whit the more for country sake'.[102] His successor painted a similar picture. In 1682, after Algiers had been bombarded and cowed by a French fleet, one report claimed that the triumphant admiral had demanded a salute be fired to honour the birth of a French prince. Babba Hassan, the dey's son-in-law and effective ruler of Algiers, was about to comply, but the dey's wife, described now as 'an old Irish woman', allegedly forbade it. One of her own slaves, an Englishman, was reported to have brought a stern message that it would be a sin for Muslims to rejoice at the birth of a Christian. Whether originally English or Irish, she had emphatically 'turned Turk'.[103]

The other wife had a better documented and still more dramatic story. Captured on a small ship sailing to Barbados in 1685, along with her mother and two other women, she was carried to Salé, where the corsair reis gave her to the sultan, Moulay Ismail. She was young and beautiful, and Ismail urged her to lie with him and convert to Islam. When she refused she was savagely beaten, first by the black women of the harem and then by the eunuchs, and was threatened with death until she eventually submitted and agreed to convert. She gradually adapted

[99] *Thurloe*, i.729; Nabil Matar, *British Captives from the Mediterranean to the Atlantic, 1563–1760* (Leiden, 2014), 107.

[100] Robert Lambert Playfair, *The Scourge of Christendom* (1884), 61.

[101] John Baltharpe, *The Straights Voyage, or, St Davids Poem* (1671), 39; Matar, *Britain and Barbary*, 98.

[102] TNA SP 71/2, f. 104; Matar, *Britain and Barbary*, 102.

[103] TNA SP 71/2, f.300. *The Present State of Algiers* (1682), a broadside, gives a different account of this episode.

to her situation, and to the new name she was given, Balqees. She later bore Ismail two sons, and for many years enjoyed a privileged status among his four wives, allowed to wear English dress and travel outside the palace. One English captive described her as 'affable, courteous, and willing to do a good turn', and admired her skill in retaining the trust of the sultan and his almost equally formidable sultana Zidana, who ruled over the harem. The British government acknowledged her position, sending valuable presents to the 'renegado queen', while a Moroccan ambassador visiting England in 1711 brought a message of goodwill from Balqees to Queen Anne.[104] Two years later, when a British envoy was despatched with presents for Ismail, he carried a rich crimson velvet sedan-chair 'for the darling Sultaness a native of England'. Another envoy in 1721 brought more gifts.[105]

Balqees' story was of course wholly exceptional. Her mother and companions vanish from the record and would have had a very different fate. A few other British women were taken into the seraglio and became, at least for a time, the ruler's concubines.[106] But such a position rarely brought the privileges enjoyed by Balqees. Margaret Shaw, or Shea, an Irish woman enslaved at Salé in 1720, had been 'tortured almost to death' to make her convert. She too had resisted until she passed out, whereupon a correspondent reported, 'they said she had turned, she is in the seraglio and so lost'. She was lost indeed. The sultan soon tired of her, and sold her to a Spanish renegade who treated her poorly. When she begged help from envoys visiting Meknes seven years later, she 'was almost naked and starved' and had 'almost forgot her English'.[107]

The English lady captured on her passage to Venice, well treated once her status was recognized, had also initially experienced far rougher usage. A young sailor captured at the same time wrote home that the corsairs had beaten her and her maid 'in such a manner that a Christian would not have abused a dog'. The poor women's 'backs were more blacker than my writing', he added ungrammatically.[108] Corsairs and renegades were a rough breed. And while *reis* and janissaries were ultimately accountable to the authorities in Barbary, the adventurers who followed in the wake of Captain Ward, in the early part of the century, had no such constraints. John Nutt and his company, who operated from Barbary, seized a bark off southern Ireland in May 1623, and raped all twelve women they found on board.[109] Even elite captives could not be certain of respect. In 1636 corsairs seized Sir Francis Godolphin, his brother Captain Godolphin, and their party as

---

[104] *Description of the Nature of Slavery*, 32; Brooks, *Barbarian Cruelty*, 27–34; Matar, *Britain and Barbary*, 99–102; Matar, 'British Captives in Salé', 530.

[105] TNA SP 71/16, fos. 95, 320.

[106] A later Irish woman was the mother of the sultan Moulay Yazid: P. G. Rogers, *A History of Anglo-Moroccan Relations to 1900* (1977), 124.

[107] TNA SP 71/16, f.309v; Matar, 'British Captives in Salé', 527, 531; John Windus, *A Journey to Mequinez* (Dublin, 1725), 95.

[108] *CSPD 1670*, 294; TNA SP 29/276, f.228v; cf. Matar, *Britain and Barbary*, 98.

[109] Eken, *Stolen Village*, 95.

they were crossing from Cornwall to the Scilly Isles. One of the corsairs attempted to 'abuse' the wife of Captain Godolphin, who responded by running him through with his sword, whereupon the corsairs promptly 'cut him into a hundred pieces' before carrying away the others into slavery.[110]

Some information also survives on a girl from another elite family that was at least partly British—or rather Irish. Comte Tobias de Bourk was an Irish officer who had joined the Jacobite exiles in France, and in 1719 his wife and two of their children sailed to join him in southern Spain, where he was serving. Their small vessel, a tartan, was captured by an Algerian man-of-war commanded by a Dutch renegade. Acknowledging that the women of the party would not be safe among his corsairs, he allowed them to remain on the tartan, which a small prize-crew would take to Algiers. In the event it was driven off course in a storm and wrecked, and the countess and most of the party were drowned. Among the few survivors were her daughter, aged almost 10, her brother-in-law, the Abbé de Bourk, and their Irish steward. They were promptly seized by Kabilye tribesmen, who threatened to shoot or burn them as infidels. According to an emotive account of their ordeal, when one tribesman held a sabre against her neck, the child vowed to die rather than renounce her faith. If true, such resolution suggests a very strict and effective religious upbringing, or perhaps the influence of the Abbé The immediate danger passed when a Kabilye sheikh took possession of the group, but she was soon facing a new danger. She had contrived to send several messages to the French consul in Algiers, on scraps of paper torn from the steward's book, and this prompted plans to ransom them. The sheikh, however, wanted to keep the girl and marry her to his own young son. It took the influence of a venerated *marabout*, substantial ransom money, and a Jewish intermediary to secure the group's safe return.[111]

European women were highly valued in the regencies. They fetched considerably higher prices at auction and attracted larger ransoms than most men. The few eventually redeemed had presumably been able to retain both their religion and their honour. But most were never ransomed. The corsairs who raided Baltimore in 1631 carried away eighty-nine women and children, along with twenty men, and very few ever returned home. James Frizzell, the English consul, wrote more than a year later that nothing had been done to secure their release. Early in 1634 he reported in disgust that the group had already shrunk from 109 to seventy. Only one woman had been redeemed, and the others now missing had probably either died or apostatized.[112] Two more Baltimore women were among the slaves redeemed by Cason at Algiers in 1646–47.[113] The rest simply vanish from the record. A raid on the Cornish coast near Fowey in 1645 was reported to have

---

[110] HMC, 63, *Egmont MSS*, i.90.

[111] Philémon de la Motte, 'A Voyage to Barbary for the Redemption of Captives', in *Several Voyages to Barbary* (1736), 14–40. Most of the information came from the steward. The French-born countess was the daughter of the Marquis de Varenne.

[112] TNA SP 71/2, fos. 115, 135.   [113] Cason, *Relation*, 20; *Account of What Captives*, 1.

seized 240 men, women, and children, with several gentlewomen among the number, and again their fates are almost all unknown.[114]

Most women would have been quickly absorbed into the world of Barbary, as domestic slaves serving the wives of Turkish officials and Moors. Their skills, especially in sewing and spinning, were said to be greatly prized.[115] They had very little freedom to interact with anyone outside the owner's house. Henry Marsh, describing slavery in Constantinople, said that a female domestic slave could leave the house only to accompany her mistress and, unlike the men, was not allowed to meet other slaves.[116] Emanuel D'Aranda, carrying water each day to the house of the Bagnio's chief guardian, found several opportunities to speak to an English female slave belonging to the guardian's wife, but once they were observed he was promptly transferred to other duties.[117] Moorish women disliked their husbands having an 'infidel' concubine, and many slaves probably always remained domestic servants or became in time the wives or concubines of renegades.[118] But one English woman, who featured in D'Aranda's story of a lapsed Spanish priest he calls Domingo, had a very different fate. Domingo had been captured with his wife and children in 1639 on their way to South America, and enslaved in Algiers. He was able to arrange the redemption of his wife and children, but then fell for an English slave in the same household and told her that if she agreed to marry him he could raise enough money to redeem them both. She consented, whereupon he tricked a rich old Moorish woman into buying her, to remove her from their owner's close supervision. Led to believe she was now free and would soon be married, she agreed to sleep with Domingo, and his web of lies and fraud was revealed only when she gave birth to twins.[119]

Another unusual story involved the unnamed wife of a renegade named Jonas Rowland, who had run away from his British master in Tangier to avoid punishment. Rowland later accompanied the Moroccan ambassador Ben Haddu on his mission to England in 1682, as an interpreter. On the voyage home he hatched a conspiracy to discredit and ruin the ambassador, but his lies were eventually exposed and he suffered a grisly execution. The Moors, perhaps surprisingly, allowed his wife to return to Tangier, where she told her story and was planning to return to England.[120] She was presumably a free woman, and had not apostatized.

---

[114] Matar, *Britain and Barbary*, 94. Thirteen men and one woman from Fowey were named in the redemption lists of 1646–47.

[115] Fisher, *Barbary Legend*, 101.   [116] Marsh, *New Survey*, 55–6.

[117] D'Aranda, *History*, 19.

[118] Eric R. Dursteler, 'Slavery and sexual peril in the early modern Mediterranean', in Hanss and Schiel, eds., *Mediterranean Slavery*, 473–500; Bartolomé and Lucile Bennassar, *Les Chrétiens d'Allah* (Paris, 2006), 345–67.

[119] D'Aranda, *History*, 109–14.

[120] William Franklin, *A Letter from Tangier concerning the death of Jonas Rowland, the renegade* (1682); *Apostacy punish'd: or, a new poem on the deserved death of Jonas Rowland, the renegado* (1682).

It is striking that no petitions survive on behalf of female captives, to set alongside the many from desperate women pleading for their husbands and sons. In many cases, a woman would have been travelling with her father or husband, and may have had no close kin to come to her aid. That was the plight of Alice Wheeler, enslaved in Algiers in 1649. Her husband and children perished when their ship was captured, and she languished for six years before being ransomed by a German merchant. Back in England, sick, destitute, and friendless, Alice was unable to repay him.[121] It is clear, however, that in debates over redemption, little attention was paid to the situation of women. The religious orders in Spain and France gave some priority to redeeming women and children, believing them in greater danger of being induced to apostatize, and a confraternity in Sicily adopted a similar approach. Even so, only 5% of ransomed Spaniards were women, with children accounting for another 8%.[122] European and British rulers alike were primarily concerned to ransom healthy sailors and soldiers. Officials urging the British government to redeem slaves generally focused on the interests of the state, arguing that 'stout' seamen enslaved in Barbary could furnish the navy with an instant supply of experienced recruits. Only one contemporary appears to have argued that redeeming women and children should be a priority. In December 1636 Giles Penn, a veteran Barbary merchant, drafted a memorandum advising on the forthcoming expedition to Salé. He urged that the fleet should take Moors and 'Turks' held in English prisons to exchange for English slaves, and start with the women and children, 'who are more weak and readier to turn to the Moors' law than men of better strength in the faith of Christ'.[123] There is no indication that his advice was heeded.

The only account we have by an early female captive is the memoir of Elizabeth Marsh, a passenger captured off the Spanish coast in 1756. Published many years later, in 1769, it stressed the perils and hardships she had endured at Salé and on the journey to Marrakesh. In reality, she and her companions had fared far better than most, for they were treated as captives rather than slaves, and were held in reprisal for the insolent behaviour of a recent British envoy. Marsh claimed that the sultan had tried to entice her to enter his seraglio, a fate she avoided by pretending to be married to one of her fellow passengers. As Linda Colley has shown, the memoir in its published form reflected the Oriental 'Other', with a barbarous population of Arabs and Moors, a fiercely handsome young sultan, and a refined young woman exposed to sexual danger—and temptation.[124] It was far removed from the experience of earlier female captives.

---

[121] *CSPD 1655–6*, 152.

[122] Friedman, *Spanish Captives*, 111, 116–17, 119, 146–7; Dursteler, 'Slavery', 679.

[123] *CSPD 1635–6*, 253; TNA SP 16/133, f.195.

[124] Mrs Crisp (Elizabeth Marsh), *The Female Captive* (1769); Linda Colley, *The Ordeal of Elizabeth Marsh* (2007).

4

Faith and Identity

Christians, Renegades, and Apostasy

Captives in Barbary lost more than physical freedom. They found themselves in
an alien culture, with different religion, customs, language, and clothes. Even those
familiar with the Mediterranean world found the shock profound. They discovered that people they had considered 'barbarians' and 'infidels' saw them in
the very same terms, abused them as 'Christian dogs', and now had them at their
mercy. In adjusting to this hostile new world, some found comfort and strength in
their faith or sense of national identity. Others, less rooted in their old identities,
were persuaded or driven to 'turn Turk', developing new identities that were often
hybrid, multilayered, and mutable. And alongside these captives there were other
sailors and soldiers who had come to Barbary voluntarily, with identities and
loyalties still more fluid.

Christian perseverance

Most British captives had been raised as Protestants, with religion an integral part
of their identity. Many sailors had only a superficial understanding of their faith,
and some only a limited attachment to it, but it was a sliver of inner freedom that
most retained even while their bodies were enslaved. For a small minority, faith lay
at the very heart of their being. When the crew of the *Jesus,* seized at Tripoli in
1584, were stripped of their possessions, the mate refused to part with his
treasured copy of the Geneva bible, until it was snatched away by a renegade.[1]
Another new captive, in Algiers, was overjoyed to find a bible in the cellar where
the slaves slept, and a friend was able to buy it for him.[2] Others, writing home, told
how their faith had sustained them. John Stocker, held at Meknes, vowed in 1716
never to apostatize, even if tortured to death. John Willdon was proud that 'God
hath hitherto given me more grace when others have turned', though the 'hitherto'
hints at anxiety about how much longer he might be able to resist.[3] There were no

[1] Thomas Saunders, *A true Discription and breefe discourse, Of a most lamentable voiage* (1587),
sig. B3.
[2] Joshua Gee, *Narrative of Joshua Gee of Boston, Mass., when he was captive in Algeria of the Barbary
pirates, 1680–1687*, ed. Albert C. Bates (Hartford, Conn., 1945), 17.
[3] TNA SP 71/16, fos. 234, 255.

British Slaves and Barbary Corsairs, 1580–1750. Bernard Capp, Oxford University Press. © Bernard Capp 2022.
DOI: 10.1093/oso/9780192857378.003.0005

shipmasters among the many captives who apostatized in Salé between 1714 and 1721. Masters endured equally harsh treatment and had a considerably higher death-rate, but they were generally older and from better-off families, and education had probably implanted a more solid faith.[4] Slaves with a strong religious commitment helped stiffen the resolve of their weaker brethren. Peter Emes, ransomed after fourteen years at Meknes, was commended as one whose faith had persuaded weaker spirits not to apostatize.[5] Thomas Pocock, chaplain of Greenwich Hospital, paid tribute to a more surprising paragon: a 14-year-old black cabin-boy named Thomas Pero, or Saphra. Captured and taken to Meknes in 1716, he had been flogged and put to hard labour, but was promised 'liberty and preferment' if he apostatized. Instead, he had remained steadfast, choosing, so Pocock claimed, to be a martyr rather than a Moorish alcaid. Pero had probably been enslaved by the British as a child; he had served as a page in the household of an English duchess, and been raised as a Christian. Pocock selected this part of his story to shame the 'unstable' seamen he condemned for abandoning their faith.[6]

Belief in divine providence occupied a significant place in the faith of most committed Protestants, and that trust could give captives the strength to endure their sufferings.[7] God's providence featured prominently in several of the slave narratives. Thomas Saunders, author of the earliest, spelled out in detail the cruelty and treachery of the 'infidels' who had seized him and his shipmates at Tripoli in 1584. But he assured readers that theirs was a righteous God who would avenge their wrongs. Within weeks of their capture, he explained, the 'king' (pasha) of Tripoli had lost half his 300 slaves, swept away by plague, while his camel train had been seized by tribesmen. Moreover, a few months after the English were freed, the 'king' had been murdered by his own soldiers, and the galley carrying his treasure and slaves to Constantinople had been captured by the Venetians, who slaughtered the Moors and renegades and liberated the Christian slaves. God had delivered stern justice on the oppressors.[8]

William Okeley, a puritan captured in 1639 on a voyage to Providence Island in the West Indies, penned a narrative years later that was also framed, appropriately, in highly providential terms. Raised in a godly family, Okeley possessed a strong and confident faith. He entitled it *Eben-ezer*, a paper 'monument' to remind readers of the monument the Hebrews had erected to commemorate

---

[4] Nabil Matar, 'British Captives in Salé (1721), in Stefan Hanss and Juliane Schiel, eds., *Mediterranean Slavery Revisited (500–1800)*, (Zurich, 2014), 523–8.

[5] *CSPD 1699–1700*, 387–8.

[6] Thomas Pocock, *The Relief of Captives, Especially of our own Countreymen* (1720), 11–12; Matar, 'British Captives', 525.

[7] Alexandra Walsham, *Providence in Early Modern England* (Oxford, 1999), provides an excellent survey, though it does not cover Barbary.

[8] Saunders, *True Discription*. On his narrative see Jonathan Burton, 'English Anxiety and the Muslim Power of Conversion: Five Perspectives on "Turning Turk" in Early Modern Texts', *Journal for Early Modern Cultural Studies*, 2 (2002), 37–45.

God's help in a time of danger (1 Samuel 7.12). The introduction proclaimed emphatically that 'This book is Protestant', and a lengthy preface spelled out the lessons readers should take from it, urging them not to be distracted by the adventure of his escape in 1644 in a flimsy boat. Worried that some would find the preface tedious, and be 'wild to come at the story of the boat,' Okeley insisted that his book was written to demonstrate the power of divine providence. God had chosen to deliver him and his companions into captivity, God had enabled them to endure it, and God alone had delivered them, through their near-miraculous escape. Every part of their experience had been divinely ordained to convey that message. Okeley spelled out for his readers how the 'gracious God, looking upon the affliction of His poor servants and considering us in our low estate, was pleased many ways to mitigate the load of our captivity'. God had shown him how to find a livelihood, freed him from his cruel first owner, and provided the spiritual comfort of a preacher. And God alone had preserved them in their perilous escape. Had they been rescued by a passing ship, Okeley reflected, the power of divine providence would have been less apparent.[9] We will never know if Okeley's trust in providence had sustained him throughout, or if he had mentally reconstructed his experience after recovering his liberty. There may be a hint of that in his reflection that miseries 'dreadful to endure are yet delightful to be remembered, and there's a secret pleasure to chew the cud and ruminate upon escaped dangers'.[10]

Okeley's narrative had a swift and enduring impact that has been largely overlooked. The earliest surviving edition dates from 1675, but it was first published in 1668, with another edition a few years later, both now lost. Others followed in 1676, 1684, and a century later in 1764. Moreover, it soon featured in the collections of providential narratives popular with godly and nonconformist readers in the period.[11] The combination of a near-miraculous story and strong moral application proved appealing.

Another former captive, identified only as 'T. R.', described briefly how under the 'merciless Turk' he too had placed his trust in God's providence. His faith had also been rewarded: he had been 'delivered out of captivity by a marvellous way unexpected, the Lord giving me grace to call on him, gave me a gracious answer, that he would never leave me, nor forsake me'.[12] But did the faith of the godly never waver? A providential faith could create stress as well as offer solace. If their suffering was divinely ordained, was God testing their faith for his own inscrutable

---

[9] *Okeley*, sig. A4-5, pp. 1–2, 18, 20–2, 40–1.   [10] *Okeley*, 12.

[11] It had been advertised by the publisher Nathaniel Ponder in John Owen, *Of the Mortification of Sin* (1668). Nathaniel Wanley reproduced the story, from a lost second edition, in *The Wonders of the Little World* (1673), 642–3, copied in R. B., *Wonderful Prodigies* (1682), 202–7, William Turner, *A Compleat History of the most remarkable Providences* (1697), 103–4, and John Janeway, *A Token for Mariners* (1698), 93–101.

[12] (Henry Walker), *The Spirituall Experiences of Sundry Beleevers* (1652), 385–6.

reasons, like Job in the Old Testament? Or must they see it as retribution for their own sins and shortcomings? When John Rawlins and his company were carried to Algiers in 1621, some 'good Christians' urged them 'to be of good cheer', for 'God's trials were gentle purgations, and these crosses were but to cleanse the dross from the gold and bring us out of the fire again, more clear and lovely'.[13] It is not clear that Rawlins was convinced, though he was happy to attribute the success of the mutiny he led the following year to divine providence. Once it was over he assembled his men to give 'praise unto God', and the narrative begins and ends with reflections on God's goodness and providential power.[14]

The fragmentary narrative of Joshua Gee, a Boston puritan captured in 1680, reveals a more complex picture of spiritual troubles and doubts. Gee frequently turned for comfort to the book of Job and other Old Testament texts, especially Psalms, Jeremiah, and Lamentations. But he was convinced that his misery must be the consequence of his own sins or inadequate faith, and this brought him close to the grave sin of despair, and sometimes longing to die. Writing home to his parents he confessed that 'I am ashamed because God's chastisements and reproofs are lasting and sharp', and signed himself 'your poor son under God's rebuke'. That his sufferings were so sharp must surely prove the depth of divine anger at his sins. At other times, 'in desperate darkness', Gee admitted, 'I greatly feared being left to distrust God', and he sometimes fell into the sin of 'complaining of God's dispensations'. Only in retrospect was he able to shape an account in which faith and trust eventually prevailed over doubt, despair, and anger. He hoped that his brief memoir, intended for private circulation among the godly, would inspire future generations to thank and praise the Lord.[15]

Gee was not alone in having his faith shaken by the trauma of enslavement. Devereux Spratt, sailing from Youghal, Ireland, in the winter of 1641–42, had been seized with more than 100 companions before their ship was even out of sight of land. Though he was a minister, he admitted years later that the disaster had undermined his trust in God so deeply that he 'began to question Providence and accused Him of injustice in His dealings with me'. Before long, however, the 'Lord made it appear otherwise'. In Algiers he found pious Englishmen longing for spiritual support, which he was happy to provide. His trust in God's providential wisdom was restored.[16]

The majority of European captives in Barbary were Catholics, not British Protestants. The Catholics enjoyed considerable freedom of worship, shared by Irish and British co-religionists, with captured priests allowed to administer sacraments at altars erected in the bagnios. The priests were generally spared manual labour, with their owners compensated for lost earnings. D'Aranda mentions that his bagnio in Algiers had a space large enough for 300 slaves to

[13] *Rawlins*, sig. Bv.   [14] *Rawlins*, sig. Ev.   [15] Gee, *Narrative*, 16, 25, 27–8.
[16] T. Spratt, ed., *Autobiography of the Rev. Devereux Spratt* (1886), 11–13.

attend Mass. On one occasion, he reports, the slaves told the great corsair Ali Pichellin (Pegelin) that they were without a priest, whereupon he promised to buy the next one captured, and outbid all rivals to keep his word.[17] Slaves were allowed to observe the festivals of Easter and Christmas, and were given respite on the major Muslim festival days. Religious provision was also available from the priests serving in the Trinitarians' hospital.

Protestants, by contrast, had almost no religious provision or support. Devereux Spratt is the only English cleric in the seventeenth century known to have served fellow captives. Pious Englishmen, Okeley among them, had begged him to be their guide, and they promised to maintain him and satisfy his owner, who consented to the arrangement. Thereafter, Spratt held services three times a week in a cellar Okeley had hired, with as many as sixty or eighty attending. Moorish neighbours left them in peace. Though Spratt was soon ransomed, he remained in Algiers at the request of his little flock, ministering for two more years. He was even able to officiate at a wedding, for a woman described as the daughter of a Scottish viscount, and later performed the baptism of her infant daughter. Okeley and his friends also consulted him over their escape plan, and received his blessing.[18]

English consuls in Algiers did not have a resident chaplain until 1706. Informal worship had sometimes been available at the consul's house, however, and four renegades who escaped in 1641 claimed to have attended household worship there.[19] Successive treaties guaranteed the consul a safe 'place to pray in', and Samuel Martin, consul in 1675, reported that English, German, and Dutch Protestants all had a place to preach and pray in his house. Frustratingly, he supplied no details. Were there separate services for each nation or were they shared? Who led them?[20] Domestic worship might sometimes also be available in a merchant's house. Lionel Crofts, a prominent figure in the redemption business in the 1680s, was said to have relieved the sick and needy, and 'those who came on Sunday to prayers to his house'. A testimonial to that effect was supplied by several former slaves back home in Plymouth.[21] At Salé, Adam Elliot was allowed on one occasion to hear an enslaved Catholic priest preach at the French consul's house.[22]

For the most part, however, Protestant captives were left to their own religious devices. They too were allowed a day's liberty at Christmas and Easter, to employ

---

[17] D'Aranda, History, 12, 258–9. In one raid in 1638, Pichellin captured an Italian bishop and thirteen nuns: Francis Knight, A Relation of Seaven Yeares Slaverie (1640), 18–19.

[18] Spratt, Autobiography, 11–13; Robert Lambert Playfair, The Scourge of Christendom (1884), 61; Okeley, 23–4, 43–4.

[19] Calendar of Treasury Papers, 1702–1707, 437, 441. The first chaplain was George Holme. Bartolomé and Lucile Bennassar, Les Chrétiens d'Allah (Paris, 2006), 217. There was no Dutch chaplain until 1726.

[20] TNA SP 71/2, f.65v; George Philips, The Present State of Tangier . . . to which is added the Present State of Algiers (1676), 93.

[21] TNA SP 71/3, f.187c.   [22] Elliot, Modest Vindication, 10.

as they wished. No service was available for the English slaves toiling at Porto Farina in 1657, so they spent Christmas day washing and mending their clothes and killing lice—neither a merry nor pious Christmas.[23] In Algiers, Joshua Gee fashioned his own exercises, praying and singing or reciting psalms, and grateful that the Catholics did not molest him. Longing for something more, he forged ties with a few like-minded companions, and on their rare days of liberty they would walk out to a private garden outside the city to spend the day 'reading and praying and praising God'. Gee had yearned for more public worship, and there is a tantalizing hint that he had aspired to serve as a religious teacher, and possibly did so.[24]

The only other evidence we have of English worship in Algiers comes from the Quakers. In 1680 George Fox wrote to encourage a group of about twenty who held regular meetings there. He also published an open letter to the 'Great Turk and his king in Algiers', condemning their inhumanity and quoting from the Qur'an to prove that in enslaving Christians they were flouting the commands of their own faith.[25] Fox himself had narrowly escaped being captured by Salé corsairs while crossing the Atlantic in 1671.[26]

Earlier in the century, the journal of William Atkins reveals less edifying behaviour among the captives at Salé. A truce between England and Salé led to a ruling that Atkins and his companions, Catholic seminary students, were to be considered captives, not slaves, which meant they could be ransomed but not bought or sold. Atkins reports that malicious English Protestants had sought to prevent them enjoying this favour, claiming that as 'Romish papists' they were not genuine subjects of James I, or that they were Irish and so not covered by the truce. Atkins, who had an Irish complexion, had a narrow escape. His journal also provides another, and darkly comic, glimpse of tensions within the Christian community. When 150 Catholic and Protestant captives were finally ransomed and on their voyage home, the two groups attempted to sabotage each other's services. English and German Protestants and French Huguenots would 'sing, hoot and scoff' during Catholic prayers, and when the Protestants were praying or singing psalms the Catholics beat a drum to drown their words.[27] We have a similar glimpse of hostility between the rival confessions at Tunis a century later. The Christian cemetery outside the city was supposedly for all, but Spanish captives objected strongly to its use by British and Dutch Protestants, and repeatedly ransacked its chapel in protest.[28]

---

[23] Coxere, *Adventures*, 62.   [24] Gee, *Narrative*, 21, 26, 28.

[25] George Fox, *To the Great Turk, and his King in Algiers* (1680); Kenneth C. Carroll, 'Quaker Slaves in Algiers, 1679–1688', *Journal of the Friends' Historical Society*, 54 (1982), 301–12; William C. Braithwaite, *The Second Period of Quakerism*, (1921), 431–2.

[26] John L. Nickalls, ed., *The Journal of George Fox* (Cambridge, 1952), 586, 592–3.

[27] Martin Murphy, ed., 'William Atkins, A Relation of the Journey from St Omers to Seville, 1622', in *Camden Miscellany*, 32 (1994), 244, 258, 264.

[28] Laurent D'Arvieux, *Memoires du Chevalier D'Arvieux* (Paris, 1735), iv.18.

Captives 'turning Turk': persuasion and duress

In 1632 a group of thirty-eight English mariners enslaved in Morocco begged Charles I to secure their freedom. After years in bondage, they wrote, 'some, through the extreme want and servitude which we daily endure, have turned Moors [i.e. Muslims], and some have endured intolerable torment for Christ his sake'. In the same year, captives in Algiers and Tunis made a similar plea, stressing their fear of being forced to apostatize, to the 'utter perdition of their souls'.[29] Many did indeed apostatize—an uncomfortable fact that other captives and their families stressed whenever they begged for help. In 1719 an Exeter couple appealed directly to the archbishop of Canterbury, describing the sufferings of their son Edward Foster and his companions at the hands of 'vile and merciless infidels'. Some had already 'embraced the foul and accursed imposture of Mahomet', they reported, and others would probably follow. They were right: their son Edward would also apostatize.[30] More than seventy of the British slaves held in Meknes in 1714–21 apostatized—a little over 25%.[31]

Letters and other accounts include numerous reports of slaves being beaten to make them accept Islam. John Rawlins, carried to Algiers in 1621, heard lurid accounts of slaves flogged, tortured, and starved until they agreed to convert. Samuel Dawkes told his sister that he had been laid on the ground and flogged on his stomach till the blood ran down.[32] Trinity House, lobbying on behalf of a slave at Salé in 1625, stressed that he had been 'cruelly misused to make him forsake Christ, and serve Mahomet'.[33] In 1632 the ruler of Morocco vented his fury at the failure of negotiations with Charles I by having eight English merchants seized, ordered to accept Islam, and forcibly circumcised. One who resisted was threatened with decapitation.[34]

In most cases, however, extreme physical abuse was designed to make captives agree to large ransom demands, not secure their conversion.[35] Joseph Pitts assured his readers that conversion by brute force was uncommon. It was against Islamic teaching and against the owners' interests, for converts could not be ransomed. Most owners, he explained, had no wish to see their slaves convert, for 'they are more in love with their money than they are with the welfare of their slaves', and wanted a profit from their investment.[36] A few owners, determined to retain a valued slave, might resort to forcible conversion to prevent his being redeemed, but such instances were rare.[37]

[29] Vitkus, *Piracy*, 359–60; TNA SP 71/1, f.113v.
[30] TNA SP 71/21, f.28; Matar, 'British Captives', 526. Foster had been mate of the *Friendship* of Bristol.
[31] Matar, 'British Captives', 515–40.   [32] *Rawlins*, sig, Bv-2; TNA SP 29/276, f.227.
[33] Harris, *Trinity House*, 66.   [34] TNA SP 71/12, fos. 208–11.   [35] See Chapter 3.
[36] *Pitts*, 181–2.   [37] Bennassar, *Chrétiens*, 214–15.

Why, then, did many slaves apostatize? Apostasy was a widespread phenom-enon throughout the Mediterranean, among free men and women as well as captives, and prompted by a wide range of motives.[38] In the case of slaves, it is evident that the majority, though not literally forced, accepted Islam under duress in the hope of alleviating their situation. As William Okeley sighed, 'How many have made shipwreck of faith that they might not be chained to the galleys?' The chaplain of Greenwich hospital lamented that 'too many unstable Christian slaves choose rather to be circumcised, than work and starve'.[39] He recognized that many sailors had little education and only a limited commitment to their religion. William Gouge thought that most apostates probably hoped to escape one day and return to their Christian faith, though he doubted that one in a thousand would succeed.[40] Apostasy did not bring liberation, but converts would usually be spared heavy labour and the galleys, and would hope to be freed eventually.[41] It is hardly surprising that some captives enduring hunger, heavy labour, and harsh discipline seized the chance of even limited relief. In 1681 the consul at Tripoli heard that 300 had apostatized at Algiers since the outbreak of hostilities three years earlier. 'Oh! Horrible, horrible shame, damned shame!' he wailed.[42] A later group of eighty half-starved captives in Morocco were reduced to such despair that a quarter had 'converted' within a month.[43]

Captives who saw no prospect of redemption might easily sink into despair, which contemporaries identified as the most powerful trigger of apostasy. And despair intensified if hopes had been raised and then dashed.[44] In 1716, slaves in Meknes were devastated that a British envoy in Gibraltar had failed to negotiate their release. One wrote home that 'all nations is provided for but the poor English has no assistance from their nation but a parcel of lies and stories to come to clear us & none will come…abundance is dead & turned Moor for want, and will abundance more without God's great mercy'. He too was to die in captivity. John Willdon was equally bitter. 'I believe all Christian people have forgotten us in England', he wrote. 'We have had many temptations to turn Moors'.[45] The collapse of talks in 1718 created further despair. The English consul in Tetuan reported that five slaves, dismayed by the news and in desperate need of clothes, lodging, and food, had 'turned Moors…expecting to remedy their misfortunes'. He feared others would follow.[46]

---

[38] For an insightful discussion see Eric R. Dursteler, *Venetians and Constantinople. Nation, Identity and Coexistence in the Early Modern Mediterranean* (Baltimore, 2006), esp. 112–15, 118–19.

[39] *Okeley*, 21; Pocock, *Relief*, 10.   [40] William Gouge, *A Recovery from Apostasy* (1639), 42.

[41] *Pitts*, 182.

[42] C. R. Pennell, ed., *Piracy and Diplomacy in Seventeenth-Century North Africa. The Journal of Thomas Baker, English Consul in Tripoli 1677–1685* (Cranbury, NJ, 1989), 132.

[43] Thomas Troughton, *Barbarian Cruelty; or an Accurate and Impartial Narrative* (1751), 32.

[44] TNA SP 71/1, f.133; SP 71/3, f.186; Nabil Matar, *British Captives from the Mediterranean to the Atlantic, 1563–1760* (Leiden, 2014), 48–9, 110.

[45] TNA SP 71/16, fos. 255v-6.   [46] TNA SP 71/16, f.300; cf. Troughton, *Barbarian Cruelty*, 103.

A captive resigned to spending the rest of his days in Barbary might well decide to make the best of his unhappy lot. And if he happened to possess any valuable practical skills, he might well be offered inducements to make 'conversion' more palatable. Edward Coxere, a master's mate, shared the degrading treatment of the other slaves, but he was quickly identified as a skilled mariner and fluent in several languages. He was then set to work as a boatswain directing other slaves fitting out a warship to serve the Ottomans, and told that if he converted he might soon be commanding a ship of his own. When he refused, explaining that he had a wife and children in England, the objection was brushed aside with the promise of another wife in Tunis. He still refused, but it is easy to see why others might be tempted by such an offer.[47] In the late 1580s Richard Hasleton had been offered far greater inducements when he fell into the hands of a warlike Moorish tribe. When his captors discovered his skill in gunnery and carpentry, the 'king' offered him a salary equivalent to £50 a year (more than many an English yeoman then earned), money for daily subsistence, a house with farmland and oxen, and a wife of his own choosing. The 'queen' and her attendants pressed him to accept, and marvelled that he still refused. But when he attempted to escape, he was flogged, clapped in irons, and thrown in prison. Slave-owners were always ready with both carrots and sticks.[48]

Most British captives had no contact with the ministers or services of the faith in which they had been raised. Those with only a limited grasp of that faith would find its hold steadily weakening.[49] For many with little education, religion was more about rituals and traditions than doctrinal creeds. The fact that contemporaries spoke of 'turning Turk' or (in Morocco) 'turning Moor', rather than 'converting to Islam', underlined the fact that apostasy was recognized as essentially about cultural identity, expressed through the externals of dress, name, and conduct. For the pragmatic, apostasy made sense on many levels, not least freedom from the ubiquitous abuse that Christians faced. The process was simple: the convert had merely to recite the Arabic words asserting that there was one God and that Mahomet was his prophet, and point his index finger towards heaven. He would then be given Moorish dress (including a turban) and a new Muslim name, and within a few days he would be circumcised. If a conversion had been genuinely voluntary, there would be music too, and a procession.[50] While such occasions were rare, a few captives were determined to convert even in the face of the owner's opposition. One report told of a French galley-slave so eager to embrace Islam that he cut off his beard and adopted Turkish dress to proclaim his new allegiance. Unwilling to lose his services, his owner had him flogged until he promised to remain Christian.[51] James Grey, originally from Weymouth, also

---

[47] Coxere, *Adventures*, 58.   [48] *Hasleton*, sig. Dii-iv[v.]
[49] Knight, *Relation of Seaven Yeares Slaverie*, 2.
[50] *Pitts*, 196–9; cf. Bennassar, *Chrétiens*, 299–318.   [51] D'Aranda, *History*, 174; cf. *Pitts*, 182.

converted against his owner's wish. He learned to read the Qur'an in Arabic, was diligent in attending mosque and performing other religious duties, and 'was looked on as a zealot'. Joseph Pitts, who knew him well, assumed he had apostatized for material gain, but that was merely speculation.[52]

Many apostates were doubtless swayed by a mixture of motives. The longing to escape beatings and privation pulled in the same direction as dreams of advancement and eventual liberty. Many went on to serve with the army or corsairs, and a few forged successful careers. In other cases, disappointment triggered remorse. One man developed feelings of guilt after failing to secure the post he coveted, and his thoughts now turned to escape.[53] In a few cases, apostasy served as a desperate move to escape punishment. Sexual relations between Christian men and Moorish women were strictly forbidden, on pain of death for both parties, and some offenders hastily apostatized to save their lives. Renegades faced no such sexual constraints. In a few other cases a trusted slave had accepted Islam in order to marry his owner's sister or daughter.[54] No instances of such apostasies have been discovered among British captives, but a few may well have occurred.

Children and adolescents

The youngest captives were inevitably the most susceptible to both pressure and inducements. Boys intended for a maritime career often went to sea at the age of only 8 or 9, and such captives were especially prized, for it was easier to mould new identities and train them to perform loyally in new roles. When corsairs captured a small fishing boat, they would sometimes indeed take only the ship's boy and let adults go free. It would have been almost impossible for frightened and bewildered children, separated from their companions, to resist physical and psychological pressure to apostatize. Some were given no choice. Roger Hurt, son of a Bristol merchant, had been captured aged 10 in 1618 by Salé corsairs; twenty years later he was described as 'chief of the English eunuchs' in the seraglio, and 'a devout Moor'.[55] William Ezer, captured aged 12, was given a new Muslim name and circumcised even before the corsairs had returned to Salé. In another case, an English renegade raised a child's hand, recited the Arabic words of conversion on his behalf, and had him circumcised. The child would have understood little of what was being done in his name.[56] Some of these youngsters

---

[52] *Pitts*, 219–21; cf. Bennassar, *Chrétiens*, 215–16.

[53] T. S., *The Adventures of (Mr. T. S.) an English Merchant, taken Prisoner by the Turks* (1670), 71.

[54] Bennassar, *Chrétiens*, 304, 313; Leila Maziane, *Salé et ses Corsaires (1666–1727). Un port de corse marocain au xviie siècle* (Caen, 2007), 98; Dursteler, *Venetians and Constantinople*, 103–29.

[55] Murphy, 'William Atkins', 246 n.70.

[56] Bennassar, *Chrétiens*, 319–37, esp. 325–8. For captured Muslims similarly baptized by signs alone, see John C. Appleby, 'The Problem of Piracy in Ireland, 1570–1630', in C. Jowitt, ed., *Pirates? The Politics of Plunder, 1550–1650* (2007), 48.

were taken into the service of the pasha or other dignitary, and were well treated. Many later became janissaries, or came to hold official positions in Barbary or the Ottoman administration. At least one achieved eminence. Samson Rowlie, the son of a Bristol merchant, had been captured in 1577, and by 1586 had risen to become Chief Eunuch and Treasurer of Algiers, serving the beglerbeg.[57] Privately owned captives might come to accept their *patron*'s family as their own, and be trained as artisans and craftsmen. Other youngsters were valued as personal attendants, comparable to the young black domestic slaves prized by European elites. And in some cases there might also be a sexual dimension. English writers often denounced the Moors as sodomites, and the charge was widely believed. Sir Thomas Allin, negotiating exchanges at Algiers in 1664, reported that it had proved difficult to release one youngster because 'his old roguish patron was loath to part from him having abused him'.[58] John Rawlins, carried to Algiers, was told of more than 'a hundred handsome youths compelled to turn Turks or made subject to more viler prostitution—and all English!' While that was merely hearsay, young captives were particularly vulnerable to pressure, whether sexual or religious. Rawlins' own cabin-boy and the ship-owner's young servant were separated from the adults, and their captors soon 'by force and torture compelled them to turn Turk'.[59] By contrast, two boys belonging to the garrison at Tangier deserted and 'turned Moors' voluntarily when a truce ended the siege in May 1680.[60]

Two captives have left vivid and revealing testimonies of 'turning Turk'. Both eventually escaped and returned to the Christian fold, insisting they had apostatized only under extreme duress. Joseph Pitts had been captured in his mid-teens, Thomas Pellow at age 11. Pellow had been given by the sultan of Morocco to one of his many sons, Moulay es-Sfa, and insisted he had yielded only after months of being beaten, starved, and shackled in irons. Even then, he had refused to adopt Moorish dress until broken by further beatings. It was perhaps this unexpected obstinacy that had fuelled his owner's rage, and made him determined to break the boy's spirit. Years later, slaves told a visiting diplomat that Pellow had 'endured enough to have killed seven men' before he yielded.[61]

By contrast, Joseph Pitts' first owner, a cavalry officer named Dilberre Ibrahim, had no particular wish to convert him. It was his brother, a zealot, who tempted

[57] Richard Hakluyt, *The Principal Navigations* (1599), part ii, 180; Gerald M. MacLean, *Looking East. English Writing and the Ottoman Empire before 1800* (Basingstoke, 2007), 101–5 (with a watercolour portrait, in Turkish dress, reproduced on 105).
[58] Nabil Matar, 'Sodomy and Conquest', in his *Turks, Moors and Englishmen in the Age of Discovery* (New York, 1999), 109–27; R. C. Anderson, ed., *The Journals of Sir Thomas Allin, 1660–1678* (Navy Records Society, 79–80, 1939–40), i.174–5; cf. Murphy, *William Atkins*, 246.
[59] *Rawlins*, sig. B-2; cf. Harris, *Trinity House*, 16.
[60] *An Exact Journal of the Siege of Tangier* (1680), 12.
[61] Thomas Pellow, *The History of the Long Captivity and Adventures of Thomas Pellow* (1751; first published 1740), 14–16; John Braithwaite, *The History of the Revolutions in the Empire of Morocco* (1729), 192.

the youngster with promises and, when these failed, pressed Ibrahim to act, telling him that as a debauchee and murderer he had no hope of paradise without some meritorious act to atone. His words hit home. Pitts was now forced into Turkish dress with his hair shorn, the outward symbols of conversion, and when he still clung to his Christian faith, 'crying and weeping', he was bastinadoed—tied to a post and beaten on the soles of his feet with a cudgel—until he finally uttered the prescribed words that signified conversion. Not long afterwards, he received a smuggled letter from his father in England, offering a ransom. He begged his owner to accept it, explaining that he was still a Christian at heart, but Ibrahim threatened to have him burned alive if he ever spoke of it again. Pitts wrote back to his father, confessing his sin and begging forgiveness. After consulting three Presbyterian minsters, his father was eventually able to reassure him that he might yet find forgiveness if he repented and could return to his Christian faith. In the event, Pitts was to remain a slave for many more years. He tells us that he often reread his father's letter in secret, to find comfort.[62]

The chaotic politics of Algiers eventually released Pitts from his first owner. Ibrahim had schemed to make himself dey, and when his plot failed he had been beheaded. Pitts had several more owners, the last a kindly man who eventually freed him, entering him into pay in the military. Pitts served with the army and also with the corsairs, clearly willing to serve against Christians. In one cruise, he reports, 'we' took a Venetian galley whose crew of 400 were all enslaved. He explains that he had opted to serve at sea in the hope of finding a chance to escape, though he acknowledges that his master believed him to be 'a true Mussulman'. His narrative describes in detail the hazardous escape plan he eventually devised. If it failed, he could expect to die; if it succeeded, he would forfeit his pay for the cruise, his share of prize money, and the generous bequest he had been promised. His *patron*, he reflected, had 'loved me as if I had been his own child, which made me sincerely to love him' and this, he admitted, had made it tempting to return to Algiers 'and continue a Mussulman'. In the event, the pull of family, home, and faith proved too strong. But even if Pitts was honest in insisting that his conversion to Islam had never been sincere, his life as a liberated renegade evidently had considerable appeal.[63]

Thomas Pellow remained a slave still longer, for twenty-three years. He too was freed from his first sadistic owner by a twist of fate, when sultan Moulay Ismail had his disobedient son strangled. The young slave now became a royal attendant, was later given a wife (and, unusually, allowed a choice), and went on to a fairly successful military career. Though twice wounded, Pellow acknowledged that he

---

[62] *Pitts*, 192–205.

[63] *Pitts*, 209–10, 216–19, 228, 239–40, 246–7. For a good discussion see Paul Auchterlonie, ed., *Encountering Islam. Joseph Pitts: an English Slave in 17th-Century Algiers and Mecca* (2012), Part 1, 60–4.

had also found much to enjoy in this way of life, and he grew fond of his wife and little children. He appears to have given little serious thought to escape until after Moulay Ismail's death in 1727, which plunged Morocco into chaos as rivals struggled for power. Pellow suffered more wounds, and recognized that his chances of long-term survival were slim. Moreover his wife and children had died, further loosening his ties; he had been fond of his young daughter, dubbing her 'the little prattler'. His eventual flight owed as much to 'push' factors as to the pull of home.[64]

Both Pellow and Pitts hoped to convince readers that they had never truly accepted the new identities forced upon them. Pellow claimed he had taught his wife and little daughter the rudiments of the Christian faith, and had told the child stories of England.[65] To a considerable degree, however, both had developed hybrid identities, however reluctant and nominal their initial 'conversion' to Islam. Both were very conscious of the suspicion they faced after returning to England. They had lived as Muslims for many years, far longer than they had been Christians. Pitts' generally respectful accounts of his hajj to Mecca, the society and culture of Algiers, and the generosity of his last owner, would have reinforced doubts. He left the painful task of explaining his apostasy almost to the end of his narrative, and acknowledged that many would judge him harshly. In mitigation he pleaded his youth and sufferings, and insisted that his godly upbringing had enabled him to resist far longer than most.[66] Many owners were able to secure the submission of boys and adolescents without having to resort to prolonged violence. Most young apostates were quickly absorbed into their new world, never returned to England, and in many cases may have lost any wish to do so.

A third narrative comes to us indirectly through the puritan minister William Gouge, and provides another example of apostasy under duress. Vincent Jukes was a young ship's cook from a somewhat disreputable family in Shropshire, and poorly equipped to resist pressure when he was carried to Algiers in 1637. He was sold to a 'negro [who] used him most cruelly: and by daily threatenings and sore beatings forced him to renounce his Christian religion'. Jukes was made to adopt Moorish dress and customs and was circumcised, but the following year he contrived to escape, and made his way back to England. Deeply troubled over his apostasy, he consulted a minister, and his case eventually reached Archbishop Laud. The outcome was a very public ceremony conducted by Gouge to receive him back into the Christian fold.[67]

Conversion under duress was not uncommon among young men like Jukes, as well as among children and adolescents. Some owners refused to brook defiance,

---

[64] Pellow, *History*, 16–17, 70–2, 83–4, 106–9, 118, 134, 158, 186.
[65] Pellow, *History*, 190, 193–4.   [66] *Pitts*, pp. xiii–xiv, 192–6.
[67] Richard Gough, *The History of Myddle*, ed. David Hey (Harmondsworth, 1982), 115; Gouge, *Recovery*; Linda Colley, *Captives. Britain, Empire and the World, 1600–1850* (2002), 82–3.

and several accounts again hint at a homosocial or homosexual dimension. Thus Thomas Saunders of the *Jesus*, enslaved at Tripoli in 1584, explained that most of the company had been put to hard labour in the quarries, but that the pasha's son 'greatly fancied Richard Burges, our purser, and James Smith, they were both young men therefore he was very desirous to have them turn Turk'. When they refused, another young slave, John Nelson, already an apostate, was directed to persuade them. And when they still refused, the pasha's son took them back with him to the island of Djerba, which he governed, and had them pinned to the ground and circumcised by force. Despite their protests, they were henceforth deemed converts. Queen Elizabeth eventually secured the release of the surviving captives, through her ambassador in Constantinople, but it was ruled that the converts must remain. Providence, as Saunders saw it, decided otherwise. When the pasha died, his son sailed for Constantinople to surrender his father's treasure and slaves to the sultan, as required by Ottoman law. The three young men were among them, and during the passage they plotted with other English slaves to seize the vessel. Their plot failed, and they were put in chains to be hanged once the ship arrived, but, as noted earlier, providence intervened once more: the ship was intercepted and captured by Venetian galleys, and the surviving slaves were freed. Burges and Smith eventually reached home safely.[68]

Reports of apostasy, whatever the circumstances, aroused deep concern in England. There were far more conversions from Christianity to Islam than in the opposite direction, which might undermine confidence in the faith itself. Apostates who were recaptured, or found their way back to England, presented another problem. One high-profile case concerned a young captive who had joined the corsairs but in 1628 was recaptured by an English warship. He was willing to return to the Christian fold, so a ceremony was arranged in his home town of Minehead, with two powerful sermons. Criticizing his 'frailty and weakness', the preachers explained that this 'piratical thief of the sea' had apostatized through a combination of fear and the lure of riches. They urged their listeners to give generously to redemption efforts to save others from similar suffering and temptation. Charles FitzGeffrey, preaching at Plymouth in 1636, said he might pity apostates who to 'free their bodies have made galley-slaves of their souls', but 'Excuse them I cannot'.[69] The following year. Archbishop Laud designed an elaborate ceremony for others seeking to return to the Christian fold—a response to pastoral concerns raised by parish clergymen.[70] William Gouge, preaching at the ceremony to restore Jukes, suspected that many apostates eventually contrived to return home without ever revealing their condition. He warned any present that

[68] Saunders, *True Discription*, sig. C2-v, C4-v; cf. Sir Godfrey Fisher, *Barbary Legend. War, Trade and Piracy in North Africa 1415–1830* (Oxford, 1957), 116–18.

[69] Edward Kellet and Henry Byam, *A Returne from Argier* (1628), sig. A2, 31–4 and *passim*; Charles FitzGeffrey, *Compassion towards Captives* (Oxford, 1637), 34–5.

[70] Reprinted in Vitkus, *Piracy*, 361–6.

they faced damnation unless they acknowledged their sin and underwent a similar ceremony, for apostasy, 'whether it be by fair or foul means, is to deny the Christian faith, and to renounce Christ himself'. He urged Jukes to persuade any he might know to come forward and, if persuasion failed, inform a minister so that the Church could try to rescue them from what he had earlier dubbed 'slavery under Satan'.[71]

Renegade corsairs

As already noted, by no means all apostates had been captives. In the early seventeenth century, many British seamen voluntarily threw in their lot with the renegade corsairs operating from Tunis and Algiers. Many of the corsairs had been Elizabethan privateers, and had refused to surrender their commissions when James I made peace with Spain in 1604.[72] One leading renegade, Peter Easton, allegedly boasted that he saw no need to obey a king for he was himself a king on the seas.[73] John Ward, a former fisherman who emerged as the most successful of the English renegades, struck a lucrative deal with Uthman Dey, governor of Tunis from 1590 to 1610. Recruiting English and European seamen and Ottoman soldiers, Ward captured a succession of prizes that brought him huge wealth and a flow of fresh recruits. He built a grand house of marble and alabaster and lived 'in a most princely and magnificent state', a visitor reported in 1615, attended by 'fifteen circumcised English runagates'. Robert Daborne's play, A Christian turn'd Turke (1612), focused on Ward's apostasy. His position had become less secure after his greatest ship sank in 1608, with the loss of about 400 'Turks' and Moors, whose families blamed him for the disaster. By converting in 1610, taking a Muslim name and a new wife, an Italian apostate, Ward was seeking to protect his standing and safety. He died of plague in 1622, but his name lived on for decades in popular ballads—an ambivalent figure, part hero, part villain.[74]

Some of Ward's lieutenants also apostatized. Sir Francis Verney had abandoned England after a dispute over his father's settlement, and by 1609 was commanding a man-of-war preying on shipping in the Mediterranean. He too married a Muslim. Verney's roving career proved short, however. He was captured, and

---

[71] Gouge, Recovery. 13, 26, 41, 62–4, 82–3, 89–90.

[72] Fisher, Barbary Legend, chaps. 8–10; James A. Larkin and Paul L. Hughes, eds., Stuart Royal Proclamations . . . 1603–1625 (Oxford, 1973), 30–2, 145–7, 203–6.

[73] CSPVen. 1610–13, 433.

[74] Greg Bak, Barbary Pirate. The Life and Crimes of John Ward (Stroud, 2006); Andrew Barker, A True and Certaine Report of the Beginning, Proceedings, and Overthrowes . . . of Captains Ward and Danseker (1609); Newes from Sea of two notorious Pyrats (1609); William Lithgow, The Totall Discourse, of the rare Adventures . . . of long nineteene yeers Travailes (1640), 357–8, 380–2; Robert Daborne, A Christian turn'd Turke (1612), reprinted in Daniel J. Vitkus, ed., Three Turk Plays from Early Modern England (New York, 2000); The Seamans Song of Captain Ward the famous Pyrate (1658–64, but first published in his lifetime).

for two years toiled as a Sicilian galley-slave before being ransomed by the Jesuits, on condition of converting to Catholicism. He died in 1615 in a Palermo hospital.[75]

Many of the seamen who joined Ward and his fellows came from the ships they had taken prize. Many did so willingly, with others merely hoping to avoid being killed or sold into slavery. Other recruits deserted from merchant ships visiting ports in Barbary, lured by the promise of easy money. One shipmaster, sent to Tunis in 1606 to persuade Ward to abandon piracy, had to explain, embarrassingly, that Ward had instead enticed away many of his own men. Many others followed.[76] A memorandum to the Privy Council in 1632 argued that it was essential to maintain a consul at Algiers to deter those 'who would leave the king's service and beset themselves to rob everybody'.[77] Youngsters too could be lured away, like an unhappy ship's boy on the Green Dragon, who voluntarily turned Turk at Tripoli in 1584.[78] A mariner's log in 1651 records a similar case. The governor of Tripoli (Aga of the janissaries) had come aboard one day, with about ten of his renegades, and took away one of the ship's boys 'and so carried him ashore and turned Turk but the boy was willing before to go'. No doubt they had filled his head with promises of adventure and riches.[79]

In the first half of the century many of Barbary's leading corsairs were European renegades. Englishmen were prominent among them in the 1600s and 1610s, and others continued to appear, less frequently, for decades thereafter. In 1626-27, for example, one of the largest Tunisian men-of-war was commanded by an Englishman named Good.[80] A few reached high positions: Sir John Lawson, negotiating with Tunis in 1662, found that his interlocutor, the Tunisian Vice-Admiral, was also an English renegade.[81] Lists compiled after the Restoration still identified up to half the reis in Algiers as renegades, with a few Englishmen among them.[82] One was commanding the Green Serpent, thirty-eight guns, in 1669, and the Julius Caesar, presumably a prize, a few years later.[83] The lieutenant of the Algerian Admiral in 1670 had formerly served in the British navy, and a decade later another man-of-war also had an English renegade lieutenant.[84] Other

---

[75] Frances Parthenope Verney and Margaret M. Verney, The Memoirs of the Verney Family (1970), i.60–8; HMC, 24, Rutland MSS, i.421; HMC, 75, Downshire MSS, ii.160; CSPVen. 1610–13, 100; Francis Cartwright, The Life, Confession, and Heartie Repentance of Francis Cartwright, Gentleman (1621), sig. D.

[76] G. E. Manwaring and W. G. Perrin, eds., The Life and Works of Sir Henry Mainwaring, Navy Records Society, 54, 56, (1920–2), ii.22–3; CSP, Ireland, 1608–10, 278–9; Harris, Trinity House, 49–1; Bak, Barbary Pirate, 59–61.

[77] TNA SP 71/1, f.116.   [78] Saunders, True Discription, sig. C2.

[79] BL, MS Sloane 3494, f.23.   [80] CSPVen. 1626–8, 117–18; cf. D'Aranda, History, 4.

[81] TNA SP71/26, fos. 15-v. The Algerian Admiral in 1651, Winter, also had an English-sounding name: HMC, 29, Portland MSS, ii.79.

[82] TNA SP 71/1, fos. 238–9, 354–5, 472; SP 71/2, f.137; SP 71/3, f.343.

[83] TNA SP 18/202, f.159; cf. CSPVen. 1657–9, 279; TNA SP 71/1, f.354; BL Sloane MS 2755, f.53.

[84] CSPD 1670, 374–5; HMC, 71, Finch MSS, ii.120–1.

renegades sailed with the corsairs of Tunis, Salé, and Tripoli. The Tunisian man-of-war that captured Coxere in 1657 had an English captain and an English gunner.[85] There were Scottish renegades too. An Algerian raider captured in 1676 near Orkney had Scottish commanders, whose local knowledge would have been essential in these waters. The company also included two English slaves.[86]

Renegade corsairs led hazardous lives, and many died in action. Tibalt Saxbridge, an Irish *reis* who had taken his small man-of-war across the Atlantic, was killed in 1609 attempting to seize a French vessel off Newfoundland.[87] A captured renegade also faced the risk of being condemned for piracy, and several of Ward's lieutenants and successors ended on the gallows. One of them, James Harris, was a former privateer who had been captured by Tunisian corsairs and endured three years as a galley-slave before being ransomed by Captain Bishop, a leading corsair. Bishop gave him a ship and crew to set up on his own account, but after enjoying considerable success Harris was trapped at Baltimore in 1609, carried to London, tried, and hanged. Better educated than most, he made a pious and penitential end.[88] The notorious Captain Sampson Denball was captured by a Maltese and Sicilian force and ended his career as a galley-slave, while Toby Glanville, another *reis*, committed suicide to escape trial.[89] Captured renegades could also face summary justice. It was left to the discretion of commanders to hang them, keep them for exchange, or return them to their native land for punishment. Sir John Lawson was reported to have hanged those he captured in 1661, and Cloudesley Shovell hanged an English lieutenant serving on a Barbary man-of-war in 1681.[90] A doughty German shipmaster went further: after capturing an Algerian galley, he freed the thirty-two slaves found on board and hanged all the renegades.[91] A corsair's life was often short, and its rewards unpredictable.

Many other renegades—Britons and continental Europeans alike—served in the military. The early adventurers were soon outnumbered by captives who had chosen to apostatize. In the regencies most then joined the janissaries, and both there and in Morocco they formed a significant element in Barbary's armed forces. Skilled gunners were especially valued. Hadj Mustapha, the highest commander under the dey of Algiers in a crushing victory over Tunis in 1694, was rumoured to be an English renegade, and ruled as dey himself for five years from 1700.

[85] Coxere, *Adventures*, 55; T. S., *Adventures*, 15; TNA SP 71/12, fos. 182, 183v, 197; Maziane, *Salé*, 193; John Baltharpe, *The Straights Voyage* (1671), 63–4.
[86] *CSPD 1676–7*, 246.
[87] C. M. Senior, *A Nation of Pirates. English Piracy in its Heyday* (Newton Abbot, 1976), 64–5.
[88] *The Lives, Apprehensions, Arraignments, and Executions of the 19. late Pyrates* (1609), sig. A2-C.
[89] Senior, *Nation of Pirates*, 96–7.
[90] Pepys, *Catalogue*, iv.538; *CSPVen. 1661–64*, 53; HMC 71, *Finch MSS*, ii.120–1.
[91] *CSPD 1680–1*, 322.

Whether or not his English origin was true, it was clearly plausible. Possibly his mother was an English concubine.[92]

Another important group of renegades occupied administrative positions. The most able of those captured as children or adolescents were sent to serve the Ottomans, or rose to positions of authority in Barbary itself. The best known, and most successful, was the eunuch Samson Rowlie, Treasurer of Algiers, who served the beglerbeg in the 1580s.[93] Older captives or army deserters might occupy roles as dragomen, or interpreters. In 1685 the new consul in Algiers was delighted to find that his new dragoman was an English renegade who 'writes both Turkish and Moorish' and appeared honest.[94] Moulay Ismail, sultan of Morocco, employed British renegades in many roles. Jonas Rowland, a deserter from the garrison at Tangier, accompanied, as interpreter, the Moroccan ambassador sent to England in 1681.[95] The role of interpreter, moreover, could easily grow into that of intermediary. Hamet Lucas, another army deserter and secretary to the alcaid of Tetuan and Tangier in the late 1690s, played a key role in negotiations with Britain. An envoy commented wryly that as interpreter Lucas 'makes us say whatever he pleases to the alcaid, or the alcaid to us'.[96] For several decades, consuls and envoys found it essential to cultivate his friendship. In charge of the customs at Tangier for many years, Lucas grew rich and was said to be worth £20,000, described as 'a monstrous sum in this country'.[97] Renegades held other significant posts too. John Brown, an alcaid in charge of the British slaves in Meknes, was sufficiently important to be brought a gift by a plenipotentiary in 1721. Andrew Flemming was described as Inspector-General of the military stores in the city. A better-known figure, James Carr or Kerr, an Irish renegade captured as a youth, had been induced to convert by Moulay Ismail with promises of money and 'fine women'. Carr's foundry was the only significant manufacturer of ordnance within Morocco, and he jealously guarded the secrets of his craft. Ismail had full confidence in his commitment to his new identity.[98] Another apostate, named Martin, occupied a very different position in Moroccan society. Obeying a message received in a dream, he had left England to join a *marabout* in Salé, and went on to become a prophet and healer.[99]

---

[92] Matar, *Turks, Moors and Englishmen*, 44–55; TNA SP 71/3, f. 290; John B. Wolf, *The Barbary Coast. Algeria under the Turks, 1500 to 1830* (New York, 1979), 279–81.

[93] Hakluyt, *Principal Navigations*, part ii, 180; MacLean, *Looking East*, 104.

[94] TNA SP 71/3, f.2.

[95] P. G. Rogers, *A History of Anglo-Moroccan Relations to 1900* (1977), 56.

[96] TNA SP 71/14, fos. 252, 255; HMC 32, *Fitzherbert MSS*, 188–9; Milton, *White Gold*, 43, 47.

[97] Braithwaite, *History*, 65–6, 81–5.

[98] *A Description of the Nature of Slavery among the Moors* (1721), 21; Milton, *White Gold*, 145–6, 190; TNA SP71/16, fos. 320, 330-v; Braithwaite, *History*, 165, 185–8; Colley, *Captives*. 60. For an English alcaid in 1638 see Boris Penrose, ed., *The Barbary Voyage of 1638* (Philadelphia, 1929), 21–2.

[99] Nabil Matar, 'Piracy and Captivity in the Early Modern Mediterranean: the Perspective from Barbary', in Jowitt, ed., *Pirates?*, 70.

Throughout the period we hear too of sailors and others who had apostatized on a whim, often to avoid punishment after quarrelling with a superior. An Elizabethan merchant's servant in Morocco, for example, had converted in pique after clashing with his master.[100] In 1681 Thomas Baker, consul at Tripoli, was informed that a gunner had gone to the dey, declared his wish to turn Turk, and pronounced the words that made him a Muslim. Baker hastened to the castle, took the 'rogue' away, and delivered him back to his ship—a high-handed intervention that would have been impossible in Algiers or Tunis.[101] Some of these casual apostates came to regret the decisions they had taken so lightly. Hezekiah Ware, for example, had apostatized on an impulse which, Baker commented, 'is no uncommon accident to our drunken hard-headed [i.e. thick-headed] sailors'. When Ware arrived in Tripoli, lamenting his 'rashness and folly', Baker provided a certificate testifying that he now wished to return to the Christian faith. This would be helpful should he ever reach home, but dangerously incriminating if it was discovered, for apostasy from Islam carried the death penalty.[102] In one notorious case, a Spanish friar, whose conversion had been celebrated as a triumph for Islam, died at the stake after reverting to Christianity—a horrific scene depicted in a woodcut in one of the slave narratives.[103] Jonas Rowland, who was judged to have insulted Mahomet, suffered an equally terrible fate: hanged naked from a gibbet for three days, covered in fish oil to attract biting insects, and then plunged into a vat of boiling oil.[104]

Conversion was a sufficiently important issue to be included in negotiations in the later seventeenth century. Articles agreed at Salé in 1676 required anyone wishing to 'turn Moor' to appear before an English official and affirm it was his free choice.[105] A treaty with Tripoli the same year required a prospective convert to appear three times before the dey, with the consul's dragoman, to confirm this was genuinely the case.[106] The proviso was modified in 1704; a proselyte would now be sent to the consul's house for three days, to see if he stood by his resolution.[107] A treaty with Tunis in 1699 prohibited seducing as well as coercing Christians to convert. There had been nothing on such issues in Admiral Herbert's treaty with Algiers in 1682, but in 1703 Shovell was directed to insert a similar clause into a revised treaty. These articles met with considerable resistance in Barbary, and in 1704 Tunis refused to renew the religious clause.[108]

---

[100] George Wilkins, *Three Miseries of Barbary: Plague. Famine. Ciuill warre* (1607), sig. B2-v; Pitts, 197; Maziane, *Salé*, 98.

[101] Pennell, *Piracy*, 126.   [102] Pennell, *Piracy*, 133–4.

[103] *Okeley*, frontispiece; D'Aranda, *History*, 196–200; Pitts, 241–2.

[104] William Franklin, *A Letter from Tangier concerning the Death of Jonas Rowland, the Renegade* (1682).

[105] TNA SP 71/14, f.150v. Moors in England received a comparable right.

[106] BL MS Sloane 2755, f. 46v.   [107] *CSPD 1704–5*, 71.

[108] *CSPD 1702–3*, 713–14; HMC, 71, *Finch MSS*, ii.170–2; *CSPD 1704–5*, 71.

The success of men like Samson Rowlie and of early corsairs like Ward has often been cited as evidence that Barbary offered ordinary Britons an enticing prospect of social advancement they could never achieve at home.[109] Some, like Ward, did become wealthy. Very few, however, remained so for long. A century later John Braithwaite, member of a diplomatic mission to Morocco, commented that despite the success of Lucas and Carr only a handful of European renegades in the entire country enjoyed decent lives. One renegade, a Norfolk man called Daws, told Braithwaite that he had apostatized in his teens, lured by promises of an easy life, but after falling out of favour was now, decades later, working in Fez as a lowly bricklayer. Most renegade soldiers in Morocco were posted to remote and dangerous garrisons, where they struggled to survive on their small wages. Braithwaite dismissed them as 'generally the most miserable creatures on earth, neglected and despised by the Moors'.[110]

Renegades, apostates, and identity

Eric Dursteler has described how for many of the inhabitants of the Mediterranean world, personal identities could be contingent, multilayered, and malleable—'a protean process rather than an apprehendable object'. The English, of course, were only outsiders in this world. Many of the leading corsairs of the early seventeenth century hoped to make a quick fortune and then negotiate a return home, and by no means all apostatized. The leading English corsairs operating from Mamora in the 1610s, Bishop, Easton, and Mainwaring, did not abandon their Christian or English identities, and indeed viewed themselves as anti-Spanish patriots.[111] But for these men too, identities and loyalties often proved contingent. With limited resources, the crown sometimes found it expedient to pardon them and even offer employment. Richard Gifford, one of the most notorious, had accepted a Florentine commission before making his peace with the crown and ending his career as an Admiralty Commissioner. Henry Mainwaring was pardoned and knighted, was also made a Commissioner, and compiled a treatise on piracy for the king. Several former corsairs served on Sir Robert Mansell's expedition against Algiers in 1620, among them Robert Walsingham, who not long before had been attacking English shipping.[112] His loyalties remained fluid. Feeling himself poorly rewarded for his services, Walsingham hatched a plan to carry away one of king's best ships and return to piracy. He was sent to the Tower, but within a few years he had been pardoned

---

[109] See, for example, Matar, *Turks*, chap. 2.   [110] Braithwaite, *History*, 150–2, 349–50.

[111] Senior, *Nation of Pirates*, 66–75, 256.

[112] *ODNB*, Henry Mainwaring; Manwaring and Perrin, eds., *Life of Mainwaring*, ii.18–19, 42–3; Hebb, *Piracy*, 83; HMC 75, *Downshire MSS*, v.102; John Chamberlain, *The Letters of John Chamberlain*, ed. Norman Egbert McClure (Philadelphia, 1939), i.331; cf. Smith, *True Travels*, 59.

again, commanded a ship on the Cadiz expedition in 1625, and remained in service for years thereafter.[113]

Ordinary mariners serving in the Mediterranean quickly became familiar with people of different faiths, and could display a similarly pragmatic spirit. Sailors were a proverbially irreligious breed and, as noted earlier, many had a limited understanding of their faith and some only a superficial attachment to it. An English commander reported with disgust in 1681 that twenty English sailors had deserted their ship at Gallipoli, 'unanimously renounced their religion and turned Roman Catholics'. They had probably been offered better wages on a foreign vessel, and viewed religion as no obstacle.[114] John Rawlins complained that some mariners 'never knew any god but their own sensual lusts and pleasures, [and] thought that any religion would serve their turns and so for preferment or wealth very voluntarily renounced their faith and became renegadoes'. Henry Byam, preaching at Minehead in 1628, suspected that 'many hundreds are Mussulmans in Turkey, and Christians at home, doffing their religion, as they do their clothes, and keeping a conscience for every harbour where they shall put in'.[115] It was a brutally frank acknowledgement of the contingent nature of religious identities.

Although ordinary seamen could not negotiate pardons, many probably slipped back unobtrusively after making some easy pickings. Gouge thought there were many sailors who 'have *played* renegadoes' in Barbary, hinting, perhaps, that they had passed themselves off as apostates without having formally converted.[116] The career of Thomas Norton, from Devon, underlined his point. Captured and enslaved in Algiers in 1620, Norton later escaped to Salé where, either an apostate or passing as one, he lived as a free man, working as a ship's carpenter and well paid at 4s a day. He also sailed as lieutenant on a man-of-war, and became notorious for his cruelty to English captives. This phase came to an abrupt end when his ship was wrecked in the Channel in 1637. After finding a passage to Dartmouth, he now reverted to his original Christian identity, setting up once more as a carpenter, until his cover was blown by former captives who had suffered at his hands at Salé. He was arrested, tried, and condemned for piracy at Exeter assizes.[117] For Norton, identity had been contingent, shaped and reshaped by changing circumstances. Only his (probable) execution brought that shifting process to an end.

Mariners were by no means alone in their readiness to ignore religious divisions. Although Christian and Muslim states regarded each other as infidels, most (including England) were willing to set religious differences aside when it was in their interest to do so, and make alliances traversing the religious divide.

[113] Chamberlain, *Letters*, ii.433; TNA SP 16/111, fos. 4–5; SP 16/251, f.80; SP 16/362, f.147.
[114] Pocock, *Relief of Captives*, 10; HMC 71, *Finch MSS*, ii.105.
[115] *Rawlins*, sig. B2; Kellet and Byam, *Returne*, 75.   [116] Gouge, *Recovery*, 16 (italics added).
[117] TNA SP 16/370, f.29.

Mediterranean trade operated through commercial networks linking Catholics, Muslims, Protestants, Jews, and Greek Orthodox, all behaving with similar pragmatism. John Harrison, a Protestant zealot, was disgusted to find English traders in Morocco ignoring the Sabbath and devoting the day wholly to business.[118] Sir Thomas Shirley, a captive at Constantinople in 1603–05, reported that it was a jest among English merchants that 'in every three years that they stay in Turkey they lose one article of their faith'.[119] There could even be friendly companionship across the religious divide. When the *Relief* called at Tripoli in 1651, for example, its master, Thomas Gallilee, welcomed the leading corsair commander aboard 'to be merry', and later returned the visit. The following year, however, would see Gallilee captured and enslaved while serving the Venetian navy against the Ottomans. The Mediterranean was a mutable world.[120]

Renegades were always viewed with suspicion by most other Muslims. Whether fear, ambition, or greed had led them to apostatize, their new loyalties and identities were unlikely to have deep roots. Religion meant little to the freebooters who joined Ward and his fellows. In 1606 a French writer described the English renegades in Tunis as drunken and debauched, squandering their money on drink, gambling and women, and tolerated only for the riches they delivered. John Smith damned English renegade corsairs as 'riotous, quarrelous, treacherous, blasphemous, and villainous', adding that 'all they got, they basely consumed it amongst Jews, Moors and whores'. Writers throughout the period reported that renegades were despised by Muslims and Christians alike.[121]

With renegade loyalties always uncertain, the corsairs of Algiers were reported in the 1610s to maintain a proportion of 120 Turks to twenty renegades (or three to one, according to another account), to guarantee their security.[122] Some renegades led or joined mutinies by Christian slaves, while one Spaniard persuaded his company of renegade countrymen to sail to Spain, sell their ship, and return to Christianity.[123] The articles that English commanders negotiated at Salé in 1626 and 1637 allowed renegades as well as slaves to return home, and it is striking that on both occasions some seized the opportunity.[124] Joseph Pitts observed that in Algiers the *coulougli* (sons of janissaries) would at the slightest provocation taunt renegades by accusing them of planning to run away, or say jeeringly, '"There is yet swine's flesh in thy teeth" meaning they still have a tang of

---

[118] TNA SP 71/12, f. 181v; cf. Simon Ockley, *An Account of South-West Barbary* (1713), 38–40.

[119] E. Dennis Ross, 'Discourse of the Turks by Sᵣ Thomas Shirley', *Camden Miscellany*, Third Series, 16 (1936), 11.

[120] BL, MS Sloane 3494, fos. 24, 25v, 29-v, and Chapter 3.

[121] Bent, *Early Voyages*, 14–15; Smith, *True Travels*, 59; Peter Earle, *Corsairs of Malta and Barbary* (1970), 50; *Pitts*, 224; D'Aranda, *History*, 102, 161–2; Clissold, *Barbary Slaves*, 101 and chap. 7, *passim*.

[122] Manwaring and Perrin, eds., *Life of Mainwaring*, ii.25; Maclean, ed., *Letters of Carew*, 61; cf. Maziane, *Salé et ses Corsaires*, 192–3.

[123] *Pitts*, 225; cf. D'Aranda, *History*, 178–80, and Chapter 5.

[124] TNA SP 71/12, fos. 128–9, 133, 138; SP 71/13, f.25.

Christianity'—which, as we have seen, might well be the case. The bey of Tunis commented in the same spirit that 'a pig remains a pig, even if they cut off its tail'.[125]

How far can we recover what apostasy meant to those who took this step? Many, as we have seen, acted in the hope of alleviating their harsh conditions. Accepting Islam required no prior instruction on its doctrines and practices. It was sufficient to recite a few formulaic words, accept Moorish clothes and a new name, and undergo circumcision. Apostasy was about externals. But with identity to a large extent socially constructed, those now dressing as Moors, eating the same food, and conforming to their customs, might well gradually develop a primarily Moorish sense of identity. There are very few instances of captives converting to Islam because they had been convinced of its superior truth. It is very likely, however, that some who had 'turned Turk' on pragmatic grounds might in time become genuinely attached to their new faith.[126] An officer named Ball, son of a commander in Charles II's navy, provides one striking example. Ball had apostatized at Algiers after quarrelling with his brother, and went on to become gunner and then lieutenant of a war galley. When he was captured, years later, he refused to abandon his adopted religion and ended his days as a galley-slave in Livorno. A traveller described him as 'very opinionated in his way by long custom, imagining himself to be in the right'.[127] A similar shift could occur among long-term captives who had remained nominally Christian, with apostasy its consequence rather than cause. Joseph Pitts tells of two former slaves who had accommodated so completely to the culture of Barbary that they found it impossible to reverse the process. One, already back in England, had returned to Algiers and 'voluntarily, without the least force used towards him, became a Mohammetan'. The other, also redeemed and waiting for a passage home, had similarly changed his plans, decided to stay in Algiers, and accepted Islam.[128] The sequence of events is highly suggestive. Their apostasy appears to have been a belated realization of how difficult it would be to return to their old English lives.

In 1638 Robert Blake, a Moroccan merchant, was able to question an English renegade about his faith, and asked if he would like to return home. To his surprise, the man appeared indifferent and wondered why Blake should care, adding that 'he lived well enough where he was'.[129] Whatever the circumstances of his apostasy, he too probably understood that returning to England would entail another stressful process of readjustment and expose him to hostility and

[125] Pitts, 224; Dursteler, *Venetians and Constantinople*, 119.
[126] Tobias P. Graf, *The Sultan's Renegades. Christian-European Converts to Islam and the Making of the Ottoman Elite, 1575-1610* (Oxford, 2017), chap. 3; Dursteler, *Venetians and Constantinople*, 117–18.
[127] Ellis Veryard, *An Account of Divers Choice Remarks, as well Geographical as Historical* (1701), 252.
[128] *Pitts*, 199; cf. Bennassar, *Chrétiens*, 368–407, 494–526.   [129] TNA SP 71/13, f.74v.

suspicion. It was easier to remain where he was, and as what he had become. While the Church considered a religious ceremony sufficient to restore lost sheep to the fold, neighbours could be less forgiving. Ministers clearly thought so, urging people not to humiliate former apostates with 'upbraidings, reproaches, twittings'. William Gouge, anticipating the problems ahead for Jukes and others like him, begged his congregation, 'upbraid not to him his apostasy ... shun not his society ... eat and drink with him, pray with him and for him'.[130] Joseph Pitts, writing thirty-five years after his return home, commented ruefully that 'I have been often reflected upon for my apostasy, which I desire to bear with patience'. Most of the abuse, he added, had come from 'ignorant or vile persons'.[131]

Religious and cultural assimilation naturally went furthest for those seized as children. In their case, almost all sense of their English and Christian origins might be lost. One, who had grown up to become a *reis*, had even forgotten his English name. Captured after twenty years and questioned by the Spanish Inquisition, he declared that Islam was far superior to Christianity. Some captured renegades even chose to live for years chained to the oars on Spanish or Italian galleys, clinging to their Moorish and Muslim identities, rather than reveal their original Christian faith or return to it.[132] Joseph Pitts encountered one such, an Irishman, on the hajj to Mecca. Captured when young, the pilgrim had apostatized and had completely lost his native language. After being recaptured he had endured thirty years as a slave on Spanish and French galleys, rather than renounce his Muslim faith. Eventually ransomed, he returned to Algiers where admiring neighbours funded his hajj. He told Pitts that God had brought him out of hell on earth to a heaven, Mecca. In this instance, assimilation to a new religious and cultural identity had clearly proved complete and lasting.[133]

Adult captives, by contrast, were more likely to develop hybrid and multi-layered identities. Margaret Shaw, captured as a young adult and enslaved at Meknes, lost most of her native language within seven years, but it was to British officials she turned for help when reduced to near destitution.[134] Most male renegades, whatever the circumstances of their apostasy, still had regular contact with Christians, whether slaves, merchants, or visiting sailors. Francis Knight, an English slave, remained a firm Christian but had renegade friends serving with the janissaries. When some of them were posted to Constantine, an old Roman town, they took the trouble to copy the Greek and Latin inscriptions they found on its walls, and brought them back for him.[135] Joseph Pitts, captured in his teens, said he had lost all track of the Christian calendar, but never lost the dream of home. Similarly, Thomas Pellow entranced his little mulatto daughter

[130] Kellet and Byam, *Returne from Argier*, 76; Gouge, *Recovery*, 81–2.   [131] Pitts, p. xvii.
[132] Bennassar, *Chrétiens*, 213–14, 216; Dursteler, *Venetians and Constantinople*, 117.
[133] *Pitts*, 153.   [134] Braithwaite, *History*, 181.   [135] Knight, *Seven Years Relation*, 11.

with tales of an England he had not seen since the age of eleven.[136] Decades after 'turning Moor', Hamet Lucas still served his guests English as well as Moorish food, and provided tables, chairs, knives, and forks. At Meknes, James Carr enjoyed fine clothes, women, and food, and owned his own slaves, but he insisted to sceptical visitors that inwardly he was 'as much a Christian as ever', and that his heavy drinking was to drown his sorrows.[137]

Many apostates continued to feel affection for their old land, and showed kindness to any countrymen they encountered. As Dursteler suggested, 'national' identity—a sense of association with one's place of birth—sometimes proved stronger than religious or political identities.[138] The musician Thomas Dallam, visiting Constantinople in 1600, was assisted by a dragoman named Finch, originally from Chorley, who proved a 'trusty friend' despite being 'in religion a perfect Turk'.[139] Similarly, British renegades at Salé offered help and advice to William Atkins and his fellow captives 'for country's sake'. Atkins had enjoyed visits both to and from 'our poor Christian countrymen, slaves or renegades'—a striking formulation that underlined the hybrid character of identities and loyalties.[140] And when the *Relief* lay at anchor at Tripoli for several weeks early in 1651, three English renegades came on board on Sundays to dine with the master, drink, and play cards. They valued a bond with their fellow countryman that outweighed political and religious differences.[141] In the case of the renegade Ramadan Reis, alias Henry Chandler, it was self-interest that led him to hire English slaves for his man-of-war at Algiers in 1621, but he promised 'good usage' to two fellow West-Countrymen, one of whom came from his own home-town in Cornwall.[142] More significantly, Samson Rowlie, alias Assan Aga, who held high office at Algiers, corresponded with Elizabeth's ambassador at Constantinople, and appears to have helped secure the redemption of captives. The ambassador, William Harborne, writing to Rowlie in 1586, professed to believe that he still had 'fervent faith' in Christ, loved his countrymen, and regarded himself a good subject of the Queen.[143]

Personal, religious, and political identities could thus be fluid, hybrid, and multilayered. To Ward and his fellows, religious and political loyalties were little more than labels to be worn or discarded, as circumstances altered. He would have remained Protestant had he been allowed to return to England, his original plan. When that was refused he sought a pardon from the Grand Duke of Tuscany, and would doubtless have become Catholic had he been permitted to settle in

[136] *Pitts*, 206; *Pellow*, 190.   [137] Braithwaite, *History*, 81–5, 186–8; Milton, *White Gold*, 145–6.
[138] Dursteler, *Venetians and Constantinople*, 18–19.
[139] James Theodore Bent, ed., *Early Voyages and Travels in the Levant. The Diary of Master Thomas Dallam, 1599-1600*, Hakluyt Society, 87 (1893; reprinted 2016), 84; cf. 79.
[140] Murphy, *William Atkins*, 244, 246–7.   [141] BL MS Sloane 3494, fos. 24, 25v, 29-v.
[142] Rawlins, sig. B3-v.
[143] Hakluyt, *Principal Navigations*, part ii, 180; MacLean, *Looking East*, 104.

Livorno.[144] Several corsairs did negotiate such arrangements, and were then happy to serve against the Turks. Peter Easton took his fortune to Savoy, where he was given a title and a wife, and adopted Catholicism.[145] Similarly, many renegades originally Protestant agreed to become Catholics when they were recaptured and brought before the Spanish Inquisition. One claimed not to understand the difference between the Catholic and Protestant faiths.[146]

Hybrid identities could develop even among captives who had remained Christians, with Joshua Gee providing a striking example. Gee served the corsairs on many voyages, and always refers to how 'we', not 'they', had fared in action. In the face of extreme danger, slaves and corsairs had a common interest in survival. And remarkably, he had no words of sympathy for the fellow Christians, some English, 'we' had captured, who would now be sold into servitude. On two occasions, indeed, he recalled with pleasure that his captain had allowed him and other slaves to enter a prize and help themselves to the sailors' clothes, to replace their own ragged apparel. It 'was a great favour to us', he added. Although Gee was a devout puritan, circumstances had diluted even his sense of religious and national identity.[147]

*   *   *

Barbary raised challenging issues of identity for captives and renegades alike. In the case of seamen who had joined the corsairs voluntarily, dominant identities and loyalties were swayed by the tides of circumstance and interest. Labels such as 'English Turk' reflected hybrid religious and national identities. Captives who apostatized under duress, like Pitts, developed more conflicted identities. Those who remained firmly Protestant might find comfort and strength in their faith and their English identity, clinging to the hope that their God and their monarch would eventually save them. But all captives had to adjust to the shock of finding themselves now abused as unclean infidels, and mocked for their appearance and clothes. And some faced the additional shock of having to labour alongside or under black Africans, or having a black owner. Abraham Browne found it profoundly disorientating that his black slave overseer refused to share a drinking vessel. 'I was despised of the most despisedst people in the world', he reflected dolefully.[148] For many renegades, identity might be something mutable and contingent; but for many captives, like Browne, enslavement delivered a deeply unsettling blow to their sense of self.

---

[144] CSPVen. 1607–10, 301, 309.   [145] CSPVen. 1610–13, 91, 178, 283, 501, 505–6, 516, 528.
[146] Bennassar, Chrétiens, 217–18; cf. 370–89.   [147] Gee, Narrative, 17, 18, 23–4.
[148] Riley, ed., 'Abraham Browne's Captivity', 41; Colley, Captives, 114–17.

5

Escaping from Barbary

Escaping from Barbary was a hazardous enterprise, beset with difficulties. Few succeeded. But raising a ransom was never an option for most captives, and while many grew resigned to their fate or sank into despair, others refused to abandon the dream of freedom, and were willing to risk their lives even after years of servitude. This chapter explores their stories, a few of which eventually found their way into print. Many other attempts failed, and the stories are forever lost.

Slave mutinies

Galley slaves, chained to their benches, had almost no opportunity to resist or escape. Captive seamen on the largest sail-driven men-of-war, numbering a few dozen at most, had equally little chance hope of overpowering several hundred soldiers. On smaller ships, where the imbalance was less extreme, mutiny became a more realistic option. The story of John Rawlins and the *Exchange* of Bristol, described in the Prologue, showed what might be possible with resolution and luck.

The corsairs were well aware of the danger, and after seizing a prize generally kept new captives below deck, chained and half-starved. There, weakened in body and spirit, they would pose little threat.[1] Even so, some hatched desperate plans to resist, especially when there were also older slaves and renegades on board, who might be persuaded to join them, unlock their fetters, and provide access to weapons. The risks were huge. It was always difficult to assess a renegade's loyalties, and most plans came to nothing. Many were abandoned when one or two captives refused to join, or lost their nerve and threatened to inform the corsairs.[2] As they all knew, failure carried a heavy price. James Wadsworth recalled that some German and Portuguese fellow captives had attempted a rising when they saw the corsairs half-drunk and 'merry' with opium. It failed, and the plotters were slaughtered.[3] Thomas Phelps, captured in 1684, also spotted an ideal opportunity when the corsairs' man-of-war lay at anchor off Salé, waiting for the tide. Some of the Moors had gone ashore, most of the others were asleep, and the *reis* was leaning over the rail, lost in thought. Phelps broached his plan to his

---

[1] See Chapter 2.   [2] E.g. Adam Elliot, *A Modest Vindication of Titus Oates* (1682), 4–5.
[3] James Wadsworth, *The English Spanish Pilgrime* (1629), 39.

British Slaves and Barbary Corsairs, 1580–1750. Bernard Capp, Oxford University Press. © Bernard Capp 2022.
DOI: 10.1093/oso/9780192857378.003.0006

shipmates, and offered to kill the captain himself. They all agreed to join, as did eleven of the twelve older slaves serving on board. But the twelfth, the steward, refused, and the others then drew back. Phelps, though strongly tempted to kill him and press ahead, reluctantly abandoned his plan. He neither forgot nor forgave, and when he came to publish his narrative he seized the opportunity to name and shame the 'sneaking varlet'.[4] Joseph Pitts, captured in 1678, recalled another aborted design. The corsairs' ship carried only thirty or forty soldiers, with twenty or thirty old Christian slaves 'to sail the ship and to do all the ship's work'. Over the course of several weeks the corsairs had captured five more small vessels—four English and one Dutch—bringing the number of new captives to almost thirty. With Christians now outnumbering corsairs, they hatched a plan to seize the ship. One of the old slaves smuggled two swords into the hold, and pincers to break the captives' shackles. But on the night of the planned rising, the Dutch master lost his nerve and the plan was abandoned. There was an unhappy coda, for the corsairs discovered the design and the prime suspect was bastinadoed on deck with a hundred blows. He confessed nothing, 'generously choosing rather to suffer himself than to bring us all under the bastinadoes also', Pitts recalled gratefully.[5] It was a sobering reminder of the risks of resistance.

The odds were better when captives were kept on their own vessel rather than being transferred to the corsairs' man-of-war. The prize-crew was usually quite small, and captives sometimes had to be brought up on deck to help sail the ship, creating opportunities that bold spirits were ready to seize. When the *Jacob* of Bristol was captured in 1621, the corsairs installed a prize-crew of thirteen to carry it to Algiers. In bad weather they needed assistance in handling the sails, and one stormy night four English youths seized their opportunity. They killed four of the corsairs, fastened the hatches to keep the rest below deck, where they had fled, and carried the vessel to St Lucar, in Spain. There they sold their former captors as galley-slaves, 'for a good sum of money'—and, in the view of the pamphleteer who reported the episode, 'a great deal more than they are worth'. He hailed the youngsters as 'darlings of valour', whose exploit had brought honour to Bristol and Britain and demonstrated God's providential power.[6]

The most extraordinary rising of the period, by contrast, was wholly bloodless. George Pattison and Thomas Lurting, master and mate of a ship homeward bound from Venice in 1663, were both Quakers, and they surrendered to an Algerian man-of-war without resistance. They ordered their men to obey the prize-crew and to co-operate in managing the ship. Delighted at such ready compliance, the corsairs were soon lulled into a false sense of security, and when they lost contact with their man-of-war in bad weather, Lurting broached the idea of a rising. The men were enthusiastic. Two promptly volunteered to cut

---

[4] *Phelps*, 6–7.   [5] *Pitts*, 4–8.
[6] *A Relation Strange and true, of a ship of Bristol named the Jacob* (1622), sig. A3v–B2.

the corsairs' throats, an offer that Lurting sternly rejected. Pattison refused to join a rising, fearing bloodshed and frightened of the consequences of failure, but Lurting resolved to press ahead, insisting there must be no violence. Two nights later, while the ten corsairs were asleep in the cabins, sheltering from the rain, Lurting's men removed their weapons and guarded the doors. Next morning the corsairs emerged, one by one, to find themselves now captives. Their captain wept, begging not to be sold into slavery, and Pattison and Lurting mulled over the options. The situation remained tense, for the two groups were equal in number and the corsairs were plainly hoping to seize back control. Lurting devised a quixotic plan to return them to Barbary, and as it was out of the question to sail into a port there, he found two men and a boy willing to help row them ashore in a deserted spot. This was almost equally hazardous, for they would be heavily outnumbered. Two sailors took the oars while Lurting and a companion sat in the bow, brandishing an axe and a boat-hook, their safety resting precariously on the fact that the corsairs did not realize he was a pacifist. He did not enlighten them. As they neared the beach, one sailor thought he could see Moors lurking in the bushes and panicked, whereupon the corsairs, sensing the fear, stood up ready to seize control. Lurting had to compromise his principles. Stepping forward, he struck the captain a sharp blow with the back of his boat-hook, and the danger passed. The corsairs waded ashore, and Lurting and his company set sail for England, to find that their story had arrived before them. By chance, Charles II and his brother were visiting Greenwich, and the royal party came to the ship's side to hear their story. The king said they should have brought their captives back to England, but Lurting replied that it had been better to return them to their own country. Charles merely smiled.[7]

This strange episode was not the only bloodless rising. The crew of the *Dexterity*, captured in 1667, also contrived to recover their ship, when the prize-crew put into a small harbour to replenish the water cask. With most of the corsairs ashore, the English captives seized control and sailed away.[8] The fact that prize-crews sometimes had to depend on the expertise and help of their captives created other inviting opportunities. In 1624 Thomas Melvin, a Scot, was able to turn the tables on the corsairs who had captured his ship and turned it into a man-of-war. He and his companions surprised and overpowered twenty-nine 'Turks', and brought the vessel into Portland road. William Rankin, a Scot captured while employed as pilot of a Spanish ship, achieved a comparable feat single-handed. The corsairs had installed a prize-crew to carry it to Barbary, but when their pilot

---

[7] Thomas Lurting, *The Fighting Sailor turn'd Peaceable Christian* (1710), 33–46. He had earlier given a shorter account, published in George Fox, *To the Great Turk, and his King in Argier* (1680), 15–20.
[8] TNA SP 71/26, f.92; *CSPD 1666–7*, 564. Cf. Pierre Dan, *Histoire de Barbarie et de ses Corsairs* (Paris, 1649), 427–8, for a case that resembles Lurting's story.

was swept overboard in a storm they ordered Rankin to take his place. Exploiting their ignorance, he carried it instead to Dublin.[9]

Successful mutiny on the corsairs' own men-of-war was very rare, but not impossible on smaller vessels. Eleven Christian slaves brought a polacre into Weymouth in 1623 after overpowering the corsairs, killing nine and capturing another sixteen.[10] Vincent Jukes, enslaved and coerced into 'turning Turk', also found an opportunity to recover his freedom when he was sent out in a small man-of-war in 1638, with a company of twenty 'Turks', two English slaves, and a Flemish renegade. Although heavily outnumbered, the four mutineers seized a favourable moment to kill ten corsairs and force the rest to surrender. Selling the ship and their captives in Spain for £600, Jukes returned to England with money in his pocket to become a hero celebrated in ballad.[11] Two years earlier, mutineers had seized a small Salé man-of-war that had sailed into the English Channel to snap up prizes and raid ashore. Its pilot, John Dunton, had been captured and enslaved the year before, while the rest of the company comprised twenty-one Moors and several Flemish and German renegades. The captain, Johann Rickles, was a Dutchman enslaved six years earlier, and now a trusted renegade. Rickles had led several previous cruises, but as soon as they put to sea he and his companions devised a plan to carry the ship to England or Holland. The crew of a fishing boat they had seized in the Channel swelled the number of potential mutineers, while several Moors were sent to man the prize. On Rickles' signal, the mutineers drove the rest into the hold and carried the ship to the Isle of Wight under a flag of truce. The authorities viewed them with deep suspicion, but their story was eventually believed. The following year, Dunton was employed as master of the *Leopard* on the expedition against Salé, and had the satisfaction of seeing a dozen of its men-of-war destroyed.[12]

Mutiny always carried the strong probability of bloodshed, however, and captives were often thirsting for revenge as well as freedom. The mutiny on the ill-named *Heart's Desire* or *Good Fortune* offers a chilling example of the carnage that could ensue. The ship sailed from Salé in October 1626, manned by sixty-four 'Turks', sixteen or eighteen renegades, and twenty-three Christian slaves, mostly French. Among them were six Englishmen, including Thomas Duffield, taken captive eight months earlier. The captain, a Dutch mariner named Hendrick Henderson, claimed later that he had accepted the position after his own ship had been wrecked. Duffield and Henderson hatched a plot almost as soon as the ship put to sea, and drew in three others. As captain, Henderson had ready access

[9] Harris, *Trinity House*, 59; *CSPD 1623–5*, 464.

[10] *William Whiteway of Dorchester. His Diary 1618 to 1635*, Dorset Record Society, 12 (1991), 43.

[11] William Gouge, *A Recovery from Apostacy* (1639), 2–5; Richard Gough, *The History of Myddle*, ed. David Hey (Harmondsworth, 1981), 115.

[12] TNA SP 16/332, fos. 44–6; John Dunton, *A Trve Iournall of the Sally Fleet* (1637), sig. A2-v and *passim*.

to weapons, and two hours before dawn on 21 October the mutineers launched a ferocious attack on the corsairs sleeping between decks, slaughtering about twenty. The rest escaped to the upper deck, but the mutineers now possessed all the ship's firearms and once it was light they shot and killed most of them. The remainder surrendered, and the mutineers then steered for the Canary Islands, planning to sell their captives into slavery and buy victuals with the proceeds. Their plan was thwarted when the islanders identified the ship as a Salé man-of-war and drove it away, whereupon the mutineers slaughtered all but two of the surviving corsairs and sailed for England. Bad weather drove them off course to Ireland—to Crookhaven, near Cork—and by another mischance an English warship arrived only a few hours later. Its commander, John Mason, seized the *Heart's Desire* as a pirate ship, and installed a prize-crew to carry it to England.

This account is pieced together from the petition that Duffield and Henderson sent to Buckingham, the Lord Admiral, their examinations by a lawyer for the High Court of Admiralty, and letters from Mason. The two chief mutineers felt deeply aggrieved by their treatment. They complained that Mason had turned them out with only the clothes on their back, whereas they had deserved a reward. They asked to be given the ship, promising to use it to free fellow countrymen enslaved in Salé. Presumably they hoped to operate as privateers, seizing men-of-war or using booty to ransom captives. Mason claimed the ship for himself, as lawful prize. He alleged it had served as a man-of-war for three years, and that the mutineers had committed acts of piracy after killing the corsairs.

It was possibly unparalleled for a captain to lead a bloody mutiny against his own crew, and uncertainty surrounds this strange episode. While Duffield had been compelled to serve, Henderson had freely accepted his employment. He had a plausible story; destitute after being shipwrecked, he had taken it in the hope of finding some way to return home. But if so, why sail for the Canaries, rather than Holland? They should not have been running short of victuals so soon, especially with most of the original company now dead. And was it really bad weather that drove them to Ireland? Irish harbours offered many opportunities for pirates, and if Mason had not appeared it is at least possible that the mutineers would have set up for themselves. It also remains unclear why two of the 'Turks' had been spared. Probably they were men of some standing whom the mutineers hoped to ransom or exchange. In the event, another party offered to buy the ship—an arrangement the Admiralty preferred. The authorities could not decide whether to treat Duffield and Henderson as heroes or pirates, so they were neither rewarded nor put on trial. Instead, months later, they were awarded £3 10s each, for relief.[13]

The British, of course, were not the only captives to rise up against their captors. In one spectacular case, four Dutch sailors left on board their vessel took

[13] TNA SP 16/21. fos. 45, 85-v; *CSPD 1625–6*, 268, 381, 405, 427.

advantage of a storm to overpower the distracted prize-crew of twenty-four, and take them captive to Cadiz.[14] Enslaved Moors occasionally performed comparable exploits. One company of Moorish slaves killed the French sailors guarding them while most of the crew were ashore, seized the ship, and carried it to Tunis.[15]

The chances of the sea

'Have patience, brother', an English renegade advised a distressed new captive, 'this is the chance of war; today for you, and tomorrow for me'.[16] Life at sea was always unpredictable, and in an age of endemic war and piracy the roles of captors and captives were easily reversed. When corsairs on the *Exchange* were overpowered in a bloody mutiny and saw their companions slaughtered, some leapt overboard, reportedly crying, 'It was the chance of war!'[17] Edward Coxere, enslaved at Porto Farina, near Tunis, was desperate to be ordered to serve at sea. On land he knew he had no chance of escape, but at sea there was at least a possibility of liberation if the corsairs encountered a powerful European warship or were wrecked on the Christian shore. Of course, he might easily be killed or drowned in such an event, but it offered a glimmer of hope and opportunity. Joseph Pitts remembered feeling 'great ease and content' during two months serving at sea, hoping the ship would be captured, and how as it sailed back to Algiers 'my heart began to be heavy'.[18] Some renegades nurtured similar hopes. In 1671 a newsletter reported the extraordinary story of an English slave (in fact almost certainly a renegade) who had joined the corsairs swarming aboard a Hamburg vessel, and had then turned on them and inspired the German crew to fight back. They killed about thirty corsairs, forced the rest overboard, and made their escape.[19] Reluctant renegades sometimes found easier opportunities to escape when a boat party went ashore on a deserted European shore to fetch water or wood.[20]

Richard Hasleton, a Barbary galley-slave, had more experience than most of the twists of fortune, both at sea and on land. In 1587 the galley was chased by a Genoese fleet and driven ashore on Formentera, a disaster that only fifteen of the 250 men on board survived. Hasleton and two other slaves were among them and fled inland to seek safety with the Christian islanders. But one of his companions

---

[14] HMC 79, *Lindsey MSS*, 27; cf. Dan, *Histoire de Barbarie*, 426–7.   [15] *Pitts*, 89.

[16] D'Aranda, *History*, 5.   [17] *Rawlins*, sig. E.

[18] Coxere, *Adventures*, 57–8; *Pitts*, 183–4; cf. C. R. Pennell, ed., *Piracy and Diplomacy in Seventeenth-Century North Africa. The Journal of Thomas Baker, English Consul in Tripoli 1677–1685* (Cranbury, NJ, 1989), 103.

[19] HMC 25, *Le Fleming MSS*, 86.

[20] Bartolomé and Lucile Bennassar, *Les Chrétiens d'Allah* (Paris, 2006), 216–17; HMC 75, *Downshire MSS*, i.201–2 (a successful rising in 1686 by Spanish renegades, with help from the Christian slaves, one of them English.)

denounced him as 'an English Lutheran', whereupon he was seized and handed over to the Inquisition on Majorca. Tortured and facing execution, Hasleton escaped this fate by breaking out from prison, stealing a small boat, and putting to sea, fashioning a rudimentary sail from his own breeches. The boat was blown back to Barbary, where he was recaptured, escaped again, was seized again, and endured several more years as a galley slave in Barbary before eventually being ransomed. Hasleton used his extraordinary story to demonstrate the power of divine providence, though many readers must have reflected that God moved in very mysterious ways.[21]

Francis Knight's escape in 1638 had a somewhat similar origin. The huge Barbary fleet in which he was a galley slave was destroyed by a Venetian force on the coast of what is now Albania. This was Ottoman territory, and most of the surviving soldiers and slaves were able to march away, but Knight, ill with fever, was left behind with the sick and wounded to recuperate under guard. One night, a group of thirteen took advantage of a drunken guard to escape. Seizing a boat, they rowed for two nights and a day to reach safety in Corfu, under Venetian control. From there Knight found passage to Venice, and an English ship eventually carried him home. He recalled wryly that a fellow slave, a Jersey man, had been drunk on the night of their escape and had refused to join them.[22]

The best chance of liberation came when a Barbary man-of-war was captured or driven ashore by an English warship. One that had ventured into the Thames in 1616 was seized shortly afterwards by Henry Mainwaring, himself a former corsair, who freed the Christians on board. Six slaves serving on board a Salé man-of-war in 1637 were similarly rescued when it was forced ashore on the coast of Morocco and destroyed—a disaster for which the *reis* paid with his head.[23] Such incidents occasionally freed far larger numbers. When the naval commander Richard Beach drove six powerful Algiers men-of-war ashore off Cape Spartel, near Tangier, in 1670 he was able to free 260 Christian slaves on board, among them sixty-two Englishmen.[24] Sir Edward Spragge, who captured an Algerine warship on its very first cruise, freed thirty-three Christian slaves, nine of them English.[25] Similarly, Cloudesley Shovell found twenty-seven mostly English Christians on a man-of-war he had chased for five days in 1670, and liberated a further thirty-nine after another fierce action in 1681.[26] In the final decades of the century, many of the corsairs' prizes were retaken by British warships.

---

[21] *Hasleton*, sig. A4v–E3v.

[22] Francis Knight, *A Relation of Seaven Yeares Slaverie* (1640), 21–7.

[23] G. E. Manwaring and W. G. Perrin, eds., *The Life and Works of Sir Henry Mainwaring*, Navy Records Society, 54, 56, (1920–22), ii.10; John Maclean, ed., *Letters of George Lord Carew to Sir Thomas Roe, 1615–1617*, Camden Society, Old Series, 76 (1860), 51; TNA SP 71/13, f.25-v.

[24] *CSPD 1670*, 394–5; TNA SP 71/1, fos. 461v–463; R. C. Anderson, ed., *The Journals of Sir Thomas Allin 1660–1678*, Navy Records Society, 79–80 (1939–40) ii.189–91; cf. ibid. i.23, ii.144–5.

[25] *CSPD 1670*, 595–6.   [26] TNA SP71/14, fos. 174–5; HMC 71, *Finch MSS*, ii.120–1.

British slaves were also liberated by other European warships, and occasionally by powerful merchantmen. A Barbary force that had captured four English ships off Ireland in 1640 was soon afterwards destroyed by a Dutch warship, which was able to free 140 English captives.[27] Eighteen captives were set ashore in Liverpool in 1681 after being rescued by a French man-of-war.[28] The master (and owner) of a Dartmouth ship seized off the Lizard by Salé corsairs in 1635 was liberated only two days later when it was recaptured by a Dutch warship. He came to an amicable agreement with his rescuers, paying £100 to have his ship restored. The crew of the *Golden Sun*, taken prize in 1660, enjoyed similar luck, freed only four days later by a Spanish man-of-war.[29] Even shipwreck might occasionally bring liberation. Five English slaves on a Salé man-of-war escaped ashore when their ship sank in 1691, and though tribesmen carried them into the mountains, they were eventually retrieved by the dey of Algiers. The English consul borrowed money to redeem them, and arranged their passage home.[30]

The bravest spirits preferred to shape their own destiny rather than wait on such chance events. One slave, serving as a carpenter on an Algerine man-of-war in the 1630s, contrived to fashion a rudimentary boat under the very noses of the corsairs. Working at night, he and his companions assembled a crude contraption 'more like a trough than a boat', using boards from the stores. It was able to bear the weight of only two men, and was almost swamped before it was carried to the Barbary shore. The two escapees were able to make their ramshackle craft slightly more seaworthy, and then put to sea again, rowing for ten days to reach the Spanish coast and safety. The carpenter never published his story, and we know of it only from a German traveller who heard it recounted by the Lord Mayor of London.[31]

Escaping from Barbary

Escape from Barbary itself was still more hazardous. Captain John Smith, best known as a colonial pioneer in Virginia, had once been enslaved by Tatars in the remote Caucasus, and had made a daring escape after killing his harsh owner in a fight. Stealing his clothes and horse, Smith rode for days until he reached a distant Russian outpost.[32] Such an exploit was impossible for the slaves in Barbary. The

---

[27] *CSPVen. 1640–2*, 63.

[28] HMC 12, *Bath and Wells MSS*, 446; cf. *CSPD 1676–7*, 408–9; *CSPD 1677–8*, 123; *CSPD 1680–1*, 322; *CSPD 1691–2*, 299.

[29] *CSPD 1635*, 396; *Calendar of Treasury Books, 1660–1667*, 326.

[30] TNA SP 71/3, fos. 229v, 231v, 235; *CSPD 1691–2*, 304.

[31] Adam Olearius, *The Voyages and Travells of the Ambassadors sent by Frederick, Duke of Holstein, to the Great Duke of Muscovy and the King of Persia* [in 1633–39] (1669), ii.227–8; a shortened version appeared in Nathaniel Wanley, *The Wonders of the Little World* (1670), 626.

[32] John Smith, *The True Travels, Adventures, and Observations of Captaine Iohn Smith* (1630), 32.

bagnios were heavily guarded, and those locked in cellars and dungeons were usually kept chained. Even if they could break out, they would have nowhere to go, facing a hostile population and with no overland route to safety. Only the boldest contemplated an escape, and few succeeded. Failure brought fierce retribution. Edward Webbe, held in a vast bagnio in Constantinople in the 1580s with 2,000 other slaves, paid dearly for a failed attempt: those involved were all flogged with 300 blows on the belly and 400 on the back.[33] William Atkins, held at Salé in 1622, witnessed the fate of a French slave who had also attempted to escape. His owner hacked off his ears, slit his nose, flogged him until he was covered in blood, and then drove him through the streets, naked, 'for an example and terror for other slaves'.[34] When Atkins and his young friends were also suspected to be planning an escape, their owners threatened to have them castrated and sent inland to serve as eunuchs in the ruler's harem.[35] This section looks at those who defied the odds and lived to tell their stories.

The simplest method of escape was to be smuggled aboard an English vessel in a Barbary port. Such incidents occurred throughout the period, though rulers considered it a deeply hostile act, and responded with fury. When five English slaves were carried away in 1607, the pasha of Algiers wrote to James I demanding that the owner be compensated in full, or the shipmaster sent back for punishment.[36] For their part, the English authorities were reluctant to jeopardize diplomatic and commercial relations for the sake of a handful of escapees. In 1627 the Privy Council intervened in a row over a shipmaster who had spirited away an English slave from Tetuan, along with a Moor and a piece of ordnance. It ordered the master and his company to pay for the cannon and return the Moor, along with ransom money for the slave. Failure to make such reparations, it recognized, would endanger English merchants and perhaps provoke an outright breach.[37] Later incidents saw similar angry demands for ransoms to be paid in full as compensation. After a merchantman carried away a slave from Algiers in 1675, it was agreed that the next English ships calling there must each pay $100 until his ransom of $800 had been met in full.[38] The Restoration government was deeply troubled by such incidents, especially if naval vessels were involved. Charles II and his council were furious when frigates carried away two slaves in 1674, and warned that those guilty of such 'crimes' would face 'the severest punishments they can inflict'.[39] There was further outrage a few months later, when a naval commander carried away a disguised slave belonging to one of the most powerful

---

[33] Edward Webbe, *The Rare and most wonderfull things which Edw. Webbe an Englishman borne, hath seene* (1590), sig. C2v-3.

[34] Martin Murphy, ed., 'William Atkins, A Relation of the Journey from St Omers to Seville, 1622', in *Camden Miscellany*, 32 (1994), 248.

[35] Murphy, 'William Atkins', 245–6; James Wadsworth, *The English Spanish Pilgrime* (1629), 44.

[36] TNA SP 71/1, f.15; HMC 9, *Salisbury MSS*, xix.34.   [37] *APC, 1627*, 191.

[38] TNA SP 71/2, f.60.   [39] Pepys, *Catalogue*, ii.363.

men in the city. The consul hastily paid $346 in compensation, to avert serious repercussions, and asked the Admiral, Sir John Narbrough, to forbid such actions. The crew of the *Holmes* fireship, who had similarly carried away a slave from Algiers, had their wages stopped, and their petition for the stop to be lifted was rejected.[40] Admiral Herbert's treaty with Algiers in 1682 stipulated that escapees were not to be protected on board British ships, and must be returned to their owners. Charles II brushed aside complaints that this would inevitably expose them to savage retribution from their *patrons*.[41] The French also forbade visiting ships to allow runaways on board, for similar reasons.[42]

Despite the prohibitions, escapees often continued to find help and protection from visiting warships and merchantmen. In 1684 several high-value slaves, disguised as Turks, were invited aboard three visiting English warships and spirited away. The incident had serious repercussions. The dey denounced it as a flagrant breach of the recent treaty. If slaves could be carried away with impunity, he declared, his head would soon be cut off by their enraged owners, the fate of Babba Hassan, his predecessor, only two years earlier. The new consul, Philip Rycaut, feared for his own life. He had to accept liability for the full ransom value of the five men, amounting to $1,829, and was allowed only three months to raise it. Rycaut begged the king to forbid naval officers to carry away slaves, and called for the master of every merchant ship calling at Algiers to enter a bond, in $550, not to do so unless their ransoms had been paid in full.[43] Such incidents continued, however, with further friction. To avert trouble, consuls generally made compensation payments to match the expected ransom, which the government later reimbursed.[44]

In time of war, a slave might also attempt to escape by swimming out at night to a warship lying offshore, or paddling out on a homemade raft. And in war-time, commanders were more welcoming. When Sandwich lay off Algiers in 1661, dozens of British slaves were able to swim out to a ketch waiting to rescue them. Allin's squadron lying off Algiers in 1669 similarly set out boats to approach as close as they dared, to pick up swimmers, and at least thirteen British slaves reached safety. One bold Portuguese escaped too, dashing for freedom in the middle of the day and fending off pursuers with a knife till he reached the water's edge.[45] Two years later, when a fragile peace had been restored, the city's rulers ordered the *Advice* to anchor well offshore, to prevent such escapes. In defiance,

[40] TNA SP71/2, f.88; Pepys, *Catalogue*, iv.383.

[41] HMC 71, *Finch MSS*, ii.172. The articles, as published, did not mention such a requirement.

[42] Gillian L Weiss, *Captives and Corsairs. France and Slavery in the Early Modern Mediterranean* (Stanford, CA, 2011), 30.

[43] TNA SP 71/2, fos. 382–9; *Calendar of Treasury Books, 1685–9*, 211–12.

[44] TNA SP 71/3, fos. 142, 193; *Calendar of Treasury Books, 1708–14*, 557–8.

[45] F. N. L. Poynter, ed., *The Journal of James Yonge [1647–1721]* (1963), 42; TNA SP 71/1, f.466; John Baltharpe, *The Straights Voyage* (1671), 20–1; Allin, *Journals*, ii.117, 119; cf. G. E. Manwaring, ed., *The Diary of Henry Teonge, 1675, 1678–9* (1927), 65–6.

one of its officers wrote secretly to several slaves, promising to pick them up in the ship's boat if they could swim out by night. Several were rescued, though one drowned. But the letter was discovered, and in retaliation the Aga seized several of the ship's crew who had come ashore. A dangerous standoff ensued until the captain agreed to return the escapees.[46]

Swimming out to a ship was thus more problematic than might at first appear, quite apart from the risk of drowning. And it carried dangers not only for the slaves. John Noades, a slave from Bristol who swam out to a warship at Algiers in 1690, had that very day asked an English merchant to negotiate a ransom with his *patron*. The merchant was held accountable for Noades' treachery, and condemned to pay a fine of $2,200. He was left to languish in prison, loaded with chains, until it was paid.[47] Masters and commanders, like politicians, were generally reluctant to jeopardize commercial and diplomatic relationships, so even if swimmers reached a ship they might not be allowed on board. If the escapees were not British, the issue became still more sensitive. When Admiral Blake's sailors contributed to the ransoming of several Dutch sailors who swam out to his ships at Algiers in 1655, the gesture was designed in part to avert hostile repercussions.[48] Two years later, an English shipmaster was so concerned to discover that two Dutch slaves had crept aboard at Algiers that he resolved to send them back from Livorno rather than jeopardize the peace.[49] Thomas Allin refused to take in sixteen Spanish slaves who had paddled out to his ships at night. He also had several acrimonious exchanges over allegations that his ships had received English escapees; the authorities demanded to search his entire squadron for one alleged runaway.[50] The duke of Grafton was similarly embarrassed in 1690 when several European slaves swam out to his ships at Algiers. He considered it against his honour to return them, but in the case of an English carpenter who had been brought out in a warship's own boat, he agreed that compensation was due, and stopped the crew's pay. The consul urged that a sum equivalent to the carpenter's ransom be paid to atone for what he described as an 'unworthy' action. The Secretary of State agreed, and directed the Treasury to pay the money.[51] The priorities were clear.

The very bravest spirits attempted to escape by constructing a flimsy raft or boat, with whatever materials they could find, and paddling out to sea in the desperate hope of reaching a European shore or encountering a friendly ship. Such ventures were possible, of course, only for those slaves enjoying some measure of autonomy. Francis Knight made two such attempts at Algiers in the later 1630s, though both failed. In one he acted as treasurer to a group of thirteen, all English,

[46] *CSPD 1671-2*, 220-1, 316-17.
[47] TNA SP 71/3, f.186; *Calendar of Treasury Books, 1693-6*, 256.
[48] J. R. Powell, ed., *The Letters of Robert Blake*, Navy Records Society, 76 (1937), 314.
[49] *Thurloe*, vi.164-5.   [50] Allin, *Journals*, ii.46, 48, 84.
[51] TNA SP 71/3, fos, 96, 98, 193, 203, 205, 212v, 218; *CSPD 1691-2*, 159-60.

who raised money to buy materials and assembled a boat in a smallholding tended by other English slaves. Their design was discovered two days before the planned escape, and they paid a heavy price; three were savagely beaten, and one died of his injuries. Knight's *patron* was more lenient, but he reflected years later that his next owner's customary practice in such cases had been to slice off the runaway's nose and ears.[52]

The best narrative records William Okeley's escape from Algiers in 1644, after five years of slavery.[53] He broached his plan to several friends, who all approved, though one felt too old for such a hazardous venture, and another was unwilling to leave behind his wife and child. Okeley assembled a group of seven, among them two carpenters. They pondered the many difficulties ahead: how to construct a boat and carry it to the shore without being detected, how to obtain provisions, and where to steer once at sea. They assembled their boat in a cellar where Okeley stored goods for his shop, bought canvas and pitch, and fashioned oars out of strips taken from barrels. Then, dismantling the boat, over the course of many days and nights they smuggled it in pieces out of town. At dusk on 30 June they rendezvoused, reassembled it in silence, and carried it to the shore. Every step had been fraught with difficulties, and they now discovered another: the boat proved too flimsy to bear seven people, so two had to back out. The remaining five put to sea, and for several gruelling days and nights they rowed against headwinds so strong that they almost abandoned their venture. The water they had brought in goatskin bags was soon contaminated, forcing them to drink their own urine and then sea-water. But on the fifth day they caught a turtle, cut off its head, and drank its blood. And then, far off, they sighted Majorca, and on 7 July they staggered ashore. Only when they stumbled on a well, Okeley admits, did they finally accept that 'God watched over us all'. A kind farmer provided bread, water, and olives, and the next day local townsfolk gave them money for clothes and shoes. It was a very different reception from Hasleton's experience sixty years earlier. Instead of being tortured by the Inquisition, they were given passage on a Spanish naval galley to Alicante and eventually found their way back to England.

Despite this exploit, the chances of a successful escape by sea were desperately poor. In *Robinson Crusoe* the hero is able to escape from Salé only because Defoe gave him the unlikely privilege of being permitted to go out in his owner's boat on fishing trips.[54] Three English slaves who escaped from Algiers by night in 1671 had no such favour; they put to sea on a flimsy raft fashioned from cow hides stretched across wooden spars lashed into an oblong, 'like a picture frame'. They would not have survived long, but had the luck to be picked up by an English warship patrolling offshore. One rescuer commented that they had taken a 'risk so

---

[52] Knight, *Relation*, 14–15.   [53] What follows is based on *Okeley*, 43–85.
[54] Daniel Defoe, *The Life and Strange Surprizing Adventures of Robinson Crusoe* (1719), 36–8.

great not likely to be heard of'.[55] Three years earlier a group of thirteen Spaniards had escaped to Majorca in a more substantial boat that they had also constructed themselves.[56] George Penticost and fourteen companions devised a different method of escape: in July 1640 they attacked a storehouse and seized weapons and a boat. By the time they put to sea they had already lost three of their number, and during a lengthy pursuit they suffered three more casualties before finally reaching safety in Majorca.[57] In a much later escape, in 1712, British mariners featured as victims rather than escapees. Thirty-four Dutch, Spanish, and Italian slaves working on a ship in the harbour at Algiers seized a merchantman that had just arrived, overpowered its crew, and carried it to Majorca. The British crew were later able to return to Algiers, their cargo still intact.[58] But most attempts to escape by sea probably ended in death by drowning or starvation, and their stories are lost. No escapes are recorded from Tunis or Tripoli.

Joseph Pitts devised a far more elaborate plan. He appears to have seriously contemplated escaping only after becoming acquainted with an English merchant in Algiers, who offered to help him sneak aboard a visiting warship. Pitts rejected this idea as too risky, and decided instead to join a corsair fleet sailing to Smyrna, where he would try to slip away and find a passage to Europe. Even with the help of a consul and merchant in Smyrna, the risks were high and he almost abandoned his design. In Algiers he had seen renegades suffer a grisly death for attempting to escape, and he heard of others who had been pursued and hacked to pieces. But the new friends he made in Smyrna provided him with English clothes, and a wig and cane, and eventually secured him a berth aboard a French ship bound for Livorno. Terrified of being betrayed if the ship was stopped and searched, Pitts never revealed his identity, pretending he could not speak any foreign language. He was too frightened to travel any further by sea. Resolving to reach home overland, he walked 500 miles from Livorno to Frankfurt, alone and in mid-winter. And when he finally landed in England, he was promptly seized and impressed to serve in the navy, and spent several days in prison before he could secure a safe conduct. Almost a year had passed between leaving Algiers and finally arriving home in Exeter. Escape was not for the weak or faint-hearted.[59]

For a time, Morocco offered a different route to freedom. Between 1614 and 1672, Spain possessed a military outpost at Mamora, on the coast about 20 miles north of Salé. If a captive could escape and evade pursuit, he would find a refuge there, provided England and Spain were at peace. James Cadman of Rye and three companions, all former shipmasters, achieved that feat in 1641, on the night before they were due to be shipped to Algiers. Picking the lock of their shackles,

---

[55] *CSPD 1671*, 455.   [56] TNA SP 71/1, f.316.

[57] Hebb, *Piracy*, 156–7, from BL Sloane MS 33178. Another English captive, known only as Richard, stole a Moorish bark and reached safety in Alicante: Bennassar, *Chrétiens*, 217.

[58] *Several Voyages to Barbary* (1736), 52–4.   [59] *Pitts*, 228–59.

they ran through empty streets, leaped down from the town wall, and raced along the shore to reach Mamora by daybreak. An hour later they were able to look down from its walls on a party of horsemen who had pursued them.[60] Three decades later, in 1670, Adam Elliot made the same flight. A young Cambridge graduate, Elliot had gone abroad as companion to a travelling gentleman, and after being captured devised an imaginative plan of escape. Feigning affection for his owner, he plied him with drink one night as they entertained one another with Moorish and English songs. When his owner, drunk and amorous, finally fell asleep, Elliot fled. Abandoning his clothes to swim across the river, he ran barefoot along the shore to Mamora, where he too received a friendly reception. And he too could soon look down on the frustrated horsemen who had followed in pursuit.[61]

This escape route was closed only two years later, when Mamora fell to the Moors. Thereafter, only the most desperate chanced their luck. One such was Thomas Phelps. Like most slaves in Morocco, Phelps was held at Meknes, about 20 miles inland, and when his ransom offer was rejected he feared he was trapped for life and resolved to risk an escape. On 31 May 1685 he fled with three companions, hoping to reach the sea and find a friendly ship. Travelling only by night, and surviving on snails, pumpkins, and a tortoise, it took them ten days to reach Salé, and several more to find a boat they could steal. Paddling out to sea at night, they spied a ship lying several miles offshore, but feared it might be a Salé man-of-war. If they hailed it and their suspicions proved correct, they would face almost certain death. It offered their only chance of survival, however, and after hesitating for several hours they took the risk, and their luck held: it proved to be an English frigate. But their adventure was not yet over. Informing the captain that two powerful Salé men-of-war lay at Mamora, Phelps offered to lead a raid to destroy them, and the captain agreed. Four boats launched a night-time attack with devastating success, burning both ships, one of them the man-of-war that had captured Phelps' own vessel nine months earlier. It was sweet revenge.[62]

The final English escape narrative of the century was published by Francis Brooks in 1693. Brooks had been enslaved for over ten years, and he described in detail the miseries endured by the army of slaves building Moulay Ismail's new capital at Meknes. He was fully aware of the risks. His account records numerous accounts of slaves arbitrarily put to death, including the story of an Englishman hacked to death by the sultan himself after a failed attempt to escape. Moreover, with Mamora now lost, the nearest refuge was now the Portuguese outpost of Meregan, 200 miles distant. Brooks' story is exceptional in that he found a Moor to serve as guide, promising that if they reached the fort he would ask its Governor to give him 40 pieces of eight. He and his two companions, one a New Englander, expected their trek to take ten days; in the event it took more than twice that, and

---

[60] *Newes from Sally* (1642).   [61] Elliot, *Modest Vindication*, 11–16.   [62] *Phelps*, 11–26.

their food ran out long before they arrived. Travelling by night they frequently lost their way, and he calculated they had eventually walked 300 miles, terrified of discovery and equally of the lions they sometimes heard prowling close by. The story ended happily for Brooks and his companions. After reaching the fort they were given passage in a Portuguese warship to Lisbon, where he had an audience with the king before returning to England. Their guide had a very different fate: on his journey home he was stopped, questioned, condemned, and burned alive. It is not hard to see why few slaves in Morocco attempted escape.[63]

A generation later, the renegade Thomas Pellow devoted over eighty pages of his own narrative to his hazardous escape from Morocco in 1737–38. Though he was fluent in the language and familiar with Moorish customs, it took him more than a year after leaving Meknes to reach safety. During his odyssey he had to devise ways to support himself, and was several times robbed, assaulted, imprisoned, shot, and on one occasion on the point of being beheaded. Pellow had apostatized more than twenty years earlier, but he was still viewed with deep suspicion by Moorish soldiers and officials. He spent months in the ports of Salé, Safi, St Cruz, and Willadea before he eventually found a shipmaster willing to risk carrying him away.[64]

'The worthy enterprise of John Fox'

The earliest escape narrative we have records the remarkable story of John Fox and his companions, who escaped from Alexandria on 1–2 January 1577.[65] This was not, therefore, strictly a Barbary episode, for Egypt was a province of the Ottoman Empire, not one of the autonomous regencies. It differs too in other significant ways. Fox devised an elaborate escape plan with a small group of companions of several nationalities, but then spelled out his design to the 266 other slaves held in the compound. This was to be a mass escape. His main co-conspirator was a Spaniard named Unticaro, who had been a slave for about thirty years. As in Algiers, some of the galley-slaves were allowed to support themselves by practising a trade between *corso* expeditions; Fox worked as a barber, while Unticaro kept a victualling house. Fox had been outwardly docile for fourteen years, winning the trust of the prison-keeper, and, for a fee, was allowed to enter and leave at will during the day, with a lock about his leg. The other plotters enjoyed a similar privilege. On the night of the rising they lured the prison-keeper to Unticaro's house, hacked him to pieces, and cut off his head. Hastening back to

---

[63] Francis Brooks, *Barbarian Cruelty* (1693), 85–118. The American's participation may explain why the work was reprinted at Boston in 1700. Jeremy Bingley, a shipwright, made another rare escape, from Salé, probably on a visiting ship: *CSPD 1699–1700*, 284.

[64] Thomas Pellow, *The History of the Long Captivity and Adventures of Thomas Pellow* (1751; first published 1740), 288–374; cf. Giles Milton, *White Gold* (2005), 253–61.

[65] What follows is drawn from Richard Hakluyt, *The Principal Navigations* (1599–1600), ii.131–6.

the prison compound, they killed the warders guarding the gate, seized weapons from the keeper's house, threw open the prison doors, and freed the captives. Some then set about constructing a rampart to prevent the gate being forced open, others carried masts, oars, and sails to fit one of the galleys for sea, and the rest held the remaining guards at bay. Unticaro was killed in the fighting, and Fox was shot three times through his clothes, though unhurt. Swarms of Turkish soldiers, mariners, and labourers rushed to the compound, but the slaves succeeded in putting to sea before they could break in. Steering only by the stars and driven about by strong and changeable winds, they were at sea for twenty-eight days, and ran out of food. Eight died of starvation. The survivors eventually reached safety in Crete, where they received generous help from Dominican friars, and then sailed on to Taranto, in southern Italy. There they sold the galley, sharing out the proceeds, and Fox then made his way to Rome, where an admiring Englishman gave him lodging and presented his deed to the pope. Armed with a papal certificate, he moved on to Spain, and served as a gunner on one of the Spanish royal galleys for two years before eventually finding his way home.

Fox's remarkable story first appeared in print in 1589 in Hakluyt's *Principal Voyages*, told in the third person, and again in 1608 in a pamphlet published by Anthony Munday. Both may have drawn on an earlier account, now lost, entered in the Stationers' Register in 1579. There are some parallels with later escape narratives, but also striking contrasts. A mass breakout of this kind was exceedingly rare.[66] There were only three Englishmen in the compound, which housed men of 'sixteen sundry nations'. Fox was clearly a Catholic, so the religious dimension of the narrative is framed in broadly Christian rather than Protestant terms. English slaves in Barbary, plotting escapes in later periods, rarely trusted men of other nationalities, and would never conspire with Spaniards. It is strange to find testimonies from the pope and the king of Spain included in a text published shortly after the Armada—another indication, perhaps, that it was based on an earlier narrative, from a period of friendlier relations between England and Spain. Fox had not lost his longing for freedom after fourteen years of slavery. The narrative states simply that he had become 'too, too weary' of his condition. No specific incident appears to have triggered his desperate action. Indeed, the keeper's last words, as reported, had an aggrieved tone: 'O Fox, what have I deserved of thee, that thou shouldest seek my death?' After Fox had killed the keeper with a single blow that split open his head, his

---

[66] A carefully planned Spanish mutiny on two galleys in 1589 killed 300 'Turks' and freed 420 captives, who sailed away to Barcelona. At Tripoli in 1601, 160 galley slaves killed their overseer and the Governor, seized the galley, and also reached Spain: Daniel Hershenzon *The Captive Sea: Slavery, Communication, and Commerce in Early Modern Spain and the Mediterranean* (Philadelphia, 2019), 37–9; Ellen G. Friedman, *Spanish Captives in North Africa in the early Modern Age* (Madison, WI, 1983), 65. For a highly embroidered account of another mass breakout at Alexandria see *A Narrative of the Adventures of Lewis Marott, pilot royal of the galleys of France* (1677), 16–37.

companions ran him through with their spits, decapitated him, 'and mangled him so that no man should discern what he was'. They reasoned that an anonymous, headless corpse would attract less attention than the body of an important official, but the blood-lust and pent-up hatred are unmistakeable. The same hatred and thirst for revenge are evident in the later narratives of John Rawlins and Thomas Duffield. Slavery dehumanized its victims as well as perpetrators.

Dramatic escape narratives provided welcome reassurance for English readers. With their providential colouring they suggested that mariners were not wholly at the mercy of cruel and barbarous infidels. That so few such accounts exist reflects in part the fact that few of those who did escape were sufficiently literate to compose a publishable account of their experiences. Fox's narrative is told in the third person, Hasleton and Okeley acknowledged assistance, and Rawlins' account switches between the first and third person. But the paucity of narratives also reflects the fact that successful escapes were extremely rare. Most captives recognized that only the payment of a ransom or intervention by the state would offer any hope of freedom.

6

Raising Ransoms

Corsairs hunted prey of two kinds: booty and captives. Rich merchandise offered the more lucrative returns, but as larger merchant ships became increasingly well-armed, many were able to deter or repel attacks. Most corsairs had to be satisfied with smaller vessels carrying corn, fish, and other commodities of less value, and their focus shifted towards human prizes. The potential value of 'ransom slavery' lay in extracting ransoms substantially larger than the price owners had paid at auction. In the early 1580s there were already complaints of owners demanding ransoms of 200–500 ducats even for 'poor ordinary mariners'.[1] In 1622 John Rawlins' owner demanded twice the purchase price, while Abraham Browne, bought for £75 at Salé in 1655, had to agree a ransom of £125 only three months later—a handsome return on his owner's investment. Later in the century Joseph Pitts' owner demanded $500—more than twice his auction price. When the English negotiators countered with an offer of $200, the owner laughed and the talks collapsed. They told Pitts that $500 was too much for them to risk; he came from a modest family, and they probably feared such an advance would never be repaid. He burst into tears at the news.[2]

As we have seen, corsairs tried to identify captives from wealthy families, knowing they would probably accept a high ransom demand and have the contacts to make the money materialize. Captives willing to co-operate might then suffer little hardship. Charles Longland, a merchant at Livorno engaged in redemptions in the 1650s, explained that most shipmasters and other officers negotiated private deals 'to avoid the hardship that others endure'. Thomas Highway, a shipmaster, was able to enjoy boiled mutton and wine at Tunis in 1657, presumably with money that he borrowed there. He was redeemed within two months, 'having good friends of the merchants at Leghorn [Livorno] and masters together'.[3] Ordinary seamen, by contrast, might languish for years or even decades. One group of captives in Morocco, petitioning Charles I in 1632, had endured between seven and twenty years in slavery. Some members of another group, freed at Tunis in 1658, had been enslaved for five, ten, and in one case thirty-two years.[4]

---

[1] Christopher Carleill, *A breef and sommarie discourse vpon the Entended Voyage* (1583), sig. A2-v.
[2] *Rawlins*, sig. B2v; Stephen T. Riley, ed., 'Abraham Browne's Captivity by the Barbary Pirates, 1655', *Colonial Society of Massachusetts*, 52 (1979), 41; *Pitts*, 189–90.
[3] *CSPD 1652–3*, 118; Coxere, *Adventures*, 57.   [4] Vitkus, *Piracy*, 359; Coxere, *Adventures*, 67.

British Slaves and Barbary Corsairs, 1580–1750. Bernard Capp, Oxford University Press. © Bernard Capp 2022.
DOI: 10.1093/oso/9780192857378.003.0007

Both market prices and ransoms were closely related to social status. Buyers made a careful assessment of whether a captive's family and friends were likely to be able to raise funds, and if so, how substantial. Ransoms for shipmasters, merchants, and passengers were far higher than for ordinary seamen, and ransoms for women generally higher than for men. The master and mate of the *Samuel*, captives at Tunis in 1624, faced demands of £240 and £140 respectively, while two ordinary sailors were ransomed there a year later for only £9 12s 6d each.[5] Six mariners from the *Ruth* of Dartmouth were freed in 1677 for sums that ranged from £15 to £150.[6] Owners generally assumed that the family of a shipmaster, merchant, or factor carried on board (the 'supercargo') would be able to raise a substantial ransom. Robert Adams, a ship-owner's son, described in 1625 how he was made to grind corn in a mill, loaded with heavy chains, and beaten every day until he agreed to an exorbitant demand of 750 Barbary ducats. Weak and barely able to walk, he wrote home that he had had no option.[7]

The slave-owners' assumptions often proved mistaken, however, for most of a captive's estate might have been ploughed into the ship and its cargo. One young merchant had sold his inheritance to buy a cargo to carry on his first voyage.[8] Women begging help frequently explained that the family's entire assets had been invested in the ship and the master's 'adventure', the goods he was trading on his own account.[9] That was also the situation of Captain William Hawkridge, seized by corsairs at Tunis in 1630. Hawkridge had been a man of some substance, owning his ship and its lading, worth in all £3,000. In losing them he had lost everything. Even so, he and his kind were far more likely to be redeemed than ordinary sailors, and far sooner. Hawkridge was freed within two years by friends in the seafaring and mercantile community who paid his ransom of £270. It was five years before his shipmaster secured his freedom (for £93), and though Hawkridge hoped to find some way to free his men, there is no indication that he ever succeeded.[10]

Once a ransom had been agreed, the captive would send a message home, begging his family and friends to do their utmost to raise the money, and spelling out his plight in graphic and emotional terms. He might also explain how hard he and his men had fought to defend the ship, to convince merchants and owners that help was genuinely deserved. And very often he would describe the relentless pressure he was facing to apostatize, which would make his family and friends redouble their efforts. Owners wanting to ransom their slaves encouraged such

---

[5] *APC, 1625–6*, 336; Harris, *Trinity House*, 60.   [6] *CSPD 1683–4*, 116–17.

[7] Vitkus, *Piracy*, 349–50.

[8] T. S., *The Adventures of (Mr. T. S.) an English Merchant, taken Prisoner by the Turks* (1670), 5.

[9] Harris, *Trinity House*, 60, 66, 70–1, 76–7; Wyndham Anstis Bewes, *Church Briefs or Royal Warrants for Collections for Charitable Objects* (1896), 117.

[10] TNA SP 71/26, f.3; Harris, *Trinity House*, 76; *CSPD 1635–6*, 302. Hawkridge was sailing with letters of marque, and had earlier commands on East Indiamen and in voyages to search for the North-West Passage.

letters, and facilitated collective petitions begging the crown to help. Nineteen shipmasters enslaved in Algiers were able to send a formal petition to Charles II in 1677 on behalf of themselves and their crews, numbering 241 in all. Such a document could only have been drawn up in Algiers with the knowledge and probably assistance of their owners. Even if it was drawn up in London—which is far more likely—their owners would almost certainly have been aware of the initiative.[11] Sending messages home from Salé, where few English merchant ships called, was much harder. But when Adam Elliot claimed he was related to Lord Henry Howard, a close kinsman of the duke of Norfolk, and would be able to secure a large ransom, his owner had a begging letter translated into Spanish and found a courier to carry it to Cadiz, with instructions for it to be forwarded.[12] A French gentleman, also enslaved at Salé, recalled being instructed to write home begging for ransom money, and provided with ink, pen, and paper.[13]

Communications between England and Barbary were always slow and uncertain. Consuls generally took the precaution of sending several copies of each letter they wrote home by different routes, in the hope that at least one would arrive, and as a further precaution often included a copy of their previous letter. A slave's letter might take months to arrive, especially if his family lived far from London or a major port. Many captives waited for months, in growing desperation, for a reply that might never come. Robert Adams wrote anxiously in 1625 that he had sent three or four letters, by various hands, without any answer. He had been given only six months to secure a ransom, and with three already passed he was close to despair.[14] Similarly, Thomas Sweet of Dartmouth explained that during six years in Algiers he had written many times to friends in London, as well as to his father and brothers. 'I could never hear whether any of you were alive or dead,' he added plaintively, 'which makes me think the letters are either miscarried or all of you deceased or gone to other places'—or that they did not care about his plight. Even when a letter did arrive, the family might have little idea how to set about arranging a ransom. Sweet and his friend did their best to help, passing on what information they had. 'We are told there is a merchant in London, one Mr Stanner of St Mary's Axe', they wrote, 'that hath a factor in Leghorn and one Mr Hodges and Mr Mico, Londoners that are dealers there, who are able to direct you in the readiest way for our redemption... There is a post in London that conveys letters into all parts'.[15]

[11] TNA SP 29/397, f.74; Nabil Matar, *British Captives from the Mediterranean to the Atlantic, 1563–1760* (Leiden, 2014), 87–8.

[12] Adam Elliot, *A Modest Vindication of Titus Oates* (1682), 10.

[13] *The Travels of the Sieur Mouette in the Kingdoms of Fez and Morocco* (1710), 9–10.

[14] Vitkus, *Piracy*, 349–50.

[15] Thomas Sweet, *Deare Friends: it is now about six yeares* (1647). He was eventually ransomed by Cason in 1647 for $98: *An Account of what captives hath been freed since the 14th of December Anno*

Poor captives, the great majority, knew their families could never hope to raise a ransom. Barely literate, many were unable even to send a message home to say they were still alive. Moreover, owners who had bought slaves for their labour might have no desire to ransom them, and forbid them to write home. Samuel Dawks, smuggling out a letter to his sister in 1670, explained that he would have been beaten with 200 stripes if it had been discovered. Thomas Goodman described writing hastily with 'one standing over me', adding there had been no previous opportunity to send any word.[16] It followed that many families had no information about missing husbands or sons, even whether they were alive. That provides the context for a broadsheet published in 1670 that listed 341 captives 'taken by the pirates of Argier, made public for the benefit of those that have relations there'. Three of the names were marked as 'killed', either at the time of capture or later. There was nothing to indicate who was behind the initiative, though most of the names had been sent from Algiers the previous year, probably by the consul, John Ward.[17] The publication gave families at least the comfort of knowing a loved one was still alive, and an incentive to do anything they could to help. A decade later another publication listed 126 Britons liberated after the capture of four Algerian men-of-war in 1681. Providing almost no information about the engagements themselves, this was another publication evidently designed primarily for the families of missing captives. Similarly, eighty years later, Thomas Troughton began his account of captivity in Morocco by listing all 183 people on board his ship when it was wrecked, and carefully recording the fate of each individual: drowned, killed after scrambling ashore, escaped, died in slavery, 'turned Moor', or survived, like him, and eventually ransomed. His work was published in 1751, five years after their capture, and he evidently assumed that many families would still not know what had happened to their loved ones.[18]

For their part, many captives found it equally hard to receive news. When John Pitts of Exeter wrote to his son, he directed the letter to Joseph's former ship-master, still enslaved in Algiers, who forwarded it to an English child-slave of the general commanding in the camp where Joseph then served. Pitts recalled that the boy had been too frightened to deliver it openly and 'slid it into my hand as he passed by me'. He had to slip away to a privy to read it. And to reply, he had to borrow pen, ink, and paper from the same boy, again in secret, and invent excuses

---

Dom. 1647 (1647), 1. Thomas Hodges and Samuel Mico were members of the committee for the redemption of captives, established by Parliament in 1645: *LJ*, vii.489–91. On Mico see also *CSPD 1661–2*, 58.

[16] TNA SP 29/276, f.227; SP 71/16, f.256v.

[17] *A List of the English Captives taken by the Pyrates of Argier* (1670); Matar, *Piracy*, 14. Samuel Dawks was among those listed.

[18] *A List of the English redeemed out of slavery by the taking of the Golden Horn* (1681); Thomas Troughton, *Barbarian Cruelty; or an Accurate and Impartial Narrative* (1751), 12–17.

to find somewhere private for a few minutes, where 'in fear [he] writ two or three lines at a time'.[19]

Raising ransoms: the issues

It was generally recognized that most poor families would never be able to raise a ransom of any sort for a husband, son, or brother. Many families were facing ruin themselves, for credit soon dried up once the main breadwinner was gone, leaving wives and children struggling to survive. Even the families of officers and small merchants were often unable to raise the funds they needed, and had to dispose of land or other assets. When Abraham Browne's father was enslaved in Algiers in the 1630s, the family's 'friends' in Plymouth proved unable or unwilling to help, and his mother had to sell her plate, gold ring, bracelet, and other possessions to raise the ransom of £150. It took her three years to secure his freedom. Ursula Phipperd of Topsham was ready to sell her house and every possession of value.[20] Poorer women might have to sell everything they had, simply to maintain themselves and their children. Some were driven to still more desperate measures. Ann Wry, married to an enslaved ship's surgeon, turned to crime, and only a royal pardon saved her from the gallows or transportation.[21]

The problems facing poor captives and their families were well known, and raised difficult questions. Were they simply to be abandoned? If not, who should be responsible for redeeming them and relieving their families—friends and neighbours, local magistrates, ship-owners and merchants, the Church, the general public, or the crown itself? But how could the crown treat with those it considered pirates without losing honour? And if it did treat, how could it possibly undertake to redeem every slave, perhaps for generations to come? Would it not be more honourable to send a naval expedition and force Barbary's rulers to liberate their captives? The huge sums involved made these issues all the more intractable, and each option was problematic.

The most coldly rational commentators argued that captives should be left to their fate. Henry Blount insisted that it would be a 'virtuous cruelty' to forbid the payment of ransoms, which would make sailors fight harder to defend their vessels and discourage them from going to sea inadequately armed. The Scottish traveller William Lithgow agreed that 'rash fellows' who had ventured into the Straits in small unarmed vessels had only themselves to blame. If men 'nakedly hazard

---

[19] *Pitts*, 200–3. Auchterlonie says the master, George Taylor, had probably been redeemed, but *A List of Ships taken* shows that he was still a captive: Paul Auchterlonie, ed., *Encountering Islam. Joseph Pitts: an English Slave in 17th-Century Algiers and Mecca* (2012), 232n.

[20] Riley, ed., 'Abraham Browne's Captivity', 32–3; John C. Appleby, *Women and English Piracy, 1540–1720* (2013), 167.

[21] *CSPD 1680–1*, 539.

themselves in known perils, without ordnance, munition and a burdenable ship', he argued, it was legitimate to abandon them.[22] The merchant community also displayed limited sympathy. Richard Hasleton's editor, writing in 1595, thanked the wealthy Levant merchant who had redeemed him but added pointedly that such generosity was rare.[23] Merchants might be ready to help ransom a ship-master, especially a part-owner with a share in the voyage, but many felt little obligation to assist ordinary seamen. Richard Doves, master of the *Zouche Bonaventure*, lost £1,000 when his ship was captured, and appealed to the East India Company in 1619 for help in meeting a ransom demand of £1,000 to free him and fourteen other masters. He did not mention their crews.[24] Merchants and ship-owners suffered too, of course, when vessels were lost, though the gradual spread of marine insurance helped soften the blow. Many merchants and ship-owners may well have considered it impossible to ransom a ship's entire company, and unreasonable to expect them to do so. The four owners of the *Mary*, captured in 1637, baulked at a ransom demand of £800 to free the crew, but did offer £100 towards it.[25]

Some contemporaries accused merchants of shuffling off their responsibilities, and even blocking the efforts of others. In the mid-1620s the Levant Company refused to honour bills of exchange drawn for the redemption of slaves in Barbary, arguing that its own well-armed ships were rarely captured and that it accepted no responsibility for the fate of West Country fishermen.[26] Merchants trading with Barbary itself could be equally unhelpful. William Okeley complained darkly that the wrongs he and his friends had suffered from Englishmen in Algiers, presumably merchants, 'had more of bitterness in it than in all our slavery'. They had probably found merchants unable or unwilling to negotiate ransom terms on their behalf. Moreover, as he and his companions were making their way home after their daring escape, they had only 'cold entertainment' from English merchants in Spain, who apparently disapproved of their exploit. The merchants' own interests and the property rights of Barbary slave-owners counted for more than the freedom of fellow Englishmen.[27]

Slaves in Morocco were more openly critical when they appealed to the king in 1632, begging him not to put 'the private benefit of a few merchants before the lives and liberties' of English captives.[28] Many merchants and economists viewed ransoming seamen as misguided and counter-productive. If captives could expect to be ransomed, they argued, they would tamely surrender their ships rather

[22] Henry Blount, *A Voyage into the Levant* (1636), 74; William Lithgow, *The Totall Discourse, Of the Rare Aduentures* (1640), 362.

[23] *Hasleton*, sig. A3-v; cf. *APC, 1600–1*, 270–1.

[24] *Calendar of State Papers, Colonial, East Indies, 1617–20*, 608.   [25] *CSPD 1637–8*, 477–8.

[26] *The Negotiations of Sir Thomas Roe in his Embassy to the Ottoman Porte* (1740), 522–3; see also Chapter 7.

[27] *Okeley*, sig. B2-v, 87.   [28] Vitkus, *Piracy*, 359–60.

than defend them. Ransoming seamen would also do nothing to compensate merchants for the loss of their merchandise, and by providing corsairs with a steady flow of ransom money would enable them to set out yet more ships, exacerbating the problem. That was an argument beyond dispute, and still familiar today in public debate on piracy, hostage-taking, and kidnapping.[29] Some of the merchants trading with Morocco also opposed moves to redeem slaves by exchanging them for commodities, complaining this would undermine their trade. One envoy sent by Charles II found his mission thwarted by the merchants' own envoy, who had arrived before him.[30] Profit outweighed philanthropy.

Raising ransoms: private and local initiatives

Families trying to raise a ransom turned first to their 'friends'—a term that in this period included kin. John Baltharpe, sailor and plebeian poet, recalled gratefully that friends had undertaken to repay the merchant in Algiers who had secured his freedom, and had not failed him.[31] Families without friends able and willing to make such a pledge had to look elsewhere. Some applied for a 'brief'—a licence from the crown to seek alms towards a captive's redemption or to save the family from destitution. The alms-seeker was then able to travel without fear of being arrested as a vagrant. Edmund Grindal, bishop of London, gave his support to an early request in 1567 on behalf of captives in Algiers. The churchwardens of Ashburton, Devon, gave 2s in 1568–69 'to one that gathered for them that be in Turkey', and numerous briefs were issued over the following century and a half, including some in Ireland.[32] Recipients ranged from the wives and close kin of merchants, ship-owners, and even gentlemen, all needing to raise substantial ransoms, to poor women attempting to stave off destitution. Some travelled in pairs or small groups, like a Mrs Smith and a party of ten in 1663, who had suffered 'great losses by Turkish pirates in ye Ile of Skirtyn'—perhaps a raid on the marshy coastal area close to Lancaster.[33] Briefs were often addressed to church-wardens, and modest payments appear in churchwardens' accounts throughout the land. One poor woman who passed through a village in County Durham in 1619 received 12d for her own maintenance, and 9d towards the redemption of

---

[29] TNA SP 71/1, fos. 100, 162; Francis Knight, *A Relation of Seaven Yeares Slaverie* (1640), 52; Henry Robinson, *Libertas, or Reliefe to the English Captives in Algier* (1642), 1.

[30] Simon Ockley, *An Account of South-West Barbary* (1713), 123–6; Joseph Morgan, *A Compleat History of the Piratical States of Barbary* (1750), 366.

[31] John Baltharpe, *The Straights Voyage* (1671), 5.

[32] *CSPD 1547–80*, 295; Alison Hanham, ed., *Churchwardens' Accounts of Ashburton, 1479–1580*, Devon and Cornwall Record Society, New Series, 15 (1970), 162; Bewes, *Church Briefs*; Harris, *Trinity House*, 16; Appleby, *Women and Piracy*, 129.

[33] 'Wirksworth Church Wardens' Accounts, 1658–1727', iii.3; cf. Iii.6, 7, xv.9 (<http://www.wirksworth.org.uk/CWA.htm>).

her husband and son, both enslaved in Barbary.[34] The churchwardens of Cratfield, Suffolk, gave 4s, an unusually high amount, towards a ransom in 1657.[35] Briefs were also issued for a host of other charitable causes, however, and some people came to view them as a public nuisance. Some proved counterfeit, while desperate recipients might trade them for ready money, with donations then diverted into the wrong hands. As a result of such abuses, requests for briefs were sometimes refused.[36]

As a simpler alternative, women might request a certificate from their parish, signed by the minister and parish officers, or (for Londoners) from Trinity House, the organization of ship-owners and master mariners. Some secured both. A parish certificate would enable the holder to approach parochial officers else-where, while one from Trinity House might give her the confidence to approach merchants and ship-owners. When Michael Fletcher, a Rotherhithe shipmaster, was carried to Salé in 1626, his wife secured a certificate from Thomas Gataker, their puritan minister, and eight leading parishioners—a certificate also endorsed by Trinity House. Mary Croft similarly turned to Trinity House in 1632 on behalf of her husband, a shipmaster enslaved in Algiers, and secured the backing of several prominent figures, including William Rainborough, who was later to lead an expedition against the corsairs. The merchants behind Croft's voyage also supplied a certificate.[37] As in these cases, the women approaching Trinity House generally belonged to families similar to those represented in the organization itself. When Trinity House provided a certificate, it has been said, it was effectively looking after its own.[38] Moses Mason, another beneficiary, was only a gunner's mate, but he was 'of honest life' and long settled in Wapping. His wife secured an impressive certificate signed by the rector, constable, and churchwardens, further support from the two part-owners of his ship, and from Trinity House.[39] Only rarely, however, did the families of ordinary sailors have the standing or connec-tions to secure such support. When Henry Hammon's brothers learned in 1616 that he was alive and could be ransomed for £80, they attempted to raise the money themselves. Such a sum proved beyond the reach of a lowly blacksmith and a tailor, and after five years they finally admitted defeat and approached Trinity House. They now faced another problem: how to prove their brother was still alive. Fortunately they found two former captives who had seen him on a Tunis man-of-war a few months earlier.[40]

---

[34] Bewes, *Church Briefs*, 106; cf. HMC 12, *Dean and Chapter of Wells*, 441–2, 444, 446, 450–1, 476–7; HMC 55, *Various Collections, VII, Dunwich*, 91, 94–100, 289; Linda Colley, *Captives. Britain, Empire and the World, 1600–1850* (2002), 85, 396, n.21.

[35] L. A. Botelho, ed., *Churchwardens' Accounts of Cratfield 1640–1660*, Suffolk Records Society, 42 (1999), 110.

[36] Bewes, *Church Briefs*, 26–32; *CSPD 1634–5*, 223–4; TNA SP 71/1, f.113v; Roe, *Negotiations*, 31, 36.

[37] Harris, *Trinity House*, 70–1, 76–7; cf. 16.   [38] Appleby, *Women and Piracy*, 142–9.

[39] Harris, *Trinity House*, 21–2.   [40] Harris, *Trinity House*, 51.

In the south-west, the region hit worst by the corsairs, some women turned to local magistrates, asking for direct help or permission to collect alms. One pleaded that her husband was in such desperate straits that he 'was ready to eat his own flesh'. Any payments provided were usually modest in scale, however; the awards granted in Devon averaged £2, which would afford only temporary relief.[41] A few other women ventured to approach the rich and powerful. In 1683 Elizabeth Newman, a widow, petitioned the earl of Bedford on behalf of her son, enslaved in Algiers, and was given £1—a generous gesture, though a small step towards the £100 she needed.[42]

Other captives and their families found hope in a more personal connection: the captured shipmaster. There were often close ties of neighbourhood or kinship among the crews of small vessels, and many masters felt a sense of responsibility towards their men. Some sent back personal information for their families. William Agle, writing from Algiers in 1633, gave his wife the names of those killed when his ship was captured, and described the condition of the survivors. He and his wife were probably the families' only source of information. Almost a century later John Stocker, writing from Morocco, similarly passed on messages from two of his shipmates to their families.[43] Some masters were willing to go much further and negotiate a collective ransom to cover the whole company. William Nelme, captured in 1621, remained in Algiers while his men were sent to the galleys, their fate depending on his ability to raise £200 to redeem them all.[44] Slave-owners, for their part, might calculate that such an arrangement would offer the best prospect of a quick return on their investment. That would explain the treatment of James Carter of Plymouth, captured in 1619 with a crew of seven, and carried to Arcila and then Tetuan. The slavers found it hard to dispose of them, and they were resold several times over the next few months. Eventually a Jewish dealer allowed Carter to return to England and try to raise a ransom of £420 for himself and his crew. Thomas Dirdo, master of a small bark captured off Ireland in 1636 and enslaved in Salé, had a similar story. When he fell sick, he too was allowed to return home to raise a ransom for himself, his small son, and his men. Similar cases recur throughout the period.[45] Such collective ransoms were hardly practicable, of course, for ships with larger crews. Three masters held at Algiers in 1633, each a part-owner, were confronted with a formidable ransom demand of more than £10,000 to free themselves and their companies, who together

[41] Appleby, *Women and Piracy*, 163–9.
[42] Gladys Scott Thomson, *Life in a Noble Household* (1950), 362.
[43] TNA SP 71/1, f.117; SP 71/16, f.235-v; cf. Harris, *Trinity House*, 76–7.
[44] Harris, *Trinity House*, 10.
[45] Harris, *Trinity House*, 43; *CSPD 1636–7*, 311–12, 472–3; cf. TNA SP 71/13, f.80; *CSPD 1689–90*, 498; *CSPD 1699–1700*, 45.

numbered over 100. Already ruined by losing their ships, they begged the crown for help, pleading that such an enormous sum was impossible to raise.[46]

Another group of captives found their ransoms supplied, unexpectedly, much closer to hand: from English merchant ships visiting Barbary. In the first part of the period, such acts were prompted by self-interest as much as compassion. The former corsair Henry Mainwaring claimed to have laid out almost 5,000 ducats liberating English slaves at Tunis, most of whom almost certainly then joined his own marauding force. Sir Kenelm Digby, who led a privateering expedition in the Straits in 1628, followed his example. Disease had left his company seriously depleted, so Digby borrowed £1,650 to ransom forty-seven English captives at Algiers to replenish it. He had no authority to negotiate redemptions, and only twenty-five years later did the Treasury finally approve his request for reimbursement.[47] But ordinary mariners in the Straits felt a genuine sympathy for the slaves in Barbary, knowing they might one day share the same fate, and were also ready to help. When the *Hercules* almost foundered in a storm, home-ward bound from the Levant in 1588, its company offered up desperate prayers and vowed to redeem a slave if they reached Algiers alive. John Sanderson, a young merchant, contributed 20s as his share.[48] In 1609 the company of the *Dorcas* redeemed Thomas Nicols, a galley slave at Tunis, and carried him to Algiers, where he found another ship to carry him home. The mariners expected the £50 they had laid out to be repaid later by his friends in England.[49] Such arrangements were not uncommon. An officer on the *Relief*, trading at Tripoli in 1651, similarly negotiated the redemption of a slave for 230 pieces of eight, and the ship's company held a collection.[50] The sailors of Blake's fleet even paid for the redemption of several Dutch slaves who had swum out to his ships at Tunis in 1655. Although the nations had been at war only a year earlier, sympathy for fellow mariners in distress outweighed national rivalry.[51] Similar acts of compassion can be found throughout the period. John Ward, consul at Algiers, reported in 1668 that the generosity of ships' masters and companies had enabled him to redeem thirteen or fourteen slaves, adding that almost every British ship calling there took away at least one redeemed in this way.[52] Naval seamen made similar gestures. William Jennings' crew gave up a month's short-allowance money to

---

[46] TNA SP 71/1, f.121.

[47] G. E. Manwaring and W. G. Perrin, eds., *The Life and Works of Sir Henry Mainwaring*, Navy Records Society, 54, 56, (1920-2), ii.10; J. Bruce (ed.), *Journal of a Voyage into the Mediterranean by Sir Kenelm Digby, AD 1628*, Camden Society, Old Series, 96 (1868), 18-19; *CSPD 1661-2*, 170; Hebb, *Piracy*, 162. On Digby's expedition see Kenneth R. Andrews, *Ships, Money and Politics. Seafaring and Naval Enterprise in the Reign of Charles I* (Cambridge, 1991), 106-27.

[48] Sir William Foster, ed., *The Travels of John Sanderson in the Levant, 1584-1602*, Hakluyt Society, Second Series, 67 (1931), 6; cf. Baltharpe, *Straights Voyage*, 5-6.

[49] Harris, *Trinity House*, 4-5.

[50] BL MS Sloane 3494, fos. 26-v. The beneficiary was Nicholas Read, a Dover man.

[51] J. R. Powell, ed., *The Letters of Robert Blake*, Navy Records Society, 76 (1937), 314.

[52] TNA SP 71/1, f.298v.

redeem seven slaves at Algiers in June 1668, while Thomas Allin reported that a collection around the fleet had raised 2,388 pieces of eight (almost £600), which was enough to free another eleven slaves.[53] With a consul on hand to assist negotiations, such initiatives could produce swift liberation for a lucky few.

Private acts of charity provided another source of ransom funds, with several wealthy and philanthropic individuals bequeathing substantial sums. Sir William Coventry, once a leading Admiralty official, left the impressive sum of £3,000 in 1686 to redeem captives in Barbary, and Sir Henry Marten, formerly Judge in the High Court of Admiralty, left £350. Archbishop Sheldon left a generous bequest, while other peers and gentlemen left sums as large as £500, or established trusts whose funds were to be devoted to the redemption of slaves.[54] Alice, Duchess Dudley (*d*.1669), bequeathed £100 a year 'for ever' to free captives from 'the hands of infidels'.[55]

On the continent, fund-raising was organized in Spain and France by two long-established religious orders, the Mercedorians and Trinitarians, while in Italy and later in the Baltic ports and Scandinavia municipal institutions were set up to raise funds.[56] No religious equivalent had emerged in England, where the problem was of more recent origin and religious orders had been swept away at the Reformation. In the early seventeenth century, several ministers in maritime communities attempted to fill the gap by launching local campaigns. At Plymouth, Charles FitzGeffrey delivered three emotional sermons in 1636 exhorting magistrates and people to give generously. Christians should redeem captives from the bondage of slavery, he urged, just as Christ had redeemed mankind from the bondage of sin. The sermons were published, for his appeal to 'travel over the whole land'.[57] In London, charitable collections had long accompanied Easter sermons at St Paul's Cross and the Spital, and by the 1570s these already included the relief of men enslaved by 'Turks' or 'other heathens'. In 1582 John Aylmer, bishop of London, wanted to see captives redeemed from 'hellish thraldom' and the 'Gulf of Mahomet' with funds to be raised by parish collections, and called on the Lord Mayor to take action.[58] A generation later William

---

[53] *CSPD 1667–8*, 423; R. C. Anderson, ed., *The Journals of Sir Thomas Allin 1660–1678*, Navy Records Society, 79–80 (1939–40), ii.50–1; cf. TNA SP 71/3, f.96.

[54] *ODNB*, Sir William Coventry and Gilbert Sheldon; *CSPD, 1686–7*, 191; Bewes, *Church Briefs*, 205; Hebb, *Piracy*, 157–8.

[55] Robert Boreman, *A Mirrour of Christianity...or...the Life and Death of...Lady Alice, Duchess Duddeley* (1669); TNA SP 71/3, f.288v.

[56] Ellen G. Friedman, *Spanish Captives in North Africa in the early Modern Age* (Madison, WI, 1983), chaps. 6–8; Daniel Hershenzon *The Captive Sea: Slavery, Communication, and Commerce in Early Modern Spain and the Mediterranean* (Philadelphia, 2019); Robert C. Davis, *Christian Slaves, Muslim Masters* (Basingstoke, 2003), 149–72. See also below.

[57] Charles FitzGeffrey, *Compassion towards Captives* (Oxford, 1637), sigs. *2, *4v, pp. 43–50.

[58] Betty Masters, *Tales of the Unexpected: the Corporation and Captives in Barbary*, Guildhall Historical Association (2005), 1–4; *APC 1597–8*, 408; Jerry Brotton, *This Orient Isle. Elizabethan England and the Islamic World* (2016), 115–16.

Gouge launched his own campaign, preaching that redeeming slaves was the highest form of charity, feeding both body and soul, and he longed to see every city establish a fund dedicated to the cause. Gouge doubted, however, that this would ever happen.[59] Away from the capital and south-west the issue inevitably had a lower profile, and England never adopted the French practice of organizing nationwide processions of redeemed captives to raise public awareness and encourage alms-giving.[60] Henry Newcome, a minister in Lancashire, admitted that he had never given much thought to the issue until his young son sailed for Jamaica in 1670. When no word came of his safe arrival, Newcome feared he had been captured or killed by the corsairs, and now anxiously scoured the newspapers. In future, he resolved, he would care more for his poor countrymen enslaved in Barbary.[61]

Urban authorities in London and several maritime towns accepted some responsibility for captives and their destitute families, and collaborated with local clerics to raise alms. The Easter collections at Paul's Cross were organized by London's twelve great livery companies, with the funds raised (£70–£100 a year in the 1570s–90s) stored in the city Chamber. The court of aldermen dispensed the proceeds, along with families' contributions, to the merchants engaged in arranging redemptions, making this a hybrid religious–secular and private–public arrangement.[62] At Plymouth, magistrates organized church collections for many years, on a monthly basis from 1617, to redeem slaves from the town and its neighbourhood.[63] At Bristol, magistrates chose to divert collections originally intended for the Palatinate to redeem local sailors held in Salé.[64] Aberdeen began organizing local collections as early as 1579. And when the Mayor of Limerick turned to the Lord Deputy for help in 1626, he felt obliged to explain that the town was too poor to redeem its own inhabitants.[65]

It gradually became apparent, however, that private initiatives would never be remotely sufficient. The scale and persistence of the problem demanded a more systematic and nationwide response.

---

[59] William Gouge, *A Recovery from Apostacy* (1639), 62–4; cf. William Sherlock, *An Exhortation to Redeemed Slaves* (1702), 17–18.

[60] Gillian L Weiss, *Captives and Corsairs. France and Slavery in the Early Modern Mediterranean* (Stanford, CA, 2011), 41–8, 53, 58–60.

[61] Richard Parkinson, ed., *The Autobiography of Henry Newcome*, Chetham Society, Old Series, 26–7 (1852), ii.186–7.

[62] Masters, *Tales of the Unexpected*, 1–4; Betty R. Masters, ed., *London Chamber Accounts, 1585–6*, London Record Society, 20 (1984), 7, 61, 81–2, 103; Matar, *British Captives*, 72.

[63] R. N. Worth, ed., *Calendar of the Plymouth Municipal Records* (Plymouth, 1893), 61, 180; FitzGeffrey, *Compassion*, sig.*2v.

[64] *CSPD 1637*, 48.

[65] Matar, 'Introduction', in Vitkus, *Piracy*, 24; *Calendar of State Papers, Ireland, 1625–32*, 170.

The state and fund-raising

Local initiatives made a significant contribution, but they could never redeem every captive, still less curb the corsair threat. Many contemporaries believed that the crown bore ultimate responsibility for both the economic damage inflicted by the corsairs and the plight of slaves and their families. Most magistrates in maritime cities and towns were merchants, and those trading to Spain and the Mediterranean suffered directly from the corsairs' depredations, as well as recognizing their wider impact. In the early decades of the seventeenth century, the Levant and Spanish Companies, Trinity House, and magistrates and Grand Juries in the south-west repeatedly called on the crown to take action. Some contemporaries felt that Barbary also raised issues of national and royal honour. In 1636 James Frizzell declared it shameful to see proud Englishmen 'by banished Spanish Moors, African cow-keepers, and neagers [negroes] with the scum of the world made their slaves and laughing stocks'. Turks and Moors, he added, assumed that the king must be unaware of their misery, for otherwise he would surely act.[66]

Calls for action from merchants and magistrates may have carried most weight, but the desperate appeals of captives' wives and mothers also piled very public pressure on the crown.[67] Both individually and collectively, women lobbied the Privy Council and the royal family itself. In 1623 James I and Prince Charles were repeatedly beset by women so importunate, a news-writer reported, that the king 'was forced sometimes to give them hard usage both in words and worse'. Royal guards had beaten off the protesters. A few years later, beleaguered Privy Councillors commanded desperate wives to cease their 'clamorous complaints'.[68] Instead, angry women went further, organizing impressively large-scale petitions to press for action. In 1626 almost 2,000 urged the duke of Buckingham, Lord Admiral and royal favourite, to free their husbands and sons at Salé, complaining that petitions addressed to the king had been ignored.[69] Others voiced anger when a fragile peace with Salé collapsed in 1631, after a rogue English shipmaster had seized one of its ships and sold the crew into slavery in Spain. With English merchants and mariners targeted once more, their wives and mothers urged the king to send an envoy to secure their release and restore peace. And when the Privy Council proved slow to respond, 1,000 women repeated their demands. They insisted that Morocco would be willing to treat—information that almost certainly came from John Harrison, a veteran envoy, who witnessed the women's

---

[66] TNA SP 71/1, fos. 150, 156.

[67] Nabil Matar, *Britain and Barbary, 1589-1689* (Gainesville, FL, 2005), 77-92, surveys petitions in the first half of the century.

[68] John Chamberlain, *The Letters of John Chamberlain*, ed. Norman Egbert McClure (Philadelphia, 1939), ii.507; TNA SP 71/1, f.37; Appleby, *Women and Piracy*, 149-62; cf. *CSPVen. 1621-3*, 393.

[69] TNA SP 16/43, f.76.

suffering on a daily basis and shared their frustration.[70] A few years later, in 1637, the womenfolk of the *Mary*'s crew secured a collective brief to help ransom them, with the merchant Nicholas Leate agreeing to handle negotiations. They were furious when it was suspended without explanation.[71]

Women continued to press for action throughout the civil war era. When Parliament met in 1640, members were repeatedly lobbied at the doors, and the Commons later ordered the fines levied on those arriving late for prayers to be distributed among the protesters.[72] In May 1653, shortly after the dissolution of the Rump, a group of women complained to Cromwell and his Council that ransom money intended to redeem their husbands in Tripoli had been diverted to fund the war against the Dutch. The money, already on board the *Worcester* in the Downs, had been unloaded. In September another petition, possibly from the same women, was brought before the Council.[73] A few weeks later the wives and relations of the forty mariners of the *Blessing*, held in Salé, delivered a similar appeal.[74] The Restoration period saw more petitions, addressed now to the crown or Privy Council. One in 1665 came from the wives and friends of eighty captives in Algiers, seized on two Plymouth vessels, with another a few years later from women in Weymouth and Melcombe Regis.[75] Women took action again when the *Bristol Merchant* was captured in 1675 and its crew of thirty enslaved in Tripoli. Two women travelled from Bristol to press their collective case at Whitehall.[76] A large-scale petition to the House or Lords in 1679 prompted an order for the Lord Chancellor to present their case to the Pricy Council. And in 1681, 'disconsolate fathers and wives' joined in a highly emotive petition to the Commons on behalf of almost 1,000 captives in Algiers.[77] Moreover, alongside these numerous collective efforts, desperate individuals also continued to press their case, several appealing directly to the king. Barbara Douglas told James II that her first husband had been killed serving with him in the Second Dutch War. Destitute, and with three children to support, she needed £240 to redeem her second husband from Barbary.[78]

A generation later, in 1717, we find the wives of slaves in Meknes equally resolute. They presented Jezreel Jones, a merchant and former envoy to Morocco, with a petition addressed to the king, along with letters from their husbands spelling out their plight. Jones forwarded the material to the Secretary of State, warning him that the women were clamorous and impatient. They would tell him that their husbands loved 'the king and the government too well to be kept in

[70] *CSPD 1631–3*, 219; *CSPD 1635*, 608; *CSPD 1635–6*, 15; TNA SP 71/12, f.187.
[71] *CSPD 1637–8*, 477–8; cf. ibid., 255.   [72] *CJ*, ii.597; cf. *LJ*, v.605; vi.16–19, 440–1, 501–2.
[73] Matar, *British Captives*, 104; *CSPD 1653–4*, 137.   [74] *CSPD 1653–4*, 319.
[75] *CSPD, Addenda 1660–1685*, 300; *CSPD 1665–6*, 88.   [76] *CSPD 1675–6*, 460, 466.
[77] *LJ*, xiii.550; *To the Right Honourable the Commons of England in Parliament assembled. The humble petition of disconsolate fathers and wives* (1681).
[78] *Calendar of Treasury Books, 1685–9*, 346; cf. *Cal. of Treasury Books, 1681–5*, 348.

slavery'. It was a skilfully crafted campaign, and helped trigger fresh government efforts.[79] From the early seventeenth century, female petitioning had developed into an effective means of applying pressure on both local and national authorities. And petitions on Barbary had particular impact because London's seafaring community was large and close to the heart of government, and because the cause enjoyed widespread public sympathy.

The crown generally had to be pressed into action, but it acknowledged its responsibilities. The commercial agreement ('capitulations') between Elizabeth and the Ottoman sultan Murad III in 1580 promised security for English traders and mariners and provided for any seized and enslaved to be promptly freed. Although such provisions were hard to enforce, especially in Barbary, the queen appealed to the sultan on several occasions on behalf of captives, with some success.[80] But as the problem swelled and Ottoman influence over Barbary waned, this approach became patently inadequate. Like other European governments, the crown was unwilling to ransom its subjects by paying 'pirates' from its own resources, which it saw as dishonourable and a potentially endless drain. A committee advised in 1632 that £50,000 would be insufficient to redeem even existing captives.[81] It was therefore essential to find some way to raise large sums without resorting to direct taxation or burdening the Treasury. Some suggested a national lottery. After the Restoration, one impoverished cavalier proposed a lottery in which he would retain two-thirds of the funds raised to cover expenses and restore his fortunes. Nothing came of it.[82] In 1679, MPs proposed an amendment to a Supply Bill that would have seen taxes used to redeem captives in Algiers, but it was voted down.[83]

With taxation ruled out, funds on the scale required would have to be raised from the public, through more ambitious and systematic charitable collections. The crown was prepared to help by guiding, facilitating, and regulating. It had already done so on a limited scale as early as 1579, when the Privy Council directed sheriffs and magistrates in four western counties to arrange collections for the redemption of mariners taken by 'Turkish' galleys.[84] It soon recognized that only the Church had the structural capacity to organize truly comprehensive nationwide collections, and that this was the institution through which it should work. In 1596 the Council urged the archbishop of Canterbury to organize collections throughout the land to ransom eight mariners languishing in Algiers. The moneys collected by churchwardens in each parish would be sent to London and employed by the Levant Company's Governor, Richard Staper, to redeem

---

[79] TNA SP 71/16, fos. 249, 251, 259, 264.

[80] Richard Hakluyt, *The Principall Navigations* (1599), part ii, 199–200; Brotton, *This Orient Isle*, 96, 100–1, 122, 137; Edward Webbe, *The Rare and most wonderfull things which Edw. Webbe an Englishman borne, hath seene* (1590), sig. C3v.

[81] TNA SP 71/1, f.100; cf. fos. 130, 139.   [82] Knight, *Relation*, 53; *CSPD 1660–61*, 182.

[83] *CJ*, ix.607.   [84] *APC, 1578–80*, 2; HMC, 55, *Various Collections*, i.68.

captives. Little appears to have come of this initiative, or another in 1600 that was restricted to London.[85] Sir Thomas Roe, sent as ambassador to Constantinople in 1621, proposed a somewhat similar scheme, urging monthly collections in churches throughout London and Middlesex, authorized by letters patent granted to the Levant and Spanish Companies. The proceeds would be sent to Constantinople, from where Roe would arrange redemptions. His plan won the approval of the archbishop of Canterbury, but went no further.[86]

Only a few years later, in 1624, the House of Lords put forward a far more ambitious scheme, prompted by a petition from desperate women on behalf of 1,500 captives in Algiers, Tunis, Salé, and Tetuan. The plan proposed a nationwide charitable campaign, with alms collected in every parish church and chapel throughout England and Wales. This time the crown gave its full support. James I issued letters patent that summarized the petition, spelling out the misery of slaves forced to toil 'in bestial manner like horses', the plight of their destitute families, and the scandal that many, especially 'the youthfuller sort', had been driven to renounce their faith and their nation. Each bishop was sent printed briefs to distribute throughout his diocese. Churchwardens and overseers of the poor were to collect contributions, note the totals on the back of each brief, and forward the money through their bishop to the archbishop of Canterbury. He would then disburse the funds, with the guidance of six peers and the Privy Council. Each peer was to donate 20s or 40s, according to rank, to set a good example to all men 'of quality'. The scheme was thus another hybrid construct, with voluntary contributions raised through the machinery of the Church, and dispensed by agents of the state. It ran for a year with moderate success, raising £2,848 3s 7d. By March 1626, £2,290 had been disbursed, and the Lords ordered the balance to be used to redeem slaves at Salé.[87]

The timing of this initiative was also linked to the fact that Roe had negotiated a settlement with Algiers in 1622 committing the crown to the redemption of all English and Welsh slaves. The money collected under the new 'general brief' would provide the funding to honour this pledge.[88] Families that had been clamouring for action were quick to respond to the initiative. In September 1624, for example, petitions from distressed wives led to sixty-four names being added to the list of those considered eligible beneficiaries—fifty-six in Algiers, and eight in Tunis.[89] Charles I issued letters patent for a similar brief for the slaves in Morocco in 1631. The proceeds were sent to London and entrusted to the Lord

[85] APC, 1596–7, 126–7; APC, 1599–1600, 157. On the background to this episode see H. R. [Henry Roberts], Newes from the Levaune Seas. Discribing the many perrilous events of Edward Glenham, Esquire (1594).

[86] Roe, Negotiations, 31, 36, 103.

[87] LJ, iii.413, 541, 738; James I, Whereas we have beene informed, aswell by a lamentable petition (1624), broadside; Bewes, Church Briefs, 117–22; CSPD 1623–5, 287; cf. HMC 55, Various Collections, i.68.

[88] See Chapter 8.   [89] APC 1623–5, 335–6.

Mayor until distributed to the merchants engaged in negotiating redemptions.[90] But Charles failed to repeat the 'general brief' for Algiers. In 1632 a group of experts advised against it, arguing that it would take two years to collect and would raise only a twentieth of the total now needed.[91]

The civil wars of the 1640s saw both crown and bishops swept away, and the Parliamentary regimes developed a different and more sophisticated mechanism to fund large-scale redemptions. An Act in 1642 provided for 'the enlargement and deliverance' of captives held in Barbary and elsewhere by imposing a surcharge of 1% (later reduced) on customs duties—a levy that became known as the 'Algiers duty'. Funding would thus now be raised by indirect taxation rather than by charitable collections, and on a systematic basis. The Act stated baldly that the proceeds would be employed to safeguard the seas and free captives, without specifying how these objectives were to be achieved. A series of Parliamentary ordinances and acts extended or renewed the Algiers duty up to the Restoration in 1660.[92] The new levy raised substantial sums, and the overseas trading companies were willing to advance funds on the strength of bonds secured by it.[93] In the event, it proved impossible to despatch fleets to the Mediterranean in the midst of civil war, and the proceeds were initially diverted to other expenses. The sum of £5,000 lent to the Navy Treasurer in October 1642 was never repaid.[94] And when London women petitioned in 1643 for action to redeem their husbands, Parliament responded with a measure that looked back to the pre-war general briefs—an ordinance for parish collections throughout London, Westminster, and Southwark for the relief of captives in Algiers.[95] Once the war ended, however, the Algiers duty could be used, as intended, for redemptions. An impressive total of £62,396 was raised between 1651 and 1659.[96] Parliament and the Commonwealth always appeared far more committed than the Stuarts to liberating captives—in part, perhaps, because of closer links to overseas merchants and maritime communities. Thomas Sweet, blocked from redemption in 1646 by his obstructive owner, won public support from eight Members of Parliament and also members of the Westminster Assembly of Divines. No doubt his puritan zeal also helped.[97]

The Algiers duty was abandoned at the Restoration, probably through pressure from the trading companies or tainted by its Parliamentary origins. In its place, the nationwide general briefs were revived.[98] New collections followed in 1662,

---

[90]   *By the King. A Licence for a collection throughout England and Wales, towards the redeeming of . . . captives under Muley Abdalwally King of Morocco* (1631); TNA SP 71/12, f.212; cf. SP 71/1, f.113v.

[91]   TNA SP 71/1, f.130.

[92]   *Statutes of the Realm, v, 1628–80*, ed. J. Raithby (1819).v.134–5; C. H. Firth and R. S. Rait, eds. *Acts and Ordinances of the Interregnum, 1642–1660* (1911–14), i.17–20, 553–4, 609–11, 731–4, ii.367–8, 824, 1129–30.

[93]   *CSPD 1657–8*, 293.   [94]   TNA SP 18/253, f.242.

[95]   Firth and Rait, *Acts and Ordinances*, i.134–5.   [96]   Matar, *British Captives*, 113.

[97]   Sweet, *Deare Friends*. The MPs—all Presbyterians excluded at Pride's Purge—included Sir Richard Price and Clement Walker.

[98]   *CSPD 1661–2*, 285, 488–9.

1668 (for two years), 1670 (for four years), and 1682.[99] A committee of the Lords and Privy Council resumed responsibility for overseeing redemptions, with successive bishops of London taking overall supervision. Leading merchants handled most of the practical arrangements. In 1668, for example, the Governor of the East India Company and Alderman John Frederick, a future Lord Mayor of London, were to receive and dispense the proceeds.[100] They in turn appointed regional collectors. John Knipe (or Nipe) was made collector for six northern counties for three years, while at Wirksworth, Derbyshire, the sum of 18s 5d collected on 28 March 1669 was 'paid to Joseph Nipe sub-collector to William Nipe of London'. Two years later, when the parish made another collection, each contributor's name was also returned to the bishop.[101] The new briefs raised substantial sums. Between November 1670 and April 1674, the commissioners received £21,530.[102] The king also contributed £600, and on this occasion it was royal officials who carried the money, negotiated terms in Algiers, and made the practical arrangements. Samuel Pepys, secretary to the Admiralty, commented that the king had done 'more than was ever done by the crown before'.[103] In 1672 Charles ordered a similar general brief to be issued in Ireland, for the crews of ships that had sailed from Irish ports, and others followed.[104] Some 450 English slaves were reported to have been brought home from Algiers by the spring of 1675, with only renegades left behind.[105] The general brief in 1682 was intended to raise £20,000, and by the end of that year £16,461 had already been made available to fund redemptions.[106]

More general briefs were authorized after the Glorious Revolution. One issued in 1691 raised £8,309, which paid for the redemption of 456 slaves in Morocco—though another 500 remained. A further £16,591 was raised between 1700 and 1705.[107] Groups outside the Anglican Church also participated. In 1700 the Jewish community ('Hebrew nation') contributed £101, and Nonconformists helped too, with congregations in Dover, Falmouth, and Bedford making small contributions.[108] When the consul in Algiers called for a new general brief in 1691, he urged that it be promoted by both Dissenting and Anglican ministers.[109] The Quakers developed their own initiatives as well as contributing to the national scheme. The Bristol Meeting gave £10 in 1674 towards the redemption of two poor Quaker slaves from the city, and a few years later offered £20 to the London

---

[99] CSPD 1667–8, 161; HMC 25, Le Fleming MSS, 54; CSPD 1671–2, 254; CSPD 1680–1, 328; Calendar of Treasury Books, 1681–5, 492; Bewes, Church Briefs, 392–3.
[100] CSPD 1668, 161; CSPD 1671, 59–60; CSPD 1691–2, 304; HMC, 45, Buccleuch MSS, ii.181; CSPD 1699–1700, 387–8 (a certificate also signed by three other bishops).
[101] CSPD 1671–2, 1; 'Wirksworth Church Wardens' Accounts', iv.11, xv.11.
[102] Bewes, Church Briefs, 198–9; TNA SP 71/2, f.9. In 1670 the earl of Bedford contributed £5 in Covent Garden: Scott Thomson, Life in a Noble Household, 362.
[103] Bewes, Church Briefs, 393–4; Pepys, Catalogue, iii.18.
[104] CSPD 1671–2, 254; HMC 25, Le Fleming MSS, 91; CSPD 1686–7, 387.
[105] CSPD 1675–6, 12.   [106] Calendar of Treasury Books, 1681–5, 670.
[107] Bewes, Church Briefs, 201, 205; Matar, British Captives, 140–1.
[108] Bewes, Church Briefs, 205; CSPD 1667–8, 161.   [109] TNA SP 71/3, f.202v.

Meeting, promising more if required.[110] Nationwide collections were no longer deemed necessary in the Hanoverian period. Only Morocco now held British captives, and its rulers wanted them to be redeemed primarily through the supply of arms. The Treasury appears to have provided the funds.[111]

The general briefs introduced in 1624 were limited to England and Wales. In Orkney, and probably throughout Scotland, friends of enslaved sailors appealed for help to their local Presbytery, which might authorize a local collection. In 1695, however, an act authorized a collection to be made throughout Scotland for the relief of nine Glaswegians in Barbary. By the second half of the century, however, the funds raised in England and Wales were also being employed to redeem Scots.[112]

The system of briefs, whether nationwide or issued to individuals, was inevitably imperfect. The letters patent issued in 1631 sought to build in safeguards against fraud, insisting that the total sum collected in each church was to be publicly notified and recorded on the back of the brief in words, which were harder to alter than numerals.[113] But not every parish contributed, money sometimes disappeared, and several bogus collectors operated with counterfeit briefs.[114] One rogue in Somerset passed himself off as a minister and produced a brief supposedly issued by a Westminster committee, stating that his brothers' ship had been carried to Salé, and that 1,500 ducats were needed to ransom its crew.[115] Shortly after the Restoration, another cheat, equipped with printed briefs bearing the royal arms, was prosecuted in Wiltshire and whipped as a vagabond.[116] In a still more elaborate fraud, a fake brief printed in 1660 claimed that corsairs had raided New England, burned Charlestown, carried away fifty-seven inhabitants, and were demanding a collective ransom of £8,000. It named nine leading puritan ministers that it claimed were supporting the appeal.[117] In Lincolnshire, confusion over counterfeit briefs led some collectors to return money to the donors, while news of a peace with Algiers in 1671 led many to believe that donations were no longer needed.[118] Parliament's Algiers duty raised very impressive sums but was similarly flawed, compromised by fraudulent officials. In 1656 Thomas Violet

[110] Kenneth C. Carroll, 'Quaker Slaves in Algiers, 1679–1788', *Journal of the Friends' Historical Society*, 57 (1982), 301–12; Russell Mortimer, ed., *Minute Book of the Men's Meeting of the Society of Friends in Bristol, 1667–1686*, Bristol Record Society, 26 (1971), 92, 141, 145.

[111] See Chapter 8.

[112] Orkney Library and Archives, OCR/4/1, Presbytery of Orkney Minutes, 1639–46, f.223; OCR/4/4, Minutes 1676–85, f.59; OCR/23/13, Shapinsay Kirk Session 1679–1765, f.38v. I owe these references to Professor Peter Marshall. See also Chapter 7.

[113] *By the King. A Licence for a collection.*   [114] *CSPD 1671–2*, 1, 322; *CSPD 1673–5*, 80.

[115] E. H. Bates Harbin, ed., *Quarter Sessions Records for the County of Somerset, 1646–1660*, Somerset Record Society, 28 (1912), 343–4.

[116] HMC 55, *Various Collections*, i.141.

[117] John Josselyn, *An Account of two voyages to New-England* (1674), 269–70; Nabil Matar, *Turks, Moors and Englishmen in the Age of Discovery* (New York, 1999), 165–6.

[118] *CSPD 1671*, 59–60.

made allegations of false accounting on a large scale, and called for a government inquiry. An investigation shortly after the Restoration identified £4,649 still in the hands of one of its administrators, John Langley, for which he could give no account. A prosecution was ordered to recover the money.[119]

Nevertheless, both the state-backed nationwide collections and the customs surcharges raised very substantial funds, supplemented by local initiatives and the briefs still issued to individuals. England and Wales had thus developed a very hybrid set of arrangements. Tavistock, in Devon, saw thirty collections of various kinds between 1660 and 1680, with individual contributions ranging from a single penny to 10s. In 1680, 730 of the town's inhabitants contributed something, underlining the issue's significance for the people of the south-west. And in December that year, in distant Westmorland, Daniel Fleming also gave 5s towards the 'redemption of English captives in Africa', in response to the general brief.[120]

Some scholars have drawn a sharp contrast between English meanness and European generosity in raising funds to ransom captives.[121] That seems doubtful. The absence of any equivalent to the Mercedorians and Trinitarians was certainly a significant early handicap, but paradoxically the English Church came to play a role as important as theirs in raising funds. The collections authorized by the general briefs covered every parish in England and Wales, far exceeding the reach of the religious orders in France and Spain. Recent historians have also shown that the friars' fund-raising efforts were far from sufficient to redeem all or even most captives. Families in Europe were expected to raise part of the ransom money by their own efforts, and in Spain could request a licence to collect alms, much like the English briefs. In every nation, ransom funds were raised from a variety of sources, including families, bequests, local authorities, and the Church. And in every nation, redemptions, especially for those of higher status, often continued to be negotiated privately through intermediaries.[122] Moreover, England and Wales enjoyed one major advantage, once the crown became involved through the issue of general briefs, for the state was far more centralized than its neighbours. The Spanish crown left organized money-raising to the religious orders, while French kings made local and provincial bodies responsible. In 1627, when Louis XIII sought funds to redeem 800 French slaves in Algiers, urban magistrates were instructed to impose a levy on each inhabitant to ransom their own citizens. Many towns tried to shuffle off their obligations, and the funds collected proved insufficient to ransom even half the captives. A generation later, in 1666-68, provincial estates in Provence and Brittany and urban magistrates proved similarly reluctant to contribute the sums demanded by Louis XIV. As Gillian Weiss has shown,

---

[119] Thomas Violet, *Proposals humbly presented to his Highness Oliver, Lord Protector* (1656), part ii, 26-9, 33; *CJ*, viii.146-8, 394-6.

[120] Colley, *Captives*, 76-8; J. R. McGrath, ed., *The Flemings in Oxford*, Oxford Historical Society, 44, 52, 79 (1904-24), i.506.

[121] Matar, 'Introduction', 29.   [122] Hershenzon, *Captive Sea*, 41-69, 76.

French monarchs wanted the glory that came from large-scale redemptions, but gave others the task of raising the funds.[123]

In the Dutch Republic—a loose association of seven provinces—a state-led approach proved almost impossible. In the first half of the seventeenth century, the task was left to private initiatives and local authorities. The Reformed Church asked repeatedly for the States-General to take responsibility, but the States were not a central government, and were unwilling and unable to take on the role. In 1651 they did call for a nationwide collection to ransom slaves at Salé, promised by a recent treaty, but left local authorities to devise their own arrangements. They followed the same course when they reluctantly authorized two further general collections in 1662 and 1681, to ransom captives in Algiers. Almost all the Dutch captives came from Holland and Zeeland, and the other provinces refused to co-operate. The proceeds fell far short of the target, and the States-General resolved never to approve another general collection. Amsterdam established a small committee to oversee future arrangements for its own inhabitants.[124] In the Nordic lands, it was again the secular authorities, rather than the Church, that generally took the lead. Hamburg, Lübeck, and Denmark established *Sklavenkassen*—bodies that provided social insurance from contributions that all mariners and ship-owners were required to pay. The sums raised were not always sufficient, and provincialism brought problems in the Danish case, with Copenhagen refusing to contribute to the redemption of the numerous captives from Bergen. Not until the early eighteenth century were the problems in the *Kasse* system finally overcome.[125] Sweden was slower to develop any mechanism for fund-raising, and followed a rather different course. From the 1720s, redemptions were funded by a surcharge on imports and exports (like the Algiers duty in England half a century earlier), and four nationwide charitable collections in churches each year.[126]

England undoubtedly lagged far behind the Mediterranean states in developing methods to raise large-scale ransom funds. The need only became acute in the reign of James I, and by its close a system of nationwide collections had been devised. Charles I failed either to sustain or replace it, and paid a significant political price, as we will see. From mid-century, however, Parliamentarian and Restoration arrangements may well have matched or even surpassed those found in European neighbours.

A different challenge remained: how to develop a reliable and effective system of employing the funds to secure the release of the slaves languishing in Barbary.

---

[123] Weiss, *Captives and Corsairs,* 28–9, 34–5, 58.

[124] Erica Heinsen-Roach, *Consuls and Captives. Dutch North African Diplomacy in the Early Modern Mediterranean* (Woodbridge, 2019), 138–56.

[125] Magnus Ressel, 'The North European Way of Ransoming: Explorations into an Unknown Dimension of the Early Modern Welfare State', *Historical Social Research*, 35/4 (2019), 125–46.

[126] Joachim Östlund, 'Swedes and Barbary Captivity: the Political Culture of Human Security, *circa* 1660–1760', *Historical Social Research*, 35/4 (2019), 148–63.

7

Arranging Redemptions

Ransom money raised in England had to be paid in North Africa, and the release of captives depended heavily on intermediaries engaged in the 'redemption business', among them merchants, consuls, Moors, and Jews. This chapter explores and assesses the arrangements that evolved.

Transporting money to North Africa was problematic. When the owners of the *Unity* arranged a voyage to redeem slaves in Algiers in 1583, they sought a safe-conduct from the Queen to afford some protection against attacks en route.[1] One ship carrying ransom money sank off Cadiz in 1645, while another was driven ashore in Sicily in 1671, paradoxically by Algerian corsairs.[2] The slave-owners, moreover, wanted to be paid in currencies widely accepted in the Straits, not in English pounds. Many demanded dollars and pieces of eight, neither readily available in large quantities in England.[3] Instead of sending specie, merchants engaged in redemptions often preferred to send cloth as payment in kind, or for sale in Barbary with the proceeds used to pay the ransoms.[4] Barbary merchants also made frequent use of bills of exchange, raising money in Livorno, Cadiz, or Barbary itself. Charles Longland, negotiating redemptions at Livorno on behalf of the state in 1652–53, recommended employing three-quarters of the funds available to buy cloth to sell in Barbary, and the remainder to repay bills of exchange.[5]

Redemption could be a protracted process. Captives might not be wholly free until ransoms and associated fees had been paid, or repaid, in full. Matthew Clarke and his men, enslaved in Algiers in 1620, were ransomed within a few weeks by an English merchant for £300, but Clarke was not freed until money was raised in England to reimburse the merchant.[6] In the case of American captives, the process could take still longer. It took seven years in the 1680s for the Boston worthy Samuel Sewell to have funds raised in London and forwarded to Algiers to free

---

[1] *CSPD 1581–90*, 124.

[2] Edmund Cason, *A Relation of the whole proceedings concerning the Redemption of the Captives in Argier and Tunis* (1647), 6–7; HMC 25, *Le Fleming*, 86.

[3] *Calendar of Treasury Books, 1685–1689*, 211.

[4] Betty R. Masters, *Tales of the Unexpected: the Corporation and Captives in Barbary*, Guildhall Historical Association (2005), 1–4; Betty R. Masters, ed., *London Chamber Accounts, 1585–6,* London Record Society, 20 (1984), 81–2.

[5] *CSPD 1652–3*, 118–19. In 1646 Cason paid to redeem slaves with cloth as well as money: *Relation*, 6, 13.

[6] Harris, *Trinity House*, 45; cf. TNA SP 71/12, f.182v.

British Slaves and Barbary Corsairs, 1580–1750. Bernard Capp, Oxford University Press. © Bernard Capp 2022.
DOI: 10.1093/oso/9780192857378.003.0008

Joshua Gee.[7] If a family then proved unable to repay a merchant or consul in Barbary, the liberated slave might have to clear the debt by working for him without pay. James Hallerd, redeemed for $200 at Tunis in 1653, worked for the consul on this basis, and John Hart spent two years serving the merchant who had redeemed him for £100. Samuel Dawks, an orphan, offered to serve any merchant willing to redeem him until the debt was paid.[8] Lodowick Bowyer was ransomed by a Hamburger in Salé, and then spent a year and a half teaching his benefactor's son to speak English and play the orfarian, a kind of lute—an idiosyncratic repayment in kind.[9] Such arrangements could be advantageous for both parties. Joseph Pitts, for example, recalled that when he first met Francis Baker, consul at Tunis, he was closely questioned about his family background, and 'whether I could write and understood arithmetic'. The answers were clearly satisfactory, for Baker then opened negotiations to ransom him, albeit without success. When they met again, some months later, Baker remarked that he had now 'bought a young man *for my purpose* for considerably less than I offered for you'. Self-interest had been part of his calculation.[10]

Redemptions were often negotiated privately by owners and individual slaves, with merchants or their factors as intermediaries. In the Elizabethan period, most were handled by a small group of London merchants, in conjunction with the Mayor and aldermen. Sometimes the ransom had been raised by family and friends, supplemented from the public collections at Paul's Cross and the Spital. On other occasions merchants used their own resources and then looked to be reimbursed, or employed both methods.[11] The crown also soon became involved, both directly and indirectly. William Harborne, a merchant who served as Elizabeth's first ambassador in Constantinople in the 1580s, negotiated the redemption of fifty-four English slaves in Turkey, the Levant, and Barbary over the course of five years, laying out £1,203.[12] A generation later, Sir Thomas Roe's peace with Algiers, confirmed in 1623, provided for a resident consul to supervise negotiations, and the following year saw a committee of peers and Privy Councillors established to oversee the allocation of the funds collected through the general brief. For several years Nicholas Leate, a prominent Levant Company merchant, dominated the redemption business. In 1624 he offered to advance £1,000 to redeem slaves in Algiers and Tunis if the Privy Council undertook to repay him from the funds raised under the general brief. It did. The following year it awarded Leate almost £2,500, to reimburse further operations.[13] Local magistrates would generally commission Leate or another merchant to redeem as many

---

[7] Joshua Gee, *Narrative of Joshua Gee of Boston, Mass., when he was captive in Algeria of the Barbary pirates, 1680–1687*, ed. Albert C. Bates (Hartford, Conn., 1945), 9–10.

[8] TNA SP 29/375, f.244; SP 29/276, f.227; SP 71/26, f.9.   [9] *CSPD 1633–4*, 215.

[10] TNA SP 71/26, f.9; *Pitts*, 187–91 (italics added).   [11] Masters, *Tales of the Unexpected*, 1–5.

[12] Jerry Brotton, *This Orient Isle. Elizabethan England and the Islamic World* (2016), 137.

[13] *APC, 1623–5*, 33–6; *APC, 1625–6*, 24, 61, 223.

captives as possible within a specified budget. Thus in 1624 Dartmouth magistrates commissioned Leate to redeem 100 slaves from the town, and Leate then gave letters of credit to a factor in Algiers, Nicholas Spicer. Over the following two years Spicer laid out £300 to bring captives home, though he was only able to free sixty within his budget.[14] James Frizzell, also Leate's factor and for many years consul in Algiers, handled most of the business on the ground, drawing bills of exchange on his master and the Levant Company. Serious friction developed when the Company decided to disengage from North Africa and refused to honour them, arguing that most captives were West Country fishermen for whom it accepted no responsibility. The Privy Council had to intervene.[15] In 1625 Roe claimed that 800 slaves had been redeemed at Algiers, adding that another 400 had been swept away by plague. Although his figures may have been exaggerated, the initiative had worked well.[16]

Arranging redemptions was always a key responsibility of the Barbary consuls. Most were merchants themselves, trading on their own account alongside their consular duties. In 1585 the London Chamberlain paid £162 to reimburse several merchants who had shipped cloths to Algiers, for the consul, John Tipton, to use for ransoms.[17] James Frizzell, appointed consul in Algiers in 1623, claimed that consuls could secure large-scale redemptions at half the cost of those arranged individually, and most contemporaries agreed. Frizzell reported proudly that he had freed and repatriated some 350 English slaves, but as Roe's peace frayed, the numbers swelled once more. By 1637, Frizzell reported, sixty-five English ships had been seized, with another 1,524 English captives sold into slavery. Charles I had neglected to authorize another general collection to raise funds, and fewer than 100 captives had been ransomed through private negotiations.[18]

Peace with Algiers was restored only in 1646. With the end of the civil war finally in sight, Parliament despatched the merchant Edmund Cason to negotiate a new agreement and free captives. Renewing the peace proved far easier than freeing the captives. The pasha brushed aside his demand for their immediate release, insisting they were private property and that owners would expect compensation. He also dismissed Cason's next proposal, for flat-rate ransoms, pointing out that captives had been sold at different prices. It was eventually agreed to set redemptions at the level of the first market price. Cason was able to compile a list of more than 650 slaves held in Algiers. Another 100 were away at

[14] APC, 1623–5, 273–4; TNA SP 71/1, f.84.

[15] APC, 1625–6, 84, 122–3, 341–2, 354–5; APC, 1627, 259, 415–16; APC, 1628–9, 269–70; CSPD, 1625–6, 451; CSPD 1625–49 Addenda, 118, 165–6, 171, 281; TNA SP 71/1, f.80; Negotiations of Sir Thomas Roe (1740), 572–4; A. C. Wood, A History of the Levant Company (1964), 62–3.

[16] Negotiations of Roe, 117–18, 376, 573; Hebb, Piracy, 195–6. The numbers held and freed at Tunis were far smaller.

[17] Masters, London Chamberlain's Accounts, 81–2.

[18] TNA SP 71/1, fos. 97v–98, 156–v. Frizzell served as consul c.1611–18 and 1624–c.1638, alongside his mercantile activities.

sea, some serving with the Ottoman fleet against Crete, others had 'turned Turk' and so could not be redeemed, and many more had died. Cason's fund of $10,000 was soon exhausted, and thereafter he could negotiate only with owners willing to accept payment in kind—the cloth he had brought. Many proved reluctant to part with slaves they valued, especially on terms that would deny them a profit. Thomas Sweet wrote home that his owner, whose accounts he kept, had hastily sold him and his companion to a contact in Tunis, vowing they would never be freed until his ransom demand of £250 was met. Sweet lamented that he remained in misery 'when others that are illiterate go off upon easy terms for cloth, so that my breeding is my misery'. Some captives were probably concealed, while others living inland were almost impossible to trace. Cason had planned to redeem first 'the better sort of people', but he was in no position to dictate terms. Algiers naturally preferred to rid itself of those worn out, sick, and of little value. He redeemed an initial 244 slaves, including three children and nineteen women, two of them survivors from the Baltimore raid of 1631. He paid an average equivalent to roughly £32 a head, with port fees and gratuities adding another £6 or so. Ransoms were highest for women and children, at around £50, for shipmasters, and for skilled carpenters, caulkers, sail-makers, and surgeons. Those freed returned home on the *Charles*, while Cason stayed on to clear the remainder, urging Parliament to send more funds. He secured a similar settlement with Tunis. Cason's mission had been the initiative of the English Parliament and, like the redemptions funded by general brief of 1624, it did not cover Scots. But at the request of the Scottish commissioners, the Commons in 1647 authorized Cason to negotiate the redemption of Scottish captives too.[19] By the end of that year Cason had redeemed another 262 captives, including Thomas Sweet, eventually ransomed for $98, far less than his owner had demanded. Several ransoms, however, were considerably larger than any of those paid the previous year. The owners had clearly driven hard bargains for the wealthier captives; their names come towards the end of the published list, suggesting that negotiations had been prolonged.[20] Cason's peace held for several years. In 1648 Parliament appointed Humphrey Oneby as resident consul at Algiers, and Thomas Browne at Tunis, while Cason remained in Algiers as a merchant. By the time of his death in 1654, he and Oneby had laid out in all more than £37,000 on redemptions.[21]

Ransom funds came now from the new Algiers duty, and from 1645 a 'committee for the preservation of customs and redemption of captives' oversaw the

---

[19] Cason, *Relation, passim*; *LJ*, vii.539; *LJ*, viii.426, *LJ*, ix.205; *CJ*, v.141; Thomas Sweet, *Deare Friends: it is now about sixe yeares* (1647); Hebb, *Piracy*, 152, 162; *CSPD 1631–3*, 217; Sir Godfrey Fisher, *Barbary Legend. War, Trade and Piracy in North Africa 1415–1830* (Oxford, 1957), 210–14.

[20] *An Account of what captives hath been freed since the 14th of December Anno Dom. 1647* (1647), 1, 7–8.

[21] Wood, *History*, 63; Fisher, *Barbary Legend*, 213–14; *CSPD 1653–4*, 52, 476; *CSPD 1656–7*, 282; *CSPD 1657–8*, 43–4; TNA SP 18/253, fos. 242–3; *Thurloe*, iii.157, 500–1.

arrangements. Its first members were merchants (including Alderman Samuel Avery and Cason), though by the mid-1650s prominent administrators such as Sir William Roberts, Adam Baynes, and Gervase Bennett had taken over.[22] During the Commonwealth (1649–60), the Council of State kept a watching brief on arrangements and dealt with major disputes. In 1656 we find Sir William Cockayne (representing the East India Company) and fifteen other merchants seeking reimbursement for £5,382 9s 11d they had laid out two years earlier.[23]

The mid-1650s witnessed saw a dramatic shift in the state's approach, reflecting its growing strength as a naval power. Negotiations over redemptions were now accompanied by the threat of force. In 1654 Cromwell sent Robert Blake to the Straits with a powerful fleet, and over the next few years he and his colleagues used this leverage to liberate captives on more favourable terms (as explored in Chapter 8). Naval pressure became still more important after the Restoration. The king's return brought further changes. In 1660 Charles referred a petition from slaves and former slaves to the Convention Parliament, and on 29 December it ordered £10,000 from excise arrears to be paid to help them. This was the Convention's last day, however, and the money failed to materialize.[24] In February 1662 a petition from 300 slaves in Algiers begged Charles to revive the Jacobean model of a nationwide collection in parish churches.[25] He consented, and this time the Church took over responsibility for distributing as well as collecting funds. Two clerics, Dr John Bargrave, a canon of Canterbury Cathedral, and John Selleck, archdeacon of Wells, were directed to carry the money to Barbary and handle negotiations. Bargrave may have been behind this new approach. He had spent much of the previous fifteen years travelling in France and Italy, and would have been familiar with the redemption missions traditional in southern Europe. Carrying £10,000 in foreign currency provided by the London goldsmiths, the two clerics arrived on 8 November on board the *Bonaventure,* and were welcomed by Admiral Lawson and his squadron. Lawson had concluded a new treaty with Algiers in April, under which ransoms were to be set at the first market price. A proclamation directed Turks, Moors, Arabs, and Tagarines to bring in their slaves, and from the 13 to 19 November Bargrave and Selleck met and negotiated with dozens of owners. They redeemed a total of 142 captives, all male, and left behind sufficient money to ransom another twenty-one living further away. Half of those freed came from London's Thames-side parishes, the rest mainly from the south-west, along with five Irishmen, one Scot, and one from St Christopher's (St Kitts) in the Caribbean. Bargrave's account also provides a rare glimpse of the emotional strain on captives as they waited to learn their fate. One man, told erroneously that his name had been crossed off the list, 'suddenly fell into a swoon and with great difficulty was recovered' Bargrave, a keen collector, brought home

---

[22] *LJ*, vii.491; TNA SP 18/253, f.243. For Roberts and Baynes see *ODNB*.
[23] *CSPD 1656–7*, 165–6.   [24] TNA, SP 29/48, fos. 123, 125.   [25] *CSPD 1661–2*, 285.

some mementoes of his mission—red leather Moorish slippers and boots—but it had also left a deeper impression. In his will, proved almost twenty years later, he directed that the chains that had once shackled one of the slaves were to be placed over his tomb. He had kept them for twenty years.[26]

This mission proved to be the only occasion on which England imitated the Catholic European pattern of redemptions. European redemptive missions are often described as exercises in 'state-building', but this operation might be better understood as an exercise in 'Church-building', or rather 'rebuilding'. A detailed account, published by royal command, praised the mission as a 'pious and seasonable work, well becoming the reverend undertakers, the bishops and cathedrals of the Church of England'. The restored episcopal hierarchy was far from popular, and it had much to gain from a mission that would enjoy almost universal support. It is unclear where the £10,000 was sourced. In June 1662 it had been described as already 'prepared to be transmitted '. Some of it probably came from the excise arrears allocated earlier, with the rest advanced by the goldsmiths, to be repaid from the proceeds of the new general brief. The published account listed by name all the captives freed (along with their former owners), explaining that this was in order to protect them and their families from fraud. If cheats pestered them for money, claiming they had paid part of the ransom and demanding to be reimbursed, they could be sent packing.[27]

The clerical mission was never repeated. Charles usually left a Privy Council committee for the redemption of captives to supervise arrangements negotiated by merchants in Barbary. Merchants, of course, saw redemptions as a business venture from which they wanted to make a good profit. So in 1671, at the close of another conflict with Algiers, Charles experimented with another and potentially cheaper method. Bypassing the merchants, he appointed his own agent, Francis Baker, aged only 22, to negotiate redemption terms.[28] Typically, however, he failed to send the funds promised until forced into action in 1675 by the threat of the renewal of war. Admiral Narbrough was now despatched in haste, with bills of exchange to raise sufficient money in Cadiz to assuage the anger in Barbary. Samuel Martin, the new consul, was told that the crown relied on his 'good husbandry' to negotiate ransoms at reasonable rates. He and his colleague John Brisbane, the judge advocate, were able to redeem 283 slaves for £22,369—about £79 each. This was more than Blake had paid twenty years earlier, but there had been considerable inflation in ransom levels, and Narbrough had brought no fleet

[26] *CSPD 1661–2*, 488–90; *CSPVen. 1661–4*, 160; *Mercurius Publicus*, 2 (8–15 January 1663), 26–32; Nabil Matar, *British Captives from the Mediterranean to the Atlantic, 1563–1760* (Leiden, 2014), 113–14; <https://www.canterbury-cathedral.org/bargrave;> *ONDB*, John Bargrave. For Lawson's treaty see *Mercurius Publicus*, 26 (26 June-3 July 1662), 401–4; George Chalmers, *A Collection of Treaties* (1790), ii.360–5.

[27] *Mercurius Publicus*, 26 (26 June-3 July 1662), 404–5; *Mercurius Publicus*, 2 (8–15 January 1663), 32.

[28] TNA SP 71/3, f.345v; SP 71/2, f.18; *CSPD, 1671*, 160.

to strengthen his hand. The crown was pleased with the terms. A newsletter reported the arrival of 182 at Deal early in 1675, adding that some 450 in all were thought to have been ransomed.[29]

Despite the state's initiatives, many shipmasters and merchants still preferred to arrange their own redemptions, through intermediaries. Even in periods of open war, redemptions could be arranged with the help of Europeans, Jews, and Moors. During the war of 1677–82 with Algiers, forty-three captured shipmasters had been redeemed before the end of the conflict. (Another forty-nine remained captives, eighteen were dead, four had escaped, and the situation of the rest, another forty or so, was unknown.)[30] Negotiating a ransom privately was generally quicker, but considerably more expensive. Those redeemed sometimes struggled to repay loans, and some then turned to the redemption commissioners for assistance.[31] Richard Sessions, for example, had commissioned a merchant to pay $976 to redeem his son in Algiers, and when he was unable to repay the advance he begged help from the commissioners, the Secretary of State, and finally the king. Clearly an adroit lobbyist, he also offered to reveal concealed redemption funds, and persuaded the king's mistress, the duchess of Portsmouth, to deliver his appeal.[32]

Jewish merchants in Barbary also played a major part in negotiating, financing, and facilitating individual redemptions, as they did for captives from across Europe, drawing on networks that linked North Africa with Italy and the entire Mediterranean world. Charles Longland, arranging redemptions from Livorno in the 1650s, viewed them as valuable partners.[33] But Barbary's Jews also helped finance corsair operations, many owned slaves themselves, and there were even allegedly a few Jewish *reis*, or commanders. Their Janus-faced role predictably attracted fierce criticism. James Frizzell fulminated in 1634 that it was 'strange that our king's majesty's subjects should be bought & sold by Jews (that sold our saviour Jesus Christ)'.[34] Francis Knight, enslaved in Algiers in the 1630s, damned them as 'a most execrable people...bloody hearted, living by defrauds'.[35] In Richard Head's proto-novel, the enslaved narrator explains that he could not tell at first whether his cruel and avaricious owner was 'man or devil...To say all in short, he was a Jew'.[36] In 1692 Thomas Baker ransomed ten slaves with funds advanced by Jewish financiers, but denounced the interest they charged, 4% per month, as a 'rapacious wolf devouring everything'.[37] Most striking of all is a printed address to Parliament in 1680, during the war with Algiers, which accused

[29] TNA SP 71/2, fos. 145–6; Pepys, *Catalogue*, ii.357, 359, 362, 380, 420, iv.119; *CSPD 1673–5*, 12; Fisher, *Barbary Legend*, 253–4. For Blake's terms see Chapter 8.

[30] *A List of the Ships taken since July 1677* (1682).   [31] *CSPD 1671*, 568.

[32] TNA SP 29/375, fos. 187–9.   [33] *CSPD 1653–4*, 167–8, 262–3, 289.

[34] John Chamberlain, *The Letters of John Chamberlain*, ed. Norman Egbert McClure (Philadelphia, 1939), i.559; TNA SP 71/1, f. 135.

[35] Francis Knight, *A Relation of Seaven Yeares Slaverie* (1640), 51.

[36] Richard Head, *The English Rogue* (1665), part iii, 79–80.   [37] TNA SP 71/3, f.235v.

Jews of controlling the corsairs' operations through a vast and sinister conspiracy. They funded the corsairs, it alleged, pressed them to demand extortionate ransoms, and encouraged them to beat captives without mercy until they agreed. There were very 'few slaves in Algiers', it added, 'but a Jew is their patron, or else hath at least a share in them'. Claiming that 'the Jews in all places are in a combination and society', it hinted that English Jews fed information on valuable targets to their friends in Algiers. It proposed a drastic solution: a new law should make English Jews liable for all English losses in Barbary.[38]

In 1681, towards the close of the war with Algiers, the government introduced a new set of redemption arrangements, which drew on and developed those operating at the end of James I's reign. The Privy Council invited Barbary merchants to subscribe to a scheme that would give them access to a fund of £20,000, to be raised by another nationwide parish collection. The Council allocated a 'bounty' of £40 for each slave, with families and friends expected to cover any costs above that figure. The commissioners for the redemption of captives would oversee the arrangements, which would continue until the fund was exhausted. A proclamation warned that captives would be ineligible if their ship had failed to take advantage of a convoy's protection.[39]

William Bowtell was by far the most prominent merchant in the redemption business at this time, and a memorandum drawn up in 1690 throws light on his operations. It named 392 slaves who had been redeemed through his factor, Lionel Crofts. A Treasury report estimated that the other undertakers, between them, had redeemed only about fifty. Lists of eligible captives were compiled based on information from Barbary and from families and friends, with certificates from provincial ports validating the names of their captives and ships. Merchants and consuls handled negotiations, and the consul sent the Secretary of State certificates listing those now freed. In a petition to the Treasury a few years later, Bowtell claimed that he was still owed £7,000 for sums laid out redeeming slaves in Algiers since 1682. The Treasury report found that by June 1693 he had been repaid £12,880 for moneys he had laid out under the scheme in the years 1681-87, but was still owed £740 for a number of other approved redemptions outside it.[40] Those engaged in the redemption business often had to resolve issues of eligibility, priority, and scheduling. In one letter Crofts explained that two poor slaves could not be redeemed at present unless a 'vacancy' arose in the lists.[41] Families, friends, and captives themselves lobbied to have names inserted, especially if they had been ignored by the factors or commissioners.[42] Such lobbying was far from new, of course. In the 1670s, for example, two Jersey women had repeatedly appealed

[38] *The Case of many Hundreds of Poor English Captives in Algier* (1680).
[39] *CSPD 1680-1*, 328; cf. *CSPD 1683-4*, 116–17; TNA SP 71/3, fos. 382–92.
[40] TNA SP 71/3, fos. 92, 382–92; *Calendar of Treasury Books, 1693-6*, 255–7; *Calendar of Treasury Papers, 1556/7-1696*, 389.
[41] TNA SP 71/2, fos. 327–8.   [42] *CSPD 1672*, 231; *CSPD 1672-3*, 191.

on behalf of their husbands and other islanders, and had begged the king to intervene.[43] Those with good connections predictably fared best. When Alderman Sir John Frederick and Sir Nathaniel Herne informed the Navy Board in 1674 of several individuals they were anxious to have redeemed, the men were promptly recommended to the 'special kindness' of Sir John Narbrough, negotiating at Algiers.[44]

The arrangements introduced in 1681 proved effective, though they were also open to abuse. By 1688 Consul Erlisman could report that few slaves now remained in Algiers, and urged the king to redeem them all, 'not by orders to merchants (wherein a great abuse) but by money to be brought from Cadiz'.[45] His successor, Thomas Baker, promised that he could redeem all those remaining, about 200, for £65 a head. It would be an honourable action, he urged, and would also furnish the navy with much-needed 'stout seamen'. By satisfying owners it would also help cement a peace that was still fragile. Although his suggestion was ignored, Baker remained actively involved in negotiating redemptions. In January 1694 he reported that he had freed more than half the remaining slaves, and a few months later appealed to the bishop of London, who controlled the funds, for money to clear the rest.[46] Early in 1695 he could finally report, with 'a great deal of pleasure', that not a single British slave remained in Algiers, Tunis, or Tripoli. In March that year he retired from his post, sailing to Gibraltar on one of the dey's own men-of-war, accompanied by his wife and children and the last forty-five slaves. It was a major milestone in the story of the British slaves of Barbary.[47]

Morocco

It was not yet the end of that story, however. Redemptions in Morocco, not covered by Roe's treaty, followed a different and far longer trajectory. There was no resident consul, so the process usually depended on merchants and brokers in Salé. In 1622, for example, a French dealer in 'slaves and other commodities' arranged the redemption of more than 150 of many nationalities, including a dozen English Catholic students.[48] Morocco was repeatedly torn apart by civil wars, making negotiations difficult, especially when Salé, the corsairs' main base, threw off royal authority and declared itself a free republic. The English crown

---

[43] TNA SP 71/2, f.440B; cf. ibid., f.454.   [44] Pepys, *Catalogue*, ii.382; cf, 385, 410.

[45] TNA SP 71/3, f.113.

[46] TNA SP 71/3, fos. 193-v, 231, 235, 239, 241v, 256, 268, 286-8. Baker generally had the approval of Sir Robert Clayton, London merchant, magistrate, and philanthropist, who was more closely involved than the bishop.

[47] TNA SP 71/3, fos. 301, 315.

[48] James Wadsworth, *The English Spanish Pilgrime* (1629), 41-2; Martin Murphy, ed., 'William Atkins, A Relation of the Journey from St Omers to Seville, 1622', in *Camden Miscellany*, 32 (1994), 246-7.

often had to engage with several warring rivals. From 1610 John Harrison traversed this diplomatic minefield as a royal envoy, travelling to Morocco eight times over the course of twenty years in attempts to promote trade and redeem captives. In 1626 he negotiated a favourable treaty with Salé that freed some 260 English slaves without the payment of ransoms.[49] But his peace collapsed in 1631, and merchants and sailors became targets once more. On Harrison's initiative, Charles I authorized a 'general brief' to raise charitable relief, but did little else to address the problem. A naval expedition was eventually dispatched in 1637, under William Rainborough, who succeeded in restoring peace with both Salé and the king of Morocco, and in liberating the slaves. Harrison—massively in debt, now out of favour, and harassed by creditors—was left begging for his salary and expenses.[50]

Truces with Salé continued to be agreed and broken throughout the seventeenth century and beyond. Rather than mount further expeditions, the state authorized Barbary merchants to handle negotiations over both trade and redemptions. During the Commonwealth, the Council of State kept a watching brief on the ransom terms they negotiated. Contracts were tightly drawn and closely monitored. When Robert Downs requested an advance of £1,000 in 1653, to redeem thirty-two slaves at Salé, the Council demanded a detailed breakdown of the costs previously allowed. A recent precedent was produced, which gave an average ransom figure of £42 a head, plus precise sums for customs charges, clothing, and diet on the homeward voyage.[51] The following year Thomas Warren was authorized to expend £1,000 on redeeming captives, and nine months later those freed were paraded before the redemption committee.[52] A decade later, Charles II commissioned Warren to negotiate a trade treaty, and the Treasury later refunded £5,500 to cover his expenses. He had also laid out substantial sums to redeem slaves, but a request for these to be reimbursed was firmly rejected. They had not been authorized, he was told. The crown always resisted using its own funds to redeem slaves.[53] In 1671 Nathaniel Lodington and other merchants trading with Salé were authorized to explore privately the possibility of redeeming English captives, especially the 'cheapest able seamen'—a clear indication of the crown's priorities.[54] The following decades saw numerous attempts by merchants, diplomats, and military and naval commanders to redeem slaves and secure a firm peace. The situation deteriorated further during the long reign of Moulay Ismail

[49] *CSPD 1627–8*, 361; TNA SP 71/12, fos. 82, 125-34v; Castries et al., eds., *Sources Inédites*, ii, *passim*; *ODNB*, John Harrison; P. G. Rogers, *A History of Anglo-Moroccan Relations to 1900* (1977), 25–30. See also my 'John Harrison, envoy to Morocco', forthcoming.

[50] TNA SP 71/12, fos. 187–206; John Harrison, *The Tragicall Life and Death of Mvley Abdala Melek the last King of Barbarie* (Delft, 1633), sig. A3-v; *CSPD 1638–9*, 254. On the expedition see Chapter 8.

[51] *CSPD 1652–3*, 338–9.

[52] *CSPD 1656–7*, 1; *CSPD 1657–8*, 34–5.

[53] *Calendar of Treasury Books, 1660–1667*, 297, 382, 393, 597, 603, 606; TNA SP 71/13, fos. 149–50.

[54] Matar, *British Captives*, 121.

(1672–1727), described in Chapter 8. Not until 1721 was a comprehensive settlement secured.

As in the Regencies, Jewish intermediaries played a prominent and contentious role. In 1671, for example, Lodington and his colleagues were instructed not to approach Jewish owners.[55] Some years later Thomas Phelps launched a bitter attack on Jewish dealers for overturning a redemption agreement with Moulay Ismail. He accused them of offering the sultan a lucrative rival deal that would leave the captives still in bondage, and denounced the Jews as 'the stench and pest of the nations of the earth, malicious to all mankind'. He was delighted that Moulay Ismail had later reneged on the deal.[56] In 1698 the Secretary of State blamed avaricious Jewish dealers for the exorbitant ransoms (£150 a head) that Moulay Ismail was now demanding.[57]

The redemption systems: an assessment

The hybrid system that evolved from 1624 had both public and private dimensions. The crown authorized nationwide church collections to raise funds, while negotiations were generally conducted by resident consuls, Barbary merchants and their factors, or naval commanders. The merchants usually bought goods to sell in Barbary, using the proceeds to ransom slaves within an agreed budget, and were reimbursed on their return home. Their profits came mainly from the difference between the sale of their merchandise and the sum they had contracted to lay out on redemptions. Processions of freed captives and thanksgiving services in St Paul's Cathedral proclaimed the crown's care of its subjects—a propaganda exercise that also helped keep the issue in the public's consciousness.[58] Although this system lapsed under Charles I, it was revived after the Restoration and brought freedom for thousands of poor captives whose families could never have raised a ransom.

The undertakers encountered numerous problems, however. It was never possible, for example, to obtain comprehensive data on the slaves—a body that was always in flux. Some had been resold or moved inland, others were away at sea, had died, or had 'turned Turk'. Owners could also be hard to locate, perhaps away on campaign, or obstructive. Nothing could be done without 'presents' (bribes) to all in authority, universally expected and demanded. Negotiators were dependent on local officials to help locate captives, and might have to pay substantial sums to induce powerful owners to part with them.[59] 'Presents' were

---

[55] Matar, *British Captives*, 121.   [56] *Phelps*, 13–14.   [57] *CSPD 1698*, 384–5.
[58] Linda Colley, *Captives. Britain, Empire and the World, 1600–1850* (2002), 78–82; see also Chapter 8.
[59] TNA SP 71/1, f.89; SP 71/13, f.80.

also necessary to secure the release of captives who had never been auctioned, having been claimed by the pasha or dey or gifted to a favourite, and so had no market price.[60] Securing documentation was also slow and expensive. Bowtell claimed to have spent more than £100 on international postage alone, with a single packet costing up to £3.[61]

The redemption arrangements also contained significant flaws—some inherent, others reflecting the shortcomings of those involved. Ransom money sometimes failed to arrive, or disappeared into the wrong hands. William Hawkridge complained of funds being used to redeem wealthy individuals who could and should have raised their own ransoms, creating such bitter resentment, he added, that he wished the money had been thrown into the sea.[62] The government's decision in 1681 to allow only £40 a head, from the funds raised by the general brief, created new difficulties. Market prices had risen sharply, and Bowtell complained that owners were demanding ransoms 50% higher than formerly. Moreover, the treaty with Algiers in 1682 did not stipulate that ransoms must be at the original market price, which left owners free to drive a hard bargain. With most ransoms well above £40, contractors might then struggle to recover the balance from the slave's friends. Bowtell listed 134 debts still outstanding, including £190 owed by the Duchess Dudley's Charity. In other cases, when a ransomed slave had died on the passage home, it had proved impossible to secure reimbursement.[63] Bowtell suffered a particularly heavy loss in 1687. He had shipped a cargo to Algiers worth £2,500, with instructions for it to be sold to fund ransoms, but the goods were seized on arrival to meet debts run up by his agent, Lionel Crofts. Not a single slave could be redeemed.[64]

The British, like other Europeans, were never able to control the terms of engagement in negotiating redemptions. The level of ransoms was only one issue. Barbary's authorities decided which captives they would permit to be redeemed, and in what order. Like other governments and the friars, the crown wanted to prioritize the 'better sort', and healthy soldiers and sailors. The slave-owners, by contrast, wanted to rid themselves of the old and sick, and might insist on their being included in any deal. Some owners refused to free the slaves on the list unless Bowtell's factor agreed to ransom others not included.[65] Moreover, rulers expected their own slaves to be ransomed first, and at a higher price. When Crofts failed to observe this custom, the dey and Babba Hassan, his co-ruler, made

[60] CSPD 1672, 250.   [61] TNA SP 71/3, f.187.   [62] TNA SP 71/1, f.133.
[63] TNA SP 71/3, fos. 182–90.   [64] TNA SP 71/3, f.188.
[65] Daniel Hershenzon, 'The Political Economy of Ransom in the Early Modern Mediterranean', Past and Present, 231 (May 2016), 68–74; Daniel Hershenzon, The Captive Sea: Slavery, Communication, and Commerce in Early Modern Spain and the Mediterranean (Philadelphia, PA, 2019), 48–56, 62–3; Calendar of Treasury Books, 1693–6, 256–7.

him pay £250 to redeem two young slaves of their own, for which Bowtell was only repaid the standard bounty of £40 each.[66]

Both sides engaged freely in sharp practices. The records of slave auctions were poorly kept and unreliable. One Jewish official in Algiers was said to enter false prices, which enabled owners to demand fraudulently high ransoms. It was alleged, too, that when a British ship arrived, some owners contrived for their slaves to escape, which allowed them to demand whatever ransom they liked, rather than the figure negotiated by the consul.[67] Sharp practices were equally endemic among British and European merchants and factors. The ethics of the redemption business were notoriously elastic. Instead of using the proceeds of the goods they brought to Barbary to redeem slaves, for example, merchants might employ them to finance further trading ventures in the Mediterranean, to increase their profits. That could leave the slaves waiting months, even years, before they were redeemed.[68] The redemption business also generated fierce competition, as merchants vied to attract 'clients' (both slaves and their owners) and maximize profits. Their behaviour provoked scorn among the 'Turks', and scandalized British officials. Philip Rycaut, consul in Algiers in 1683–84, was disgusted by the practices of Robert Cole, who pressed slaves to accept greatly inflated demands, which naturally delighted their owners. Rycaut begged in vain for officials in London to stop his 'tricks'.[69]

The fiercest criticism was directed at Bowtell's factor Lionel Crofts. In 1682 the consul John Neville called him unfit to be trusted, accusing him of entering false figures and adding Dutch and French slaves, some already redeemed, to the lists. Such frauds, Neville grumbled, had 'put a great many forty pounds into his own pockets'. His practices had been exposed by a slave who refused to accept his own redemption, unwilling to commit to repaying more than the ransom actually paid. Crofts retaliated by undermining Neville's position, persuading Babba Hassan that he lacked proper credentials.[70] Still more damaging charges surfaced a few years later, in 1686. A new consul, John Erlisman, accused Crofts of redeeming thirty or forty English slaves and then making them serve with the corsairs to raise the additional money he needed to pay their ransoms in full. The 'world cries shame on us', the consul declared, 'that free Christians should assist these people to make Christian prizes'. Summoned home to answer the charges against him, Crofts replied airily that he would be too busy to leave Algiers for many months.[71] He never did return; in January 1689 he was killed in a brawl, leaving debts of £5,000 outstanding.[72]

---

[66] TNA SP 71/2, 325; 71/3, f.186; *Calendar of Treasury Books, 1693–6*, 256.
[67] Cason, *Relation*, 11; TNA SP 71/2, fos. 45v, 353v.
[68] The best account is in *The Travels of the Sieur Mouette in the Kingdoms of Fez and Morocco* (1710), 78–80.
[69] TNA SP 71/2, f.374-v.   [70] TNA SP 71/2, fos. 333, 353v.
[71] TNA SP 71/3, fos. 65, 69–70; *CSPD 1685*, 96; *CSPD 1685–6*, 61.
[72] TNA SP 71/3, f.119; *Calendar of Treasury Books, 1693–6*, 257.

The sharp practices of the 'redemption business' could also spread to the captives. The most prominent alleged offender, Seth Sothell, had been captured in 1678 on his way to take up a post as Governor of Carolina, and was initially sold to a mason in Algiers. His situation deteriorated sharply when his identity became known. Loaded with chains, he was now presented with an impossible ransom demand of $50,000, allegedly through the machinations of Robert Cole and Jewish dealers, who spotted an opportunity for huge profit. Sothell's plight was brought to the notice of Charles II, and the Privy Council decided to secure his release by exchanging him for two captured corsair *reis*. Money was always demanded to supplement an exchange, however, and Sothell was not allowed to leave without also paying a ransom. Cole borrowed 3,000 pieces of eight from the Jews in 1681 to ransom Sothell and another captive, with Sothell engaging to repay his debt once back in England. Instead, he repudiated his bond and appealed to the king, accusing Cole and the consul of conspiring with the king's enemies. In retaliation, the consul, Nicholas Parker, denounced Sothell as a 'damned Presbyterian' who would 'glory in washing his hands in the king's blood'. The Jews, wanting their money, turned to Babba Hassan, who ruled that the consul would be held accountable. The Privy Council had to intervene once more. Lionel Crofts was directed to repay the ransom using bounty money Bowtell had just received for other redemptions. Sothell sailed for America, leaving a debt he would never honour. No one emerged with credit from the episode.[73]

Consuls, diplomacy, and redemptions

Barbary consuls operated far from home, and as they might receive no letters or instructions for many months they often had to act independently and go beyond their official remit. Consuls in Tunis, for example, intervened when corsairs from Algiers or Salé brought prizes and captives to sell there. John Erlisman helped one crew in 1669 by redeeming six sailors with his own money, 'three of them being youths who else might have been undone both in body and soul'. He had received permission from the city's rulers to buy captives before they were brought to market, and wrote home that he could secure much better terms if he had ready funds available for such situations.[74] Similarly, Samuel Martin and a partner used their own resources to redeem fifteen English captives brought by a Salé man-of-war to Algiers, which had a bigger and better market.[75]

The consuls' duties went far beyond redeeming slaves. They were expected to defuse tensions, resolve disputes, and preserve the peace. When Thomas Baker

---

[73] TNA SP 71/2, fos. 233v, 263, 300-v, 333; SP 71/3, fos. 186–9; *CSPD 1680–1*, 458; *Calendar of Treasury Books, 1693–6*, 256.
[74] TNA SP 71/26, fos. 141, 144.   [75] TNA SP 71/2, f.49.

was invited to serve at Algiers in 1690, he demanded an annual salary of £500, plus another £500 for each year that he succeeded in maintaining the peace.[76] Successive treaties had still left open contentious issues over passes, flagging, Britons captured on foreign vessels, and the ownership of the goods carried on British ships. Whenever a ship was seized and brought into port, the consul would try to prevent the vessel, cargo, and crew being condemned as prize. He would press the most favourable interpretation of the relevant articles, stress the crown's displeasure should a ship be condemned, exploit ties of friendship with influential figures in the divan, and distribute covert bribes as necessary. When Samuel Martin summed up his achievements in 1676, he claimed that in clearing the *Leopard* and its rich cargo he had saved the owners and the nation £150,000. Over the course of four years, he added, he had cleared thirteen ships with cargoes worth in total almost half a million pounds, and had saved their crews from slavery and the burden of ransoms. A few judicious bribes had been a small price to pay.[77]

There was no shortage of applicants for consular posts, which were evidently viewed as potentially lucrative. Most consuls were still active in commerce, sometimes in partnership, and the position gave them a status and connections they could turn to advantage. The salary of the consul at Algiers rose from £100 per annum in the mid-seventeenth century to £600 by its close.[78] Yet the office almost always proved precarious and fraught with danger. Consuls often felt forgotten by ministers preoccupied with European problems they considered more important.[79] The fees payable on goods imported or exported by British merchants could prove difficult to collect, while salaries were often poorly paid until later in the century, and many consuls ran up large debts. Moreover, for much of the period consuls were held answerable in Barbary for any acts its rulers judged hostile or dishonest, whether committed by shipmasters, merchants, naval officers, or the British government. Several were imprisoned, chained, and mal-treated, and had their money and goods seized. In 1626 James Frizzell begged to be replaced, pleading that his life was in 'daily hazard' from both Turks and embit-tered English slaves. Sir Kenelm Digby, visiting Algiers early in 1628, reported that only a few weeks earlier Frizzell had been 'brought out to be burned and hardly 'scaped'.[80] Half a century later, in 1671, John Ward was widely reported to have been murdered by a mob—a rumour that lived on for decades. His successor feared being burned alive, joking bleakly that he was perhaps 'too lean to be

[76] HMC 71, *Finch*, ii.304, 314.

[77] TNA SP 71/2, fos. 118-24v, 172-v; cf. *CSPD 1672*, 362–4; HMC 71, *Finch*, iv.104.

[78] *Calendar of Treasury Books, 1689–92*, 816.

[79] E.g. TNA SP 71/1, f.93; SP 71/2, f.134v; SP 71/3, fos. 202, 316.

[80] TNA SP 71/1, f.72; *Negotiations of Roe*, 574; J. Bruce (ed.), *Journal of a Voyage into the Mediterranean by Sir Kenelm Digby, AD 1628*, Camden Society, Old Series, 96 (1868), 17.

roasted'.[81] At Tunis, John Goddard (d.1711) was treated with contempt and eventually went mad, while his successor was threatened with execution after an English privateer attacked a Barbary vessel.[82]

The crown never devoted sufficient time or resources to Barbary. Leaving consuls largely to their own devices, it was happy to judge them by results. Bribes and sharp practices proved essential, and only those with quick wits and flexible morals prospered. The earliest consuls, operating primarily as merchants, included some shady as well as shadowy figures. John Tipton, consul at Algiers from 1585, was described (by an admittedly malicious contemporary) as 'a wicked atheistical knave' who had poisoned a rival. He was later murdered by one of his own employees.[83] Some consuls demanded a fee from every slave they helped to redeem—a practice that Philip Rycaut (not a merchant) defended in 1683 as a legitimate perquisite. Charles II disagreed, and prohibited it.[84] Those engaging in trade on their own account faced hostility from rival merchants. Samuel Martin operated a partnership with James Bowtell for some time, but after it collapsed acrimoniously in 1675–76 he raged that his 'blood boils with passion' and damned his former partner as 'one of the greatest villains that ever breathed this Barbary air'.[85]

Several consuls faced still more serious accusations. Admiral Herbert held the dishonest practices of consuls engaged in trade largely to blame for former wars.[86] Equally serious was an allegation in 1694 that Samuel Goodwin, consul in Tunis, had forged a letter in the name of the late dey of Algiers, with the collusion of the consul in Tripoli. The Privy Council ordered a local investigation and also pursued the matter in London. Goodwin's friends denied the charge, but admitted that he had persuaded the dey to write the letter. He and a partner had advanced $800 for redemptions, they explained, and had wanted this recorded because they believed Consul Baker of Algiers would try to cheat them. They retaliated by hinting that Baker had forged the new dey's letter of complaint. As a minister remarked of a later dispute, it was impossible at such a distance to establish the facts, and impracticable to summon the parties home. In the event, all three remained in post.[87] The crown generally decided that experience and expertise outweighed consular failings and sharp practices.

Consuls without experience of Barbary and its commercial and political culture struggled to cope, and were soon begging to resign. Nicholas Parker and John

---

[81]   TNA SP 71/2, f.3v; *CSPD 1671*, 234–5, 249, 435, 455; HMC 25, *Le Fleming*, 84, 86; Fisher, *Barbary Legend*, 244, 245; *Calendar of Treasury Books, 1708–14*, 285.

[82]   *Calendar of Treasury Books, 1708–14*, 261–2, 285; HMC 29, *Portland*, x.246.

[83]   Sir William Foster, ed., *The Travels of John Sanderson in the Levant, 1584–1602*, Hakluyt Society, Second Series, 67 (1931), 10–12; cf. Fisher, *Barbary Legend*, 114–15, 118–20.

[84]   TNA SP 71/2, fos. 376, 378.

[85]   TNA SP 71/2, fos. 95v, 124, 168, 172, 201A, 202A; Fisher, *Barbary Legend*, 249–50. Crofts was Bowtell's nephew. On their alleged malpractices see also HMC 75, *Downshire*, 247.

[86]   TNA SP 71/3, f.315.

[87]   TNA SP 71/3, f.315; *CSPD 1695*, 130–1; *CSPD 1699–1700*, 80; HMC 45, *Buccleuch*, 274.

Neville—naval officers installed as consuls in Algiers against their wishes—both hated the position. Parker described it as 'a continual confinement and slavery', surrounded by 'barbarous and unruly people' and beset by 'importunate complaints and solicitations' from those who really were slaves. Neville, too, longed 'to get out of this cursed place'.[88] Even Thomas Baker, a Barbary veteran, came to share their sentiments. Feeling neglected and ill-served by the government, he wrote home in 1691 that 'it must be my fate to die an old fool and a beggar at my return home'. When France and Spain redeemed more than 1,200 slaves in Algiers in 1692, and the crown failed to take similar action, British slaves turned their anger on Baker. He reported nervously that some had 'lately threatened and waited opportunity to assassinate me'. He had agreed to serve for only three years, and longed for permission to leave.[89]

Successive consuls accused the merchant Robert Cole of sharp practices. He had established himself as the leading slave-broker in Algiers, exploiting his connections as a close associate and relative of James Bowtell, and winning the favour of the dey. Despite the accusations, Cole's experience and contacts made him indispensable. In 1694 we find Thomas Baker reluctantly supporting the dey's wish for Cole to succeed him. Cole went on to hold the consular office for eighteen years, proving tough, bold, and effective, and winning accolades from the Treasury itself for his 'fidelity, resolution and vigilance'. Even Baker later paid tribute to Cole's 'unparalleled services' in the most 'perplexing and hazardous' circumstances.[90] It was a classic instance of poacher-turned-gamekeeper.

Despite their plentiful shortcomings, consuls played an essential role in securing the redemption of several thousand English slaves and preventing the sale of many others. Operating in a venal world, with minimal support from home, they inevitably absorbed something of its character. Without it, they could not have succeeded.

Redemptions by exchange

Ransoms were not the only way to liberate captives. Contemporaries repeatedly urged the crown to employ force, although naval expeditions (examined in Chapter 8) were hugely expensive and success was far from assured. Another possible option was to free slaves by exchange, which would have the added attraction of being cost-neutral. But the number of Barbary captives in England was always small, and Algiers almost always preferred cash to captives. Exchanges

---

[88] TNA SP 71/2, fos. 262, 311.   [89] TNA SP71/3, fos. 202, 239, 286–7.
[90] TNA SP 71/2, fos. 374v-375; SP 71/3, fos. 111, 146–7, 156, 168, 175, 182–9, 345; *Calendar of Treasury Books, 1708–14*, 491; Fisher, *Barbary Legend*, 281–7; J. S. Bromley, 'A Letter-Book of Robert Cole, British Consul-General at Algiers, 1694–1712', in Bromley, *Corsairs and Navies, 1660–1760* (1987), 29–42.

played only a limited role in all European states.[91] Slave-owners in Barbary wanted a return on their investment, which a simple exchange would deny, and while a pasha or dey might occasionally be open to an exchange for his own slaves, for political reasons, he could rarely force them on private owners.

Several bizarre solutions were suggested to address one problem: the numerical imbalance. In 1636 an anonymous seaman urged Charles I to round up 'whores, harlots and idle lascivious' women 'of the female sect' and send them to Barbary to exchange for English slaves. Each woman, he claimed, would secure the redemption of six young male captives 'who are made slaves to fulfil the lustful desires of the heathen Turks'.[92] The idea, probably prompted by the new practice of despatching 'idle' young women to the American colonies, found no response. The civil war brought another odd proposal. The earl of Stamford, a Parliamentary commander in Cornwall, complained of being overburdened with royalist prisoners of war and suggested exchanging them in Barbary for English slaves, who could then be made to serve in Parliament's forces. This idea was also poorly received.[93]

English warships did not regularly operate in the Straits until mid-century, and merchant vessels wanted to escape the corsairs, not capture them. Moreover, if any did fall into English hands there was nowhere in the Mediterranean to hold them. In 1636–37 a group headed by Sir Thomas Roe suggested attacking Ottoman shipping in the Levant and raiding the coast of Barbary to seize men, women, and children. They could then be exchanged for British slaves in Algiers, or sold in Spain to raise ransom money. The project was never pursued.[94]

Exchanges did nonetheless play a limited part in the organization of redemptions. Once corsairs began to operate in the seas around Britain, they increased the risks to themselves. A man-of-war might be driven ashore or a prize recaptured, and such incidents increased the number of Moors and 'Turks' in British hands.[95] The peace with Algiers in 1623 provided for the release of captives by both sides, though the number of Muslim captives was put at only forty. The pasha of Algiers promised James I that once they were returned he would free the remaining English slaves and compensate their owners from his own resources. In the early summer of 1626, 121 Moors and 'Turks' were reported to be held at St Ives and Padstow, with another thirty-seven at Plymouth.[96] The following year, John Harrison took several Moors from Salé with him when he sailed to Morocco to negotiate a peace. But with several hundred British slaves at Salé, simple

[91] See e.g. Ellen G. Friedman, *Spanish Captives in North Africa in the Early Modern Age* (Madison, WI, 1983), 156–60. Nabil Matar is mistaken in stating that exchange played a prominent role: Matar, 'Introduction', in Vitkus, *Piracy*, 25–6.

[92] *CSPD 1635–6*, 143.   [93] *CSPVen. 1642–3*, 241.

[94] *CSPD 1637–8*, 192; TNA SP 71/1, f.162.

[95] Nabil Matar, *Britain and Barbary, 1589–1689* (Gainesville, FL, 2005), 118–24.

[96] TNA SP 71/1, f.43; *CSPD 1625–6*, 379; *Negotiations of Roe*, 140, 376; HMC, 13, *Westmorland and others*, 542.

exchanges would not go far, and Harrison was also authorized to transport arms. Exploiting the internal divisions he found there, he secured the release of 260 slaves without paying ransoms. Salé's governors laid out £12,000 from their own resources to compensate owners and, still more remarkably, freed some boys who had already apostatized. They even promised to free adult slaves who had converted out of 'weakness', explaining they would have to act covertly to avert popular fury.[97] Circumstances were never again so favourable.

Exchanges also featured in the plans of naval commanders. The preparations for Rainborough's expedition against Salé in 1637 saw some discussion on whether he should try to capture Moors to exchange, or sell in Spain to raise ransom money.[98] In the 1660s Thomas Allin was authorized to pursue this course. His ships recaptured several prizes, and at Algiers he was able to free a number of Barbary captives in exchange for his own, sweetening the deal with gifts of gunpowder.[99] Allin offered more exchanges when he returned in 1669, but this time he was rebuffed. During the war that followed, it became standard practice to sell captured corsairs in Spain or Italy. Allin recorded 186 sold in this way, with several delivered as presents, including one to the English consul in Alicante. Among the captives were fifty-four black African slaves, also sent to be sold—or rather resold—in Cadiz. No-one thought of liberating or repatriating sub-Saharan Africans.[100] Returning to Algiers in March 1670, Allin once again offered to exchange his captives for British slaves, who by now numbered 257, but the pasha refused even to consider the idea unless offered favourable peace terms.[101] Later commanders sent their captives to be sold in Spain and Italy as a matter of course, using the proceeds to reward their captains and crews, with the crown's full approval.[102] Only for a few important captives did the regencies show any interest in exchanges. In Morocco, as we will see, exchange played a more prominent part in government initiatives, with Moorish captives bartered together with commodities and arms to secure a truce or treaty and the release of British slaves.[103]

Many features of the 'redemption business' were shared by all the European states involved. Merchants, and Moorish and Jewish intermediaries, always played a major role. Even in Spain, where the Mercedorians were heavily involved, intermediaries were also active, and indeed before 1609 they redeemed more

[97] TNA SP 71/12, fos. 125-33v, 190; Castries et al., *Sources inédites*, iii.10–13, 30–60; Hebb, *Piracy*, 212.

[98] TNA SP 71/13, f.1; *CSPD 1636-7*, 172–3.

[99] R. C. Anderson, ed., *The Journals of Sir Thomas Allin 1660–1678*, Navy Records Society, 79–80 (1939–40), i. 170, 173–8, ii.217; *CSPD 1668-9*, 179–80.

[100] Anderson, ed., *Journals of Allin*, ii.113, 115–17, 127, 242–3.

[101] Anderson, ed., *Journals of Allin*, ii.160.

[102] C. R. Pennell, ed., *Piracy and Diplomacy in Seventeenth-Century North Africa. The Journal of Thomas Baker, English Consul in Tripoli 1677–1685* (Cranbury, NJ, 1989), 88; HMC 71, Finch, iv.388.

[103] Chapter 8.

captives than did the friars. The secular authorities frequently tried to shape the pattern of redemptions. The friars had to seek permission for a mission from the crown, which closely regulated their activities. Rulers everywhere wished primarily to ransom members of the elite and healthy soldiers or sailors. In 1691 the Swedish crown ordered that priority be given to 'the best, the most functional, the youngest and purest Swedes'. The old and worn out had little value. Negotiators faced common obstacles, with Barbary's authorities imposing their own rules on proceedings. Many negotiations failed, and merchants and missionaries alike often redeemed far fewer captives than they had hoped or expected.[104]

Comparing success rates is problematic, for there are no reliable statistics on those who died in captivity.[105] Historians have shown that in the first half of the seventeenth century, more Spanish, French, Italian, and Dutch captives died in Barbary than returned home, and the same is true of the British. Britons' prospects improved greatly in the second half of the century, however, while those of Italians, for example, deteriorated.[106] For Britain and France, moreover, the problem itself had almost disappeared by the end of the century, except in Morocco. That development owed much to the power of their navies (the subject of Chapter 8). Only during the eighteenth century did the other European states find other ways to end attacks, mainly by agreeing to pay regular tributes equivalent to the corsairs' prizes.

Coda: life after redemption

Slave narratives and government reports invariably ended with the captives' liberation and return home. But freedom, however it was achieved, brought with it a new set of challenges. How were former captives to readjust, perhaps after years of servitude, reintegrate, and rebuild their lives? One scholar has argued that many would have been suffering from what we now call Post-Traumatic Stress Disorder.[107] Many were penniless and in poor physical condition, while many families had been forced to sell property or borrow heavily to raise a ransom. The newly redeemed had to find employment, and some had substantial loans to repay. It is striking that a petition to Charles II in 1660 was presented in

---

[104] Gillian L. Weiss, *Captives and Corsairs. France and Slavery in the Early Modern Mediterranean* (Stanford, CA, 2011); 34–5, 47, 50, 80; Erica Heinsen-Roach, *Consuls and Captives. Dutch North African Diplomacy in the Early Modern Mediterranean* (Woodbridge, 2019), 49–51, 77–95, 102–3, 118–37, 149; Hershenzon, *Captive Sea*, 47–93, 170; Joachim Östlund, 'Swedes and Barbary Captivity: the Political Culture of Human Security, *circa* 1660–1760', *Historical Social Research*, 35/4 (2019), 148–63 (quote at 150); Friedman, *Spanish Captives*, 105–64.

[105] For a good discussion see Robert C. Davis, *Christian Slaves, Muslim Masters* (Basingstoke, 2003), 170–3.

[106] See n.98, and Davis, *Christian Slaves*, 172–3 and chap. 5 *passim*.

[107] Robert Spindler, 'Identity Crises of Homecomers from the Barbary Coast', in Mario Klarer, ed., *Piracy and Captivity in the Mediterranean, 1550–1810* (Abingdon, 2018), 128–43, esp. 131.

the name of former as well as current slaves, and the families of both groups. Charles passed it to the Convention Parliament, which established a committee to investigate who had been ransomed, by whom, and for how much. The issues may well have included harassment and fraud as well as hardship.[108] Many of those redeemed found it impossible to pick up the threads of their old lives, and the experience of captivity overshadowed the rest of their lives. One mariner proposed a fund for the relief of former slaves and shipwrecked sailors, with every seaman paying 12d at the port from which his outward voyage had begun. Nothing came of his proposal, which may have been inspired by the North German and Danish *Sklavenkassen*.[109]

Many of the newly liberated were in poor shape. Robert Cole's consular accounts include outlays on clothes, shoes, and blankets, and sometimes the cost of maintenance for several months until he could arrange their passage home.[110] Most were totally dependent. One group of women petitioners, seeking help from the king in 1635, explained that they had been able to raise enough to redeem their husbands and sons but could not pay for their passage home.[111] Some of those freed found ways to work their passage, joining any ship bound for a European port, though it might take weeks or even months to find a suitable berth.[112] During the First Anglo-Dutch War (1652–54), English shipping was driven out of the Mediterranean and some former captives found themselves unable to leave Algiers. One group eventually secured a passage to Majorca, in the hope of reaching home overland. Cason, who had lodged them in his house for several months, had found them troublesome guests.[113]

Some of those freed proved too sick and weak even to survive the voyage home, while others suffered fresh misfortunes on the passage. One of them, William Wood, was a ship's surgeon enslaved at Tunis for three years in the early 1620s until redeemed by Nicholas Leate. On the voyage home he was captured again, this time by corsairs from Algiers, leaving his father still obliged to repay the £73 12s that Leate had laid out. His story was far from unique.[114]

Sailors made up the great majority of captives freed, and those sufficiently healthy usually returned to the sea. Seamen liberated by the navy were often distributed among its ships, and would eventually arrive home with a modest wage. One of the state's main considerations in promoting redemptions, especially in time of war, was indeed to tap into this resource of experienced seamen. More than half the slaves redeemed by Bowtell in the 1680s then served with the navy,

---

[108] TNA SP 29/48, fos. 123, 125.   [109] *CSPD Addenda 1660–1685*, 491.
[110] *Calendar of Treasury Books, 1699–1700*, 178–9.   [111] *CSPD 1635*, 476.
[112] Pennell, ed., *Piracy and Diplomacy*, 136, 140, 142–3.
[113] *CSPD 1653–4*, 52; TNA SP 18/57, f.121.
[114] Nabil Matar, 'British Captives in Salé (1721)', in Stefan Hanss and Juliane Schiel, eds., *Mediterranean Slavery Revisited (500–1800)*, (Zurich, 2014), 528; *CSPD 1625–6*, 210; Harris, *Trinity House*, 16; TNA SP 71/2, f. 327.

and Thomas Baker assured the government in 1691 that the 200 left in Algiers were 'all very expert sailors and very few worn out men among them'.[115] Captives themselves, aware of the state's priorities, sometimes had their petitions framed accordingly. An appeal to Charles II in 1662, from 300 slaves in Algiers, stressed that most were young and 'all of us capable and desirous to serve your Majesty in the most hazardous employment'. John Baltharpe, also ransomed from Algiers, was happy to serve in the navy thereafter, eager for revenge.[116] A handful, blessed with connections, talent, and good fortune, went on to enjoy successful naval careers. Peter Mootham became a commander under both Cromwell and Charles II, and enthralled Samuel Pepys with tales of his life as a slave in Algiers. The Restoration Admiral Sir Edward Spragge had also been enslaved as a young man in Algiers, long enough to become proficient in the language.[117] More typical was the experience of Abraham Sampson, formerly a master's mate, who later found comparable berths in the navy as a boatswain and master's mate.[118]

The more dramatic career of Edward Coxere illustrates the vicissitudes of a sailor's life after redemption. Coxere was also happy to serve with the squadron that had freed him, hoping that Cromwell's war with Spain would provide plentiful opportunities to recoup his losses. He seized every chance that came for plunder, but within a few months he had been captured again, this time by Spaniards, and he was totally destitute by the time he eventually reached home. His wife, he recalled in his memoir, 'did begin to keep shop, there being a necessity for something to be done for a livelihood'. Coxere knew he would soon need to go back to sea and, pitied by friends and neighbours, he was able to borrow £5 to buy clothes, instruments, and books, and another £10 'for a venture'—commodities he could trade privately. This voyage ended successfully, and he cleared more than £50, sufficient to pay off his debts and provide a stock for his next venture. This time his ship was intercepted by corsairs, but his luck held; England was now at peace with both Algiers and Tunis. The corsair officer who inspected the ship's pass behaved honestly, and eventually revealed himself to be 'an old renegade named Wood, but in Moorish Balam', and like Coxere, originally from Dover. 'We parte[d] very good friends', Coxere remarked. Coxere belonged to a well-known and respected family, and it was his ability to borrow from friends, along with luck, that enabled him to rebuild his life.[119]

Most ordinary sailors lacked such resources, few possessed Coxere's drive and initiative, and many had less luck. Serving in the navy was certainly no guarantee of security. Rowland Hobson, a former slave, survived all the major battles of the First Anglo-Dutch War, but by 1659 he was begging for a cook's place—a position

---

[115] Calendar of Treasury Books, 1693–6, 257; TNA SP 71/3, fos. 195–6.
[116] TNA SP 29/51, f.47; John Baltharpe, The Straights Voyage (1671), 6.
[117] The Diary of Samuel Pepys, ed. R. C. Latham and W. C. Mathews (1971–83), ii.33–4; F. N. L. Poynter, ed., The Journal of James Yonge [1647–1721] (1963), 41.
[118] CSPD Addenda, 1625–49, 438.   [119] Coxere, Adventures, 57–64, 80, 84–5.

generally reserved for the maimed and destitute. John Hawker, a gunner formerly enslaved for eleven years, lost an arm in battle and by 1657 was in prison, charged with fraud.[120] Another former slave was killed in action, leaving a widow still obliged to repay the ransom she had raised to free him, and now facing a debtors' prison.[121]

Shipmasters had much further to fall in terms of social and economic status. Some, like John Rawlins, appear to have bounced back. But Rawlins had suffered only a short period in captivity and, having escaped, had no ransom to repay.[122] In other cases, the loss of money, goods, and earnings, and the burden of repaying ransoms, made their fall irreversible. If their families had been obliged to sell most of their property to raise or repay a ransom, they might have little left to maintain themselves.[123] William Hawkridge had invested his entire estate in his ship and its lading, to the value of £3,000, all lost when it was seized at Tunis in 1630. Unable to repay the ransom advanced by his friends, he begged letters of marque to repair his fortunes, offered his services in vain to the English navy and then to the Genoese, and in desperation requested a patent to supervise pilots around the English coast. Nothing materialized.[124] Edmund Berryman had similarly invested everything in his ship and its cargo, and was reduced to begging a licence to run a ferry at Barnstaple.[125] Other former masters and merchants sought places ashore in the Customs service.[126] John Spurrell of Ratcliff., who endured ten years of slavery before being ransomed by friends for £400, pleaded seven years later that he was still unable to repay them, and could barely maintain his family.[127] Even those without a ransom loan to repay often struggled to rebuild their lives. Richard Hunt explained in 1634 that he had been a shipmaster with forty years' service at sea, and had once commanded 1,000 men. But he had been taken three times by the 'Turks', ransomed at great expense, and then captured by Spaniards and forced to serve them at sea for six more years. Despite having contrived to escape during the English attack on Cadiz in 1625, he was very poor and begged for employment.[128] James Hales of Dover, once master of a good ship, had also escaped after nine years 'in a place remote from the sea', but at the age of 60 he

---

[120] *CSPD 1657-8*, 496; *CSPD 1659-60*, 537.   [121] *CSPD 1652-3*, 587.

[122] His name appears twice (perhaps father and son) in a declaration by radical brethren of Trinity House in June 1648: *The Humble Tender and Declaration of many well-affected Mariners* (1648).

[123] *CSPD 1638-9*, 243; Hebb, *Piracy*, 157 n.3.

[124] TNA SP 71/26, f.5; *CSPD 1633-4*, 357-8, 528, 547; *CSPD 1635*, 33. In March 1642 Hawkridge was appointed Master of the 702-ton *Marten,* hired as part of the fleet to be sent to Ireland: *The True List of his Majesties Navie Royall* (1642); see also *CSPD 1648-9*, 239, 293.

[125] *CSPD 1634-5*, 223-4.

[126] *Calendar of Treasury Books, 1685-9*, 171; *CSPD 1699-1700*, 387-8; cf. *CSPD 1660-1*, 159.

[127] W. J. Hardy, ed., *Middlesex County Records. Calendar of the Sessions Books 1689 to 1709* (1905), 179, 288.

[128] *CSPD 1634-5*, 223.

was scraping a living on a small hoy with a crew of one man and a boy. He begged for them not to be pressed into the navy.[129]

Joseph Pitts and Thomas Pellow, authors of successful published accounts, also struggled to integrate themselves back into English society. They had unusually high obstacles to overcome, for both had been captured when young, had spent many years in Barbary, and had 'turned Turk'. Neither possessed any maritime skills, and their military experience in the armies of the Maghreb was of no interest to the British army. Pitts spent the rest of his life mostly in Exeter, where he still had family, and married, dying probably in 1739. He mentions that a senior Treasury official had been interested in his story and had offered to help him find a post—an offer he had declined 'for some private reasons'.[130] Pellow had wanted to find employment, but his narrative ends on a sour note. He knew no-one in London, and his hope of securing letters of recommendation in his native Cornwall came to nothing. His dream of being presented to the king also failed to materialize, and he commented bitterly that he had found a warmer welcome from the Moroccan ambassador than from his own countrymen. He too disappeared into obscurity.[131]

Pellow was fortunate, however, compared to an unnamed Cornishman a century earlier. This man, a native of Perin, had led a picaresque career as a pirate, Barbary galley-slave, and ship's surgeon in the East Indies before eventually returning home in 1618, now quite rich, after an absence of sixteen years. His family failed to recognize him, and the hints he dropped unwisely about his wealth led to a calamitous result: his father, in debt and urged on by a grasping stepmother, murdered him as he slept, only to then kill himself when he discovered that he had slaughtered his own son. The sensational tale reached the royal court, and was long remembered. Moralizing writers spelled out its providential lessons—the terrible wages of sin and greed, and the dangerous temptations presented by women in general and stepmothers in particular.[132]

Gilbert Anderson also belonged to the poorly documented number of ship's surgeons captured and enslaved. By 1660, he explained, he had spent thirty-five years at sea, traversing much of the known world, including North Africa and the Americas, and for twelve years had served Venice in its long war with the Ottomans over Crete. Although he had lost his hearing during his time as a

[129] TNA SP 18/42, f.222. Another James Hales of Dover and his son Hugh had been redeemed in 1647 for $1,700 and $1,535 respectively: An Account of what Captives, 7.

[130] Pitts, pp. xvi–xvii; Paul Auchterlonie, ed., Encountering Islam. Joseph Pitts: an English Slave in 17th-Century Algiers and Mecca (2012), 55.

[131] Thomas Pellow, The History of the Long Captivity and Adventures of Thomas Pellow (1751; first published 1740), 384–8.

[132] Newes from Perin in Cornwall (1618); Strange & bloody news from Perin in Cornwall (1675); Sir William Sanderson, A Compleat History of the Lives and Reigns of, Mary Queen of Scotland and... James (1656), 464–5; R. B., Wonderful prodigies of judgment (1682), 155–6.iztory fo the Lives and rweigns of Mary Queemn oif Acotland and...James (1656), 464–5; jjj

slave, he explained that God had compensated him with the gift of revelation. Back in England by the Restoration, which he claimed to have prophesied, Anderson begged (probably in vain) for a meeting with a royal official to reveal more. He went on to pursue a lengthy and successful career as a physician and surgeon in London, and briefly in Sweden, his hearing presumably restored.[133] Surgeons' professional skills may have made it easier for them to recover from the disaster of captivity than it was for merchants or shipmasters, whose position was bound up with the ship and its cargo.

Alongside the liberated mariners were a much smaller number of merchants and passengers. Many merchants had been able to ransom themselves, and with luck they could return to trade, perhaps on a smaller scale. Abraham Browne's father had resumed his cross-Channel trade, while Browne himself, captured twenty years later, went on to modest success as a merchant in Boston. Two former Jamaican merchants enjoyed far more remarkable careers. Captured by Salé corsairs on their passage home to England around 1684, and enslaved for several years, they were eventually able to purchase their own redemptions. Instead of returning to England they chose to remain in Morocco, and a visitor who encountered them in Tetuan in 1727 reported that they were said to be more prosperous than when they had been captured.[134]

The very few passengers whose later careers we can follow were a very miscellaneous group, and had equally mixed fortunes. Seth Sothell was able to take up his post as Governor of Carolina, where his oppressive regime eventually provoked his violent overthrow. Despite his personal experience of enslavement he was a notoriously avaricious plantation-owner.[135] Jeffrey Hudson, once Queen Henrietta Maria's dwarf, had been banished from France after a duel and endured years of harsh treatment as a slave in Algiers. Eventually ransomed and pensioned by the second duke of Buckingham, he retired to his native Rutland.[136] William Atkins, a Catholic seminary student, ministered for many years as a Jesuit missionary in Staffordshire. He was captured and condemned to death during the furore over the Popish Plot, but reprieved on account of his age and died in prison in 1682.[137] Elizabeth Marsh's captivity, which had lasted only a few months, affected the rest of her life. As a young woman of twenty who had lived with a male 'friend', passing herself off as his wife, she would inevitably face difficult questions. Within a few weeks of reaching safety in Gibraltar, a hastily arranged marriage to her 'friend', James Crisp, had turned her into his real wife, to

---

[133] TNA SP 29/1, f. 222; Gilbert Anderson, *All Praise and Glory be given to God alone* (1680).

[134] Stephen T. Riley, ed., 'Abraham Browne's Captivity by the Barbary Pirates, 1655', *Colonial Society of Massachusetts*, 52 (1979), 31; John Braithwaite, *The History of the Revolutions in the Empire of Morocco* (1729), 67. He names them as Nash and Parker.

[135] Mattie E. E. Parker, 'Seth Sothel, *d.*1693 or 1694', in *Dictionary of North Carolina Biography* (<https://www.ncpedia.org/biography/sothel-or-sothell>).

[136] *ODNB*, 'Jeffrey Hudson, 1619–82', and sources there cited.

[137] Murphy, ed., 'William Atkins, A Relation', 200.

salvage her reputation. The marriage set her life on a very different course from the one she had planned.[138]

Most former slaves probably wanted no more than to pick up the lives that had been so cruelly disrupted. Those able to do so now relished the freedom they had once taken for granted. Thomas Phelps explained in 1685 that 'although my circumstances are otherwise but indifferent, yet I am affected with extraordinary emotions and singular transports of joy'. Freedom, he added, could be appreciated fully only by those who had endured captivity and slavery.[139] Many former captives struggled, weakened in health and strength, and burdened with debt or simply penniless. William Berriman, preaching at St Paul's in 1722 to celebrate the redemption of captives from Morocco, stressed their urgent need for relief "till such time as they shall be able to look out and make provision for themselves'.[140] That might prove a long time. The itinerants begging relief on the road, armed with a brief or certificate, were as likely to be destitute former slaves as wives trying to raise a ransom. In 1642 Cratfield's churchwardens gave 2s to John Brown and four others 'taken by the Turks', and another 2s to Edmond and Mary Blake 'spoiled by the Turks'. Perhaps their goods had been plundered at sea, or they had been forced to sell everything to raise a ransom. The churchwardens recorded other small payments to impoverished itinerants whose certificates testified they had lost more than £1,000 each 'by Turkish pirates'.[141] Almost all the Barbary relief paid by the churchwardens of Devizes in the second half of the century went to former captives, redeemed but destitute.[142]

All too often, slavery proved a blow from which even the once prosperous might never recover. And most captives, of course, had never been prosperous. John Kay, an illiterate soldier, was arrested for begging soon after his arrival back in England. Thomas Troughton and his companions received £5 apiece from George II when they reached home after several years in captivity. It was valuable as temporary support, and Troughton found work as a plasterer and in other trades—but he was nonetheless to die in a workhouse.[143]

---

[138] Linda Colley, *The Ordeal of Elizabeth Marsh* (2007), 87–90.

[139] *Phelps*, 'Preface to the Reader'.

[140] William Berriman, *The great Blessing of Redemption from Captivity* (1722), 25.

[141] L. A. Botelho, ed., *Churchwardens' Accounts of Cratfield 1640–1660*, Suffolk Records Society, 42 (1999), 33, 35, 100; cf. 33–4, 122. Cf. HMC 12, *Dean & Chapter of Wells*, 441–2, 444, 450–1.

[142] Alex Craven, ed., *Churchwardens' Accounts of St Mary's Devizes, 1633–1689*, Wiltshire Record Society, 69 (2016), 175, 194, 212, and *passim*.

[143] Thomas Troughton, *Barbarian Cruelty; or an Accurate and Impartial Narrative* (1751), 182; Linda Colley, *Captives. Britain, Empire and the World, 1600–1850* (2002), 85, 91.

8

Government Action

Gunboats and Diplomacy

The crown recognized a moral obligation to protect its subjects, and commerce, by curbing the Barbary corsairs. It was always painfully conscious, however, of the huge resources required, and the many risks. Samuel Pepys commented ruefully in 1675 that 'every former expedition into the Straits hath been of more than double the charge it ought to have been, besides the infamy brought thereby upon the honour of the king's service and disappointment to the designs thereof'.[1] Moreover, the crown, invariably short of funds, always had far more pressing demands on its attention and resources. The 1620s, 1650s, 1660s, 1670s, and 1690s saw wars against Spain, France, or the Dutch, while in the 1640s Britain was torn apart by civil war, and the 1680s ended with another revolution. Conflicts with European rivals always took priority.[2] Only slowly did the state develop the determination as well as the strength to curb the corsairs and liberate their captives.

English trade in the Mediterranean had grown rapidly from the 1580s. The Levant Company, founded in 1581 under government regulation, forged highly profitable links with the eastern Mediterranean, protected by a commercial agreement between Elizabeth and the Ottoman sultan. An extensive trade also developed with Morocco, largely unregulated except during the short-lived monopoly of the Barbary Company in 1585–97. As the volume of trade grew, so did the threat from Barbary corsairs. In 1584 complaints from the English ambassador in Constantinople, William Harborne, prompted the sultan to order Algiers, Tunis, and Tripoli to free captives and stop molesting English ships. They took little notice. In 1602 the Lord High Admiral complained to Algiers that ships and cargoes were still being seized, and though Algiers freed ten English slaves as a goodwill gesture, complaints generally proved ineffective. By 1608 the Levant Company was calling for an expedition to crush the corsairs.[3] A decade later,

---

[1] Pepys, *Catalogue*, iii.39.

[2] John B. Wolf, *The Barbary Coast. Algeria under the Turks, 1500 to 1830* (New York, 1979); chaps. 9–12; Hebb, *Piracy, passim*; cf. Sari R. Hornstein, *The Restoration Navy and English Foreign Trade, 1674–1688* (Aldershot, 1991).

[3] *Calendar of State Papers, Foreign, 1583–4*, 536; *CSP, Foreign, 1584–5*, 269; *Calendar of Documents relating to Scotland, 1509–85*, 431; HMC 9, *Salisbury*, xv.251; TNA SP 71/1, fos. 9–10; *CSPD 1603–10*, 469.

British Slaves and Barbary Corsairs, 1580–1750. Bernard Capp, Oxford University Press. © Bernard Capp 2022.
DOI: 10.1093/oso/9780192857378.003.0009

with corsairs now also operating in the Atlantic and the seas around Britain, pressure steadily mounted.

James possessed only modest naval resources, and knew that any expeditionary force would face daunting operational problems. Unlike France or Spain, England had no Mediterranean base to supply and refit its ships, which would thus have limited time to achieve their objectives. There was no safe anchorage off Algiers, so any blockade would be broken whenever bad weather drove them from their station. It was also unlikely that the corsairs could be brought to a decisive battle. English warships, though powerful, were too slow to overhaul the corsairs or prevent them slipping in or out. Attacking Algiers itself was not a realistic option. In 1600 it was as large as London, and had far stronger defences. Moreover, as the economist Henry Robinson observed in 1642, in the highly unlikely event of its rulers being overthrown, England lacked the resources to take possession or install a more compliant regime.[4]

The crown was very conscious of these constraints. The first treaties with Algiers, in 1622 and 1646, were secured by diplomacy alone, and when naval forces were despatched to the Straits commanders were generally left free to decide whether to attack or negotiate. Naval pressure procured new treaties in 1655, 1660, 1662, 1664, 1672, and 1682, but, as this list suggests, they proved short-lived and British naval superiority was far from total. A lasting peace with Algiers was always problematic, for its political economy demanded a steady flow of prizes, plunder, and slaves. Moreover, Barbary often had legitimate grievances against English merchants and shipmasters, and even when its rulers wanted to preserve peace, their authority was precarious.

Early Stuart endeavours

Early Stuart attempts to assert naval pressure were limited in scope. James I lacked the means to suppress Barbary corsairs or even British pirates—categories that initially often overlapped. Diplomats and merchants warned of the dire consequences of inaction, and in 1610 John Awdeley, formerly consul in Algiers, complained that English commerce in the Mediterranean could soon be totally destroyed.[5] The government eventually responded by planning an expedition in 1615, and though this project was abandoned, the idea did not go away. In 1617 James directed his council to canvass opinion on the best course of action. Advisors dismissed an attack on Algiers itself as unfeasible, and recommended that a naval force should try to destroy the corsairs at sea or pin them in its harbour. An international operation would stand the best chance of success, and

---

[4] Henry Robinson, *Libertas, or Reliefe to the English Captives in Algier* (1642), 1–3.
[5] TNA SP 71/1, f.17.

James opened negotiations with the Dutch and Spain. Both were willing in principle to participate but they failed to overcome their mutual suspicions, and James resolved to press on alone.[6]

The force that eventually sailed in September 1620 comprised six royal warships and twelve hired merchantmen, under the command of Sir Robert Mansell. Arriving off Algiers in November, Mansell opened negotiations with the pasha, demanding the restitution of 150 English ships and cargoes seized over the preceding five years, and the release of English captives. The pasha countered that most of the ships and goods had been sold, and that many of the captives were dead. He also demanded that English losses be set against earlier losses inflicted by English pirates. But he promised to restore English ships still in the Mole, and free all surviving slaves except those who had converted to Islam. In the event, only eighteen were returned, and no ships. The mood soured and the English negotiators were placed under guard, along with the eighteen slaves. It became plain that the pasha did not intend to honour his promises, and he now claimed, wildly, that a hundred slaves had escaped and were being sheltered in the fleet. Mansell withdrew to refit over winter in Spain, returning in May 1621 and determined this time to attack. But his attempt to fire the corsairs' men-of-war in harbour failed, further attempts proved impracticable, and he was eventually recalled home. His force had remained abroad far longer than any before it, but the results were meagre. His ships could not overhaul the corsairs' men-of-war, and he lacked the fast, shallow-draught vessels essential for an effective blockade. A news-writer commented sourly that Mansell and his fleet 'have done just nothing', and the expedition had merely underlined the scale of the challenge.[7]

Richard Ford, left behind as consul, was able to negotiate the redemption of a further thirty English slaves, but soon exhausted his money and credit. His efforts were also overtaken by events, for the corsairs intensified their attacks and by autumn 1621 were said to be operating seventy men-of-war. Ford reported in November that since Mansell's departure they had brought in forty-eight English ships and 400 captives. Within a few months, the number of English slaves had swollen further to an estimated 800–1,000, and Ford added that two other ships' companies, seventy men in all, had been put to the sword.[8] With the corsairs now also active in the seas around Britain, maritime communities in the south-west wailed that ship-owners were too nervous to send their vessels to sea, and sailors too frightened to go. Weymouth magistrates reported in 1622 that the number of its fishing boats sailing to Newfoundland had slumped from thirty-nine to eleven.[9]

[6] Hebb, *Piracy*, chaps. 3–4.

[7] On Mansell's expedition see Hebb, *Piracy*, chaps.5–6; TNA SP 71/1, fos.21–9; (John Button), *Algiers Voyage [in a Iournall or Briefe Reportary of all occurents]* (1621); John Chamberlain, *The Letters of John Chamberlain*, ed. Norman Egbert McClure (Philadelphia, 1939), ii.350.

[8] TNA SP 71/1, fos. 31, 33; *CSPVen. 1621–3*, 337–8.   [9] *CSPD 1619–23*, 385.

Faced with renewed demands for action, James turned to diplomacy. Refusing to negotiate directly with the 'thieves' of Barbary, he sent a new ambassador to Constantinople in 1621, to urge the sultan to assert his authority over the regencies. Sir Thomas Roe was an accomplished and resourceful diplomat. Calling at Messina on his outward journey, he persuaded the authorities to free thirteen former Barbary galley-slaves the Spaniards had rescued and consigned to their own galleys.[10] But in Constantinople Roe found that Mansell's failure had left him with very little leverage. The sultan agreed to send an envoy to Algiers and Tunis to demand the release of English captives and immunity for English shipping, but Algiers countered by sending commissioners to Constantinople to present its own grievances. After complex negotiations Roe was able to secure a compromise settlement. English slaves would be ransomed and delivered to a new resident consul, and Roe promised that England would secure the release of forty Moorish captives, many of them now held in Spain. While English ships would henceforth be protected, there was an uneasy compromise on those carrying the goods of Algiers' enemies. English ships were not prohibited from transporting such goods, but the cargoes would be lawful prize, which implicitly conceded the corsairs' right to stop and search any ship they judged suspect.[11] English ships trading to the Straits made much of their profit by carrying other goods between Mediterranean ports before returning home, and many foreign merchants viewed them as providing the safest carriage. Conceding the corsairs' right to seize such goods risked undermining the whole trade.

James disliked the agreement and appeared ready to repudiate it, partly because it offended Spain, and because he baulked at treating with pirates. Roe explained that his agreement was formally with the Ottoman sultan, who would impose it on Algiers, not with the corsairs themselves, but an envoy from Algiers found a cold reception when he arrived to complete the deal. As losses mounted, however, the king's attitude softened. Nicholas Leate, a leading Levant Company merchant, wrote in July 1623 that English slaves in Algiers now numbered 1,000. He argued that Roe had achieved miracles, and that a consul could negotiate ransoms far more cheaply than those arranged privately. The peace was confirmed and James Frizzell, a veteran merchant in Algiers, returned as consul.[12] Frizzell soon negotiated the release of 240 slaves for £1,815—only about £7 10s a head—using bills of exchange drawn on the Levant Company. More followed, bringing the total to at least 350 and possibly as many as 800, for an outlay far less than the cost of Mansell's expedition.[13]

---

[10] *Negotiations of Sir Thomas Roe* (1740), 8–9, 11. Twelve were English, one a Scot.
[11] Hebb, *Piracy*, chap. 8; *Negotiations of Roe*, 117–19, 128–30, 139–40, 177; Sir Godfrey Fisher, *Barbary Legend. War, Trade and Piracy in North Africa 1415–1830* (Oxford, 1957), 193–6; *CSPVen. 1623–5*, 107.
[12] Hebb, *Piracy*, 187–92; TNA SP 71/1, fos 37–8; *Negotiations of Roe*, 162, 177, 279–80.
[13] Hebb, *Piracy*, 195–6; TNA SP 71/1, fos.45, 91; *CSPVen. 1623–4*, 107; *CSPVen. 1625–6*, 23–4.

For a few years the corsairs broadly observed the terms of the treaty. Some moved their operations to Salé, however, and the fishing fleets returning from Newfoundland proved especially vulnerable. American colonists began to suffer too. In 1625 a ship with a cargo of valuable furs, despatched from Massachusetts by Edward Winslow, was seized as it approached Plymouth and carried to Salé. The corsairs sold its crew into slavery, and disposed of the valuable beaver pelts for a paltry 4d each.[14] Moreover, in Algiers the pace of redemptions soon slowed. Leate claimed in 1625 that 500–600 English slaves still remained there and at Tunis, and by the following year the peace was already starting to break down. The corsairs and their backers, including the pasha, had a vested interest in resuming the operations on which their wealth depended and, as Leate and Frizzell acknowledged, there had been provocations by the English too. It did not help that the Algerian envoy had been denied an audience by the new king, Charles I. Roe himself had always viewed his mission as a temporary expedient, and wrote home that he would have much rather have seen Algiers and Tunis 'burned in their own ashes'. Even before reaching Constantinople he had urged another attempt to organize a joint attack with Spain, convinced that force alone could provide a lasting solution.[15] Contemporaries recognized, moreover, that Ottoman influence over the regencies was rapidly declining, which the sultan did not deny. Many suspected he was happy to see the corsairs inflicting heavy damage, knowing that he could avoid all responsibility by accusing them of disobedience.[16]

Several years passed before any further attempt to address the problem. The wars with Spain and France in the later 1620s devoured all the government's resources and energy. Roe was informed that while the cries of captives 'come daily to his majesty's ears' the exchequer was empty, and that urgent business left not 'an hour's leisure' for Barbary.[17] Anxious to avoid another conflict, Charles issued a proclamation in 1628 forbidding attacks on Barbary shipping, and even toyed with the idea of co-operating with Morocco against Spain, now their common enemy.[18] That possibility disappeared when he made peace with Spain in 1630, and over the following decade merchant shipping continued to suffer heavily. The West Country was worst affected, with the Newfoundland fishing fleets suffering most. Merchants, magistrates, and seamen and their wives heaped pressure on the crown to take action. Petitioners from Exeter, Dartmouth, Plymouth, and other towns complained that their coasts were infested by pirates from Salé and Algiers. One group of petitioners reported that they had lost

[14] William Bradford, *Of Plymouth Plantation, 1620–1647*, ed. S.E. Morison (New York, 1952), 176.
[15] TNA SP 71/1, fos. 52v, 56, 80-v, 85–6, 91–3; *CSPVen. 1625–6*, 29; Hebb, *Piracy*, 191–5; Fisher, *Barbary Legend*, 199–204; *Negotiations of Roe*, 33, 140.
[16] Henry Blount, *A Voyage into the Levant* (1636), 72; Francis Knight, *A Relation of Seaven Yeares Slaverie* (1640), 34.
[17] *Negotiations of Roe*, 4–6, 29.
[18] *CSPVen. 1626–8*, 296, 302; *CSPVen. 1628–9*, 395–6; Larkin and Hughes, eds., *Stuart Royal Proclamations*, ii.209–10; P. G. Rogers, *A History of Anglo-Moroccan Relations to 1900* (1977), 25–8.

eighty-seven ships, with cargoes worth almost £92,000. Some 1,160 seamen had been enslaved and local economies crippled, with merchants and ship-owners not daring to trade. In 1635 Dartmouth magistrates complained of the intolerable burden of poor relief to support the families left destitute. In Cornwall, justices reported that East and West Loo alone had lost almost seventy seamen to the corsairs, and that fear had paralysed the local economy, with sixty vessels lying idle and 200 sailors unemployed.[19]

The tide of complaint finally pushed the crown into action, and in 1633 it began planning for another expedition against Algiers. London's merchant community, however, proved very reluctant to help finance it. Leading traders told the Privy Council bluntly that they 'were secure and have naught to do with the western parts'.[20] The plans had to be abandoned, and the government switched its focus to Salé, by now the greatest threat to the western fishermen. In 1636 Charles resolved to dispatch an expedition under the command of William Rainborough, a seaman with both naval and mercantile experience.[21] His force, though much smaller than Mansell's, was better designed for its task, with two fast pinnaces able to intercept corsairs and operate in shallow inshore waters. Rainborough's orders were to capture or destroy the corsairs' men-of-war and free the slaves. Salé consisted of Old and New Towns on opposite sides of the Bou Regreg river, and a decade earlier it had thrown off the authority of Morocco's ruler at Fez. The New Town, the corsairs' base, was at odds with the Old, which was under the sway of al-Ayyashi, a powerful *marabout* (holy man) and warlord. Arriving in March 1637, Rainborough imposed a tight blockade and made a tactical alliance with al-Ayyashi to besiege the New Town. The English carried their ordnance ashore, and by the end of July they had destroyed all the men-of-war anchored in the river. The New Town was eventually starved into surrender, and agreed to free some 340 English slaves without the payment of ransoms. Although many more slaves had been shipped to Algiers shortly before his arrival, Rainborough had liberated those remaining and had annihilated Salé's fleet, destroying thirteen men-of-war in the river and four at sea, and capturing two others. He had also thwarted plans for another major *corso* expedition, saving hundreds more seamen from probable capture. Moreover, al-Ayyashi and the corsairs both now agreed to recognize the authority of the Moroccan ruler at Fez. Building on his success, Rainborough sent envoys to Fez to negotiate a treaty, and brought home a Moroccan ambassador who agreed a formal treaty incorporating its articles.

---

[19] *CSPD 1625–49, Addenda*, 45, 546; *CSPD 1635*, 398; *CSPD 1635–6*, 15, 143, 302; *CSPD 1636–7*, 4, 60, 111.

[20] *CSPD 1633–4*, 97, 102.

[21] This paragraph and the next are based on Hebb, *Piracy*, chap. 11; Kenneth R. Andrews, *Ships, Money and Politics. Seafaring and Naval Enterprise in the Reign of Charles I* (Cambridge, 1991), chap. 7; Adrian Tinniswood, *The Rainborowes* (2014), 30–44; John Dunton, *A True Journal of the Sally Fleet* (1637); TNA SP 71/13, fos.1–32; *CSPD 1637*, 7, 87, 351, 430–1, 533; Edmund Waller, 'Of Salley', in *Poems* (1646), 67–8.

Rainborough's triumph was celebrated in London in magnificent style. A hundred coaches escorted the ambassador to his lodgings, watched by an estimated 10,000 citizens, and he was brought to Whitehall with similar pomp. A pamphlet account stressed Morocco's former and potential future greatness, underlining the embassy's importance, while also informing its readers that the liberated slaves had suffered a misery even 'worse... than the Egyptian bondage under Pharaoh'.[22] The pamphlet, like the ceremonies, thus served to proclaim both Charles' power and his benevolence. After years of public anger and frustration, the expedition's success offered reassurance that his Ship Money levies could deliver glory and tangible benefits. Never again did Salé match the threat it had posed in the 1620s and 1630s, though it was to remain a significant corsair base for another century. The cheering crowds would not have realized how much the triumph owed to the exceptional circumstances that Rainborough had found there.

This success naturally prompted calls for similarly decisive action against Algiers. A letter brought by the Moroccan ambassador even raised the possibility of joint assaults on Algiers and Tunis, which it dismissed as 'dens and receptacles of... inhuman villainies'.[23] Charles turned to his experts for advice. In response, Sir Thomas Roe summarized a report he had drawn up several years earlier with Sir Kenelm Digby, Sir Paul Pindar, and other leading merchants. It called for a fleet to attack Ottoman merchant shipping near Alexandria, putting pressure on the sultan, and seize captives on Barbary's coast to exchange for English slaves.[24] Rainborough proposed a more ambitious version of his recent expedition. Ten good ships, periodically rotated, would blockade Algiers for several years, long enough to destroy its piratical economy and render its ships rotten and useless.[25] By 1638, however, Charles was already facing domestic problems that would soon trigger the collapse of his Personal Rule. Neither plan was ever implemented, and both would almost certainly have failed.

Barbary and the Civil Wars

It was by no means obvious in 1640 that England was about to slide into civil war. With the corsair menace reaching new heights, both king and parliament recognized the need for action. It was reported that between May 1639 and January 1640 more than sixty-eight English ships had been captured, along with 1,222 mariners and passengers. Eighty men-of-war were said to be cruising off Spain's

---

[22] *The Arrival and Intertainements of the Embassador, Alkaid Jaurar Ben Abdella* (1637), 9–11, 26–7 and *passim*.

[23] *A Letter from the King of Morocco to his Majesty the King of England, Charles I* (1680; reprinted 1682 in both London and Edinburgh). It was presumably copied from a 1637 edition, now lost.

[24] *CSPD 1637–8*, 192; TNA SP 71/1, fos. 130-2v, 162.   [25] *CSPD 1637–8*, 187.

Atlantic coast, with another ten infesting the English Channel. The coast itself was again under threat, and a raid near Penzance was reported to have seized sixty men, women, and children. Any government unable to protect its subjects on its own territory would quickly forfeit both credit and authority. A further humiliation was the capture of the *Rebecca* in January 1640, carrying 400 chests of silver, worth £260,000, to Flanders. When Parliament met in April, the government's own ministers urged the need for action.[26] Pamphleteers added to the pressure. Francis Knight appealed for the king to liberate the English slaves in Algiers, estimating their number at 1,500. He suggested, optimistically, that it might even be possible to capture Algiers and use its riches to recoup the costs. Henry Robinson urged a very different course: sending a fleet of forty ships to lie off Constantinople and sever its vital supply routes. Once the starving population took to the streets, he argued, the Ottomans would be forced to accept a treaty meeting English demands. His project, wildly over-ambitious, failed to recognize that the Ottomans now had little ability to impose their will on Algiers.[27]

The Long Parliament that assembled in November 1640 also devoted considerable attention to Barbary in its first months. It heard that between 3,000 and 5,000 English slaves remained in Algiers and Tunis (an exaggeration), and that the corsairs were planning to set out another huge force of sixty men-of-war. A bill proposing a new expedition was introduced in March 1641, though it failed to reach the statute book. Members were more attuned than royal ministers to public opinion, and the king's failure to safeguard the seas and liberate captives was one of their many sources of resentment. On 1 December the Commons complained in their catalogue of grievances, the Grand Remonstrance, that Ship Money levies had been imposed 'upon pretence of guarding the seas', but had left merchants still exposed to 'Turkish pirates', with thousands of mariners in 'miserable slavery'. A revised bill was passed later that month and received royal assent in mid-January 1642, only days after Charles' attempt to seize the Five Members, his leading critics. Reports spoke of a plan to send twenty ships against Algiers, serving for three years or as long as required—a variant of Rainborough's proposal—and funded by a new duty on imports and exports. Henceforth the financial burden of dealing with corsairs and pirates would thus be borne, albeit indirectly, by the whole nation.[28]

In the event, the outbreak of civil war prevented any direct action against Barbary for more than a decade. Parliament did not forget the issue, and in July 1643 it sent an envoy, Lewis Hodges, to Algiers to demand the release of English slaves, authorizing him to threaten force if necessary. Although that was as yet an empty threat, he was able to redeem 112 English captives, and more two years

[26] Hebb, *Piracy*, 140–1, 266–8.   [27] Knight, *Relation, 55*; Robinson, *Libertas*, 8–9.
[28] Hebb, *Piracy*, 268–73; Nabil Matar, *Britain and Barbary, 1589–1689* (Gainesville, FL, 2005), 65–9; *CSPVen. 1640–42*, 172, 289–90; 16 Car. I, c24, 25 (*Statutes of the Realm*, ed. J. Raithby, v (1819), 134–5.

later.[29] In 1645, with victory finally in sight, Parliament despatched Edmund Cason on a more ambitious mission, and the following year he succeeded in renewing the treaty of 1622 and ransoming several hundred captives (as described in Chapter 7). The new peace held for several years, and Parliament built on his efforts by appointing resident consuls at Algiers and Tunis.[30]

Cason had brought only money to the table, but once the civil wars were ended the application of naval pressure became a realistic option. Parliament had greatly expanded England's navy, and Oliver Cromwell, as Lord Protector, continued that process.[31] After making peace with the Dutch in 1654, Cromwell felt free to employ the navy to assert British interests in the Mediterranean. The fleet he despatched later that year under Robert Blake was a show of strength to Barbary as well as to Spain and France. Tunis, rather than Algiers, had re-emerged as a threat. A conflict had been provoked by the behaviour of an English shipmaster named Stephen Mitchell, who had contracted to carry Muslim passengers from Tunis to Smyrna. When his ship was intercepted by Maltese galleys, he had permitted them to be seized and carried to Malta, where they were made galley-slaves. Tunis reacted with justifiable fury. The pasha held the English consul, Samuel Boothhouse, accountable and sequestered his property until he secured their release. Boothhouse laboriously negotiated a collective ransom, but the Maltese rejected it as inadequate.[32] To break the impasse, Blake was directed to demand the release of all British captives along with the *Princess*—a vessel which Tunis had seized in retaliation—and to employ force if necessary. Both sides nursed a legitimate sense of grievance. The Muslim captives claimed that Mitchell had sold them to the Maltese, a charge he strongly denied. Boothhouse conceded that Mitchell was greatly to blame for allowing the Maltese to search his ship and seize them, but protested that Tunis had no right to seize English property, ships, and sailors.[33]

Reaching Tunis in February 1655, Blake met with a blunt refusal, though the Tunisians professed their readiness 'to make a firm peace for the future'. He complained that in further talks he had found only 'insolence' and 'barbarous provocations', and resolved to settle the matter by force. On 4 April his ships sailed into the harbour of Porto Farina, under heavy fire from shore batteries, and

---

[29] *LJ*, vi.122; Fisher, *Barbary Legend*, 208–9; BL MS Add. 5489, fos.85, 87v-88; Nabil Matar, *British Captives from the Mediterranean to the Atlantic, 1563-1760* (Leiden, 2014), 100, 218. Hodges was directed to locate James Frizzell in Algiers and work in partnership with him. Whether Frizzell was still alive is unclear.

[30] Edmund Cason, *A Relation of the whole proceedings concerning the Redemption of the Captives in Argier and Tunis* (1647); *LJ*, ix.205; Fisher, *Barbary Legend*, 210–14.

[31] Bernard Capp, *Cromwell's Navy. The Fleet and the English Revolution, 1648-1660* (Oxford, 1989), chaps. 1–3.

[32] Samuel Boothhouse, *A Brief Remonstrance of Several National Injuries and Indignities* (1653); Fisher, *Barbary Legend*, 215–17.

[33] J. R. Powell, ed., *The Letters of Robert Blake*, Navy Records Society, 76 (1937), 271; Boothhouse, *Remonstrance*, 10–13 and *passim*.

burned the eight Tunis men-of-war at anchor there, along with the *Princess*.[34] His operation matched Rainborough's success at Salé, and in far more difficult circumstances, but it achieved very little. Blake feared, indeed, that it might provoke retaliation, for the ships had been intended for the service of the Ottoman sultan. He wrote in haste to the ambassador at Constantinople, Sir Thomas Bendysh, to explain his actions, and wrote again to the dey, demanding the captives' release but also offering to refer the issue of English losses to the sultan. The dey sent a contemptuous reply, and despatched his own messenger to Constantinople. Rumours soon swirled that Bendysh had been beheaded as retribution, though in reality the sultan had no wish to be drawn into a conflict. The captured English seamen remained, of course, enslaved.[35]

Since entering the Mediterranean, Blake had also been scouring the sea for French and other privateers. One excited pamphleteer claimed that 100 had been captured within a month, while another proclaimed that Blake 'rides triumphant in the Levant Ocean'.[36] Although such claims were wildly inflated, his presence had a significant impact. In one striking example, four Algerian men-of-war made a Salé ship surrender its English captives and delivered them to Blake. An English officer commented happily that 'we are not only a terror to the French and Spaniard but also the Turks seek to get into our favour'.[37] Blake found a respectful reception when he arrived in Algiers a few weeks after the action at Porto Farina. He was able to replenish supplies and confirm Cason's treaty, with a new article that extended protection to ships from Ireland and Scotland. He also redeemed twenty-seven slaves (English, Irish, and Scots) for £1,435—about £53 a head. On departing, he left the merchant Robert Browne to fill the place of consul, vacant by Oneby's death.[38]

Peace with the regencies was always precarious. When he returned to the Mediterranean in 1656, Blake found Algiers already less co-operative. Cromwell had neglected to confirm Browne's appointment, and Blake suspected that the corsairs were looking for an excuse to resume attacks. Only the presence of his fleet, he reported, restrained them.[39] With England now at war with Spain, he had no opportunity to return to Tunis. He and his partner Edward Mountagu, in joint command, did briefly confront the corsairs of Salé. Its governor appeared ready to negotiate after two of his men-of-war were run ashore, but he refused to free any slaves without the payment of ransoms, a demand they rejected as dishonourable.

---

[34] Powell, *Letters of Blake*, 288–9, 291–5, 317–21.

[35] Powell, *Letters of Blake*, 295, 318–19; W.C. Abbott, ed., *The Writings and Speeches of Oliver Cromwell* (Oxford, 1937–47), iii.759; *Thurloe*, iii.512–13, 550.

[36] *A Message sent from His Highness the Lord Protector, to the Great Turk* (1654), 7–8 and *passim*.

[37] J.R. Powell, ed., 'The Journal of John Weale 1654-1656', *The Naval Miscellany, 4*, Navy Records Society, 92 (1952), 94.

[38] *CSPD 1655–6*, 129; *Thurloe*, iii.422, 463, 526–7; Powell, *Letters of Blake*, 296–7, 362.

[39] Powell, *Letters of Blake*, 362. Algiers sent an envoy to England in 1656–57: HMC 29, *Portland*, i.544.

There were in fact only twenty-four English slaves then at Salé, and most new captives were transferred inland to Meknes or Fez or sent to be sold in Algiers. Blake later agreed a settlement with Salé, in 1657, after ransoming the slaves,[40] and in August that year, John Stokes, commanding the squadron that remained when Blake sailed home, concluded a peace with Tetuan and installed a consul there.[41]

The dispute with Tunis was also eventually settled. The Muslim slaves held in Malta were released in April 1657, after England had paid ransoms to the Knights who ruled the island.[42] Stokes sailed to Tunis in February 1658, announcing that he was ready to make peace once the English slaves were also freed. The pasha replied nonchalantly that he could have them at the rate Blake had paid at Algiers. After reconnoitring Porto Farina, Stokes judged it now too heavily defended to attack, but the pasha did not relish the prospect of the English threatening his ships for weeks or months, and the two sides came to an accommodation. Some seventy-two English slaves, among them Edward Coxere and three women, were ransomed for $11,250, or about £40 each—better terms than Blake had secured. Stokes claimed that their current market value would have been $30,000.[43] Blake and Stokes were both able to negotiate flat-rate ransoms, rather than a different price for each individual as Cason had been obliged to do a decade earlier. Both commanded powerful naval forces, which greatly strengthened their bargaining position. One article in the treaty agreed by Stokes promised that in future, British ships carrying Tunisian passengers would be required to defend them and their goods; there would be no excuse for another Stephen Mitchell. For its part, Tunis promised not to target British ships, and gave them the right to buy supplies and refit in its harbours. Stokes immediately took advantage of this privilege at Porto Farina, and wrote home that it would be an invaluable supply base for operations against Spanish shipping and privateers, his main targets. During the course of the summer, Stokes also made a treaty with Tripoli.[44]

Naval pressure was finally bearing fruit. This was far from the end of the story, however. Stokes had to return to Tunis in April 1659 after an incident almost wrecked the new peace. A salute fired by an English ship had accidentally killed a sailor on a Tunisian man-of-war, whose captain, an English renegade, exploited the mishap to inflame passions. After restoring calm, Stokes reported, he was moving on to Algiers 'to see if I can quiet those people', always eager, he thought, to break the peace.[45] The treaty with Algiers had not resolved old tensions over

[40] Abbott, *Writings and Speeches*, iv.417; *Thurloe*, i.729, v.285, 421; Powell, *Letters of Blake*, 462; Matar, *British Captives*, 107.

[41] Abbott, *Writings and Speeches*, iv.597, 919–21; *Thurloe*, vi.633.

[42] Alan G. Jamieson, *Lords of the Sea. A History of the Barbary Corsairs* (2012), 138.

[43] *CSPD 1657-8*, 307–10; TNA SP 18/179, fos. 143-v; *Thurloe*, vi.846. Stokes paid $156 a head, Blake $213½. One of Stokes' officers said the total ransom was $14,000 but that Stokes paid only $10,000; 'the Dey and Bey will pay the odd four thousand' from their own resources: Powell, ed., 'Journal of Weale', 156.

[44] *CSPD 1658-9*, 92, 140; Matar, *British Captives*, 110.   [45] *CSPD 1658-9*, 338–9.

foreign goods carried by British ships. As the consul explained, the corsairs complained this had cost them millions, and that merchant vessels of 'all nations whatsoever' now flew the English flag for protection. The corsairs were determined to assert their right of search, and take prize offending ships and cargoes. Several English sailors had been seized, with Consul Browne placed under house arrest.[46]

Very often both parties could legitimately feel aggrieved. Plunder and ransoms formed an integral part of Barbary's political economy. They were essential to pay the janissaries' wages, and unpaid soldiers were always quick to resort to violence. It was easy for Barbary's rulers, under domestic pressure, to point to a breach of the articles, deliberate or accidental, and repudiate a treaty. Throughout the century, English commanders and consuls insisted that it was essential for warships to show the flag, regularly and in strength, to persuade the regencies to honour their agreements. Peace was against the interests of the corsairs, the janissaries, the *armadors* who set out the men-of-war, and the rulers themselves, who received a share of the spoils. Cromwellian gunboat diplomacy had secured peace in Barbary, but it remained fragile.

The Restoration years

The later 1650s had witnessed an increased presence of English fleets and convoy escorts in the Mediterranean, and this trend continued after the Restoration. The convoy system proved crucial in protecting merchant shipping, while the growing strength of the English, French, and Dutch navies left the corsairs increasingly outgunned.[47] They still posed a substantial threat, however, and European rivalries continued to prevent any concerted action against them. Algiers could not afford to maintain peace with all three maritime states, which would leave the corsairs with too few targets. It remained heavily dependent on a ransom and plunder economy, and if the flow of prizes and captives dried up, its political establishment was always likely to collapse.[48]

These structural problems made a lasting peace unlikely, while a host of specific grievances triggered new conflicts throughout this period. Perennial issues remained: the right to search English ships for goods belonging to 'strangers', and ships sailing under false English colours and with English passes illicitly acquired. Corsairs complained that almost every ship they met claimed to be English, and insisted on their right of search. The government admitted that Algiers had legitimate grievances, with passes often issued for foreign-built ships and to masters ineligible. It admitted too that its warships sometimes allowed

---

[46] *Thurloe*, vii.566; *CSPVen. 1657–9*, 289; *CSPD 1659–60*, 337.
[47] Hornstein, *Restoration Navy*.   [48] Wolf, *Barbary Coast*, chaps. 11–12.

foreign ships to sail under the protection of English convoys. It countered that the corsairs frequently ignored treaty articles, sometimes torturing sailors to make them 'confess' to being Italian, or that their cargo belonged to 'strangers', and was therefore prize. Moreover, any British sailors and passengers found on board most foreign ships were considered legitimate targets.[49] Even periods of peace thus saw a steady trickle of new captives sold into slavery.

Charles II received an unwelcome reminder of such problems at the very outset of his reign. A few months earlier, the earl of Inchiquin—a prominent royalist who had entered military service under the Portuguese—had been captured on his way to take up his command. He and his son, Lord O'Brian, who lost an eye in the fight, were taken to Algiers, along with their entourage. The earl was by far the most eminent British captive ever taken. The Algerian authorities soon allowed him to return home, on a British warship, to raise the huge ransom they had set for him and his son: $7,500. His son remained a hostage. Charles ordered some of the ransom money to be provided out of public funds, and a warship conveyed it to Algiers to bring him home.[50]

There were further difficulties when the earl of Winchelsea called at Algiers in November 1660, on his way to Constantinople to take up his post as ambassador. His instructions were to finalize the earl's ransom and renew the treaty. He reported that the Aga (whom he dubbed 'the Cromwell and tyrant of Argier') had just been assassinated, and that chaos now reigned. The new rulers refused to accept an article that allowed corsairs merely to inspect passes, not search for foreign goods or passengers, declaring they would rather have war than accept such terms. Winchelsea grudgingly agreed a provisional article conceding their rights on this issue until the king's pleasure was known. Writing home, he made clear his loathing for this 'barbarous' and 'piratical nation'. He did not expect the peace to last, and hoped the king would be able to send a powerful fleet to impose better terms.[51]

Charles refused to accept the provisional concession, and despatched a fleet to demand the surrender of any right of search, the restitution of British ships and cargoes, and the release of enslaved seamen. Its commander, Edward Mountagu, now earl of Sandwich, wrote home in August 1661 that Algiers' rulers had flatly refused, declared their treaty with Cromwell no longer valid, and reiterated that they would choose war rather than concede the right of search. When they opened fire on his fleet, Sandwich retaliated by bombarding the city, though his plan to fire ships in the harbour was thwarted by adverse winds. One brazen pamphleteer published a far more exciting narrative—a detailed account of a wholly fictitious

---

[49] Pepys, *Catalogue*, ii.396, iii, pp. xviii–xxii, 341–2, iv.189, 246.
[50] *CSPD 1659–60*, 357; *CSPD 1660–1*, 183,193, 199, 355, 402; TNA SP 71/1, f.179v; HMC 71, *Finch*, i.133, 142–3; *CSPVen. 1659–61*, 137, 194, 222, 228.
[51] TNA SP 71/1, fos. 177–192; HMC 71, *Finch*, i.85–9.

victory, in which the English had supposedly destroyed eighteen men-of-war and liberated 1,100 slaves. It was an extraordinary piece of fake news. In reality Sandwich had withdrawn, sailing for Lisbon to carry home the king's new bride.[52] The squadron he left behind, under Sir John Lawson, enjoyed greater success. Lawson captured or destroyed several men-of-war, selling hundreds of captives into slavery in Spain, and one of his ships also recaptured an English merchantman laden with valuable silk. It had been 'but nine hours in possession of the Turks', he reported happily. These heavy losses triggered dismay and violent unrest in Algiers, and the clamour for peace enabled Lawson to impose a new treaty in April 1662 that removed the corsairs' right of search. He secured similar terms at Tunis and Tripoli. Henceforth, corsairs might demand to inspect a pass issued by the Lord High Admiral, but were not to search ships with a pass or even without one if more than half the crew were British.[53]

Lawson's success was greeted with delight in Whitehall. He also brought home eleven captives he had ransomed, and the Bargrave–Selleck mission a few months later redeemed 142 more.[54] The treaty proved short-lived, however, and the corsairs were soon bringing in a stream of new prizes. The consul, Robert Browne, reported that while the 'soberer sort' in the divan wanted peace, the 'perfidious' corsairs and their backers would rather have war than surrender their right of search. Browne faced repeated abuse, his servants were arrested and flogged, and he wrote home that his presence served little purpose. Algiers had its own grievances. It took a year for the English government to issue instructions about passes and supply blank forms, and trying to establish the nationality of every crew-member was almost bound to create confusion and disputes.[55]

The Aga and divan wrote to the king in September 1663 repudiating Lawson's treaty, just after it had been formally confirmed by the Ottoman sultan, and Lawson was sent back to the Straits to exact retribution. Algiers agreed to release eighteen prizes and their crews but refused to return their cargoes, whereupon Lawson opened hostilities. His force captured or destroyed several more men-of-war, and when he was summoned home in 1664 on the outbreak of war with the Dutch, a squadron remained under Thomas Allin to pursue the campaign.[56] Naval pressure eventually forced Algiers to renew Lawson's treaty, including its key provisions on searches and the safety of foreigners and their goods. Algiers also

---

[52] *The Demands of his gracious Majesty…sent by the Lord General Montagu* (1661), 6–8; R.C. Anderson, ed., *The Journal of Edward Mountagu, First Earl of Sandwich*, Navy Records Society, 64 (1929), 91–4; HMC 71, *Finch*, i.142–3; *CSPVen. 1659–61*, 266.

[53] Fisher, *Barbary Legend*, 231–4; Anderson, ed., *Journal of Sandwich*, 98, 105, 132–3, 140; George Chalmers, *A Collection of Treaties* (1790), ii.360–5; TNA SP 71/1, fos.225–6; *CSPVen. 1661–4*, 51, 53, 67.

[54] Pepys, *Diary*, iii.89. On the mission see Chapter 7.

[55] TNA SP 71/1, fos. 227–37; HMC 71, *Finch*, i.243, 276; *CSPVen. 1661–4*, 266, 271–3; Fisher, *Barbary Legend*, 234–5.

[56] HMC 71, *Finch*, i.281–2; Pepys, *Diary*, iv.369–70.

agreed to free its captives, though ransoms had to be paid for those already sold. The articles were published, together with a preface that boasted how England's naval might had forced Algiers to sue for peace, and how the treaty demonstrated the king's tender care for his subjects. The printed text also included a certificate, signed by Algiers' rulers, conceding that the breach had been occasioned by rogue corsairs, 'for which we have drowned one, banished another', and imprisoned others.[57] It was a gratifying success for gunboat diplomacy, and splendid propaganda for the crown.

The new peace, however, proved as short-lived as its predecessors. Old grievances remained, and England's military outpost in Tangier, ceded by Portugal in 1662, created fresh sources of contention. The crown regarded everyone living there as its subjects, regardless of origin, and demanded safe passage for the vessels ferrying supplies to the garrison from Spain. Their crews were mostly Spanish, and the corsairs viewed them as legitimate prizes, despite the passes they carried. Even the consul considered the arrangements ill-judged and provocative. A particular storm broke over some British and Spanish seamen seized off Tangier in 1668 and carried to Algiers. Allin returned with orders to secure their release, if necessary by force. Algiers agreed to release the British captives (though not the Spanish), but its corsairs continued to seize British ships and Allin railed at 'the perfidiousness of these villains'. For its part, Algiers continued to complain about British ships without passes and with largely foreign crews, and insisted on its right to seize any ship if more than half its crew were 'strangers'. Further negotiations failed. One English participant fumed that 'Never any one met with such wilful dissembling hypocritical traitors in this world'.[58]

Charles II, deeply dissatisfied, was reported to have declared that he now wanted to see Algiers 'reduced once and for all'. In July 1669 Allin was sent back with a stronger force and with orders to reopen hostilities. The war that followed started badly, and in March 1670 the consul John Ward reported gloomily that the corsairs had seized thirty-two English ships and 385 mariners.[59] Allin's subordinates, however, were soon to achieve some major successes. In August a squadron under Richard Beach destroyed five of Algiers's best men-of-war off Cape Spartel—a force carrying over 2,000 men and 200 guns. It was a heavy blow. In April 1671 Sir Edward Spragge, commanding the squadron left behind after Allin returned home, destroyed all ten men-of-war he found in the harbour at Bougie, with heavy losses among the commanders, seamen, and

---

[57] *Articles of Peace between his Sacred Majesty, Charles the II, and... Algiers* (1664). Anderson, ed., *Journals of Allin*, i.171–4 and *passim*; Pepys, *Diary*, v.141, 332.

[58] TNA SP 71/1, fos. 297–302, 344-v, 357-v, 377, 432–3, 438; Anderson, ed., *Journals of Allin*, ii, pp. x–xl, 45–51, 77–82, 227–30; *CSPVen. 1666–8*, 327; Pepys, *Diary*, ix.427–8, 473, 492.

[59] TNA SP 71/1, fos. 414, 424–33, 448; Anderson, ed., *Journals of Allin*, ii, pp. xli–xlviii, 109–98, 230–4; *CSPVen. 1669–70*, 75, 126, 168, 189, 201.

soldiery.[60] These disasters helped trigger another revolution in Algiers. The Aga was murdered, and power passed into the hands of the *reis* (corsair captains), whose leader ruled henceforth as dey. The new ruler negotiated a treaty with Spragge in November 1671, which provided for all British slaves to be redeemed at the first market price. Like its immediate predecessors, the treaty stipulated that British ships were not to be molested, even if without a pass, if more than half the crew were British subjects.[61]

In the event, Charles failed to reform abuses over passes, and the corsairs continued to seize ships with passes they claimed were forged or invalid, or with mainly foreign crews, and to enslave British sailors captured on foreign vessels. There was also great resentment in Algiers over the issue of redemption. The soldiers were furious that ransoms fixed at the first market-price would not yield them a profit, and they had been forbidden to sell their slaves or take them to camp. Moreover, prominent figures given slaves as presents would receive nothing. The dey faced dangerous several mutinies, slaves were ill-treated by resentful owners, and the consuls—Ward and his successor Samuel Martin—faced threats and abuse. There was also no sign of the ransom money, which Spragge had apparently promised would arrive without delay.[62]

In September 1674 the dey sent an ultimatum threatening to reopen hostilities unless the money arrived soon. This had the desired effect. Anxious to avert renewed war, the king despatched Sir John Narbrough in haste with sufficient funds to defuse the crisis. Narbrough and Martin swiftly agreed terms for the redemption of 283 slaves for £22,369—an average of £79 each.[63] They were directed not to redeem any of those captured on foreign vessels, to discourage mariners from taking such employments. Charles indeed agreed to prohibit sailors from serving on foreign ships, and to require passengers on such vessels to carry passes covering themselves and their goods. A proclamation issued in December 1675 warned that any captives who had ignored these commands could expect no assistance. Another proclamation required all British ships in the Straits to carry a pass that would be issued only for ships with a British master and largely British crew.[64] These measures were intended to reduce friction, but they were poorly enforced, and it frequently proved difficult to establish mariners' nationality. Moreover, the corsairs interpreted a measure that was designed to prevent foreigners acquiring passes as a licence to seize any British ship without one. The

---

[60] *CSPVen. 1669–70*, 278–9, 285–6; *ODNB*, Beach, Spragge; *A True and Perfect Relation of the Happy Successe... at Bugia* (1674); *CSPD 1670*, 394–5, 595–6; HMC 79, *Lindsey*, 207.

[61] Fisher, *Barbary Legend*, 244–5; *Articles of Peace... between Charles II and Algiers* (1672); BL MS Sloane 2755, fos.50–52v.

[62] Pepys, *Catalogue*, ii.357; Fisher, *Barbary Legend*, 245, 255–8; TNA SP 71/2, fos. 9, 14, 22, 87.

[63] Pepys, *Catalogue*, ii.362, 380, 420, iv.119.

[64] Pepys, *Catalogue*, ii.380, 420; iv.261–2; HMC, 25, *Le Fleming*, 115; *By the King. A Proclamation relating to the articles concluded between his Majesty, and the government of Algiers* (1675); Fisher, *Barbary Legend*, 258–60.

crown denounced this as a 'manifest perverting' of the treaty, and relations soured once more. The consul, Samuel Martin, explained that many of the corsairs had been reduced to 'a desperate condition', returning home empty-handed, and were now longing for war to resume. Martin faced repeated threats and abuse as he attempted to secure the release of ships, seamen, and cargoes seized in apparent breach of the treaty. His goods were confiscated, and he wrote home that he was half-expecting to be hanged, drowned, or burned alive.[65]

In 1677 Narbrough returned with orders to demand the immediate release of ships, goods, and slaves, and if necessary reopen hostilities. Once again, the war that followed proved initially fruitless.[66] Narbrough's primary responsibility was to convoy merchant shipping, and the force he stationed off Algiers was too weak to enforce a blockade. Arthur Herbert, who took over with a smaller force in 1679, enjoyed far greater success. Deploying his ships near the mouth of the Straits, well placed to intercept the corsairs, he inflicted heavy losses during his three years in command, destroying or capturing sixteen men-of-war. By the end of the conflict the corsairs' forces had been halved.[67]

Herbert's success pushed Algiers into negotiating peace in 1682. Charles II was equally eager to end an expensive war he had never wanted. Over the course of five years, more than 153 British ships had been captured and more than 1,850 seamen enslaved. The crown had spent £300,000 on naval operations, and an estimate put the probable cost of ransoms at £275,000.[68] The consequences of the war extended beyond the economic. Seth Sothell, newly appointed governor of Carolina, was seized on his way to take up his post, while a Massachusetts official explained apologetically in 1681 that the colony could not send an agent to London because it could not find anyone suitable willing to serve. Its last agent had also been captured, and with the colony unable to pay his ransom his fate had proved a powerful deterrent. New York was later to launch public collections to redeem its own enslaved citizens.[69]

The treaty of 1682 made only modest changes to earlier settlements. It reaffirmed the requirement for ships to show a valid pass, and phased out the arrangement protecting those without one if most of the crew were British subjects. Searches were forbidden and, as before, only two corsairs were authorized to inspect a pass. Nothing was said about British sailors serving on the ships

[65] Fisher, *Barbary Legend*, 262–3; Pepys, *Catalogue*, iii.134, 152, 229–31, 241–2; TNA SP 71/2, fos.78, 159, 162, 203-v, 206, 211.

[66] Fisher, *Barbary Legend*, 263–4; Pepys, *Catalogue*, iv.454–5.

[67] TNA SP 71/2, fos.243-v, 247-v; HMC 71, *Finch*, ii.107, 124–5, v.816.

[68] *A List of Ships taken since July 1677 from his Majesties subjects, by the corsairs of Algiers* (1682). The list included five American ships—four from Boston or New England, and one from New York. A later memo put the number of ships at 157 and captives at 3,000: *Calendar of Treasury Papers, 1702–07*, 251.

[69] CSP Colonial, *America and West Indies, 1681–5*, 126; ibid., *1693–6*, 1743, 1998. For Sothell see Chapter 7.

of Algiers' enemies, implicitly conceding the corsairs' right to enslave them along with, in future, those on ships that lacked a valid pass. One significant article declared that the crown recognized no obligation to redeem captives taken during or before the war, and left owners free to decide whether or not to ransom them. This article created some dismay in Algiers, shattering the assumption that a treaty would bring ransom money flowing to owners. It dismayed the slaves still more, of course, and provoked criticism even within the British government. Possibly the intention was to send a message that war no longer guaranteed large-scale ransom money when it ended, which might make it less appealing in future. New redemption arrangements had been established the previous year, and the crown was content to work through these.[70]

Unlike its predecessors, the new treaty was to endure for more than a century. This owed much to the navy's successes. Herbert boasted with some justice that no force sent against Barbary had achieved so much, even though several had been larger.[71] It was far from clear at the time, however, that his treaty would last. The negotiations had been tough, and Herbert had to promise sweeteners and pledge to return fifty 'Turkish' slaves within three months. Moreover, it was concluded in the absence of the most powerful figure in Algiers, Babba Hassan, who was away on campaign. English merchants and officials warned that he strongly opposed the treaty and would undermine it on his return. Over the following months, it came very close to breakdown.[72] Its survival, paradoxically, owed much to the French. Louis XIV had resolved to crush the corsairs forever, and in 1682 and 1683 his fleets bombarded Algiers with explosive shells, inflicting massive destruction. Public fury led to Babba Hassan's overthrow and murder, and the British consul, greatly relieved, wrote home that trade would now be secure 'as long as they have war with France, which God continue'. Louis renewed the war in 1687, with more bombardments that left a third of the city in ruins, and Britain was again the beneficiary. Reluctant to contemplate war with both major naval powers, Algiers was infused with a hatred of France that was to endure for generations.[73]

The later 1680s saw Algerian corsairs hunting Dutch prizes in the English Channel and North Sea, but not molesting British shipping or goods. James II, acceding to the throne in 1685, confirmed Herbert's treaty. When bad weather drove an Algerian ship into Harwich, James authorized the payment of £446 to redeem five English slaves serving on board. Leaving them in bondage would have been a public scandal, but it is striking that they were ransomed rather than freed by force, and the king even ordered a supply of fresh victuals for the rest of the

---

[70] *Articles of Peace & Commerce between...Charles II...and Algiers* (1682); HMC 71, *Finch*, ii.170–4; TNA SP 71/2, fos. 288–289v; Fisher, *Barbary Legend*, 264–5; Chapter 7.

[71] TNA SP 71/2, f.247v.   [72] TNA SP 71/2, fos. 278-v, 288-9v, 294, 300-301v.

[73] Wolf, *Barbary Coast*, 243, 258–67; Gillian L Weiss, *Captives and Corsairs. France and Slavery in the Early Modern Mediterranean* (Stanford, CA, 2011), 72–5, 81–2; *The Present State of Algeir* (1682); TNA SP 71/2, fos. 304v-5.

corsairs' men. Preserving the recent peace was clearly his primary concern.[74] The corsairs were able to buy supplies in English ports, under the terms of the treaty, and they even sought permission to sell prizes in England, though this was refused. Captured Dutch ships with Barbary prize-crews soon became a familiar sight at Portsmouth—an embarrassing development for James. In 1687 he assured his Dutch son-in-law, William of Orange, that Algiers had now promised to keep its ships out of the Channel, but admitted that he could not be sure they would do so. He added wryly that if France forced Algiers' rulers to make peace, 'then of course they must fall out with me, though they have already war with you'.[75]

After the Glorious Revolution of 1688 William now ruled both Britain and the Netherlands, with Algiers paradoxically still at peace with one and at war with the other. The British, Dutch, and French were to be locked in conflict for most of the next twenty years, and Algiers was happy to see them fighting each other and competing for an offensive alliance. William and Mary authorized bribes of up to $10,000 to induce Algiers to break with France, but though the gifts were accepted, no alliance followed. British consuls warned that Herbert's treaty remained precarious. As they pointed out, Algiers respected treaties only when naval power was visible, and with the navy fully committed elsewhere this was no longer the case. Gunboat diplomacy counted for nothing without gunboats close at hand. In the event, the treaty survived because Algiers also had other preoccupations, waging wars against Tunis and Morocco. Slavery and redemptions remained an issue for several more years, with a trickle of new captives continuing to arrive— mainly sailors captured on foreign vessels or ships without a valid pass. In 1695, however, the consul reported proudly that no British slaves remained in Algiers.[76]

Relations with Tunis were usually friendly in the Restoration period, and Tripoli, the smallest and weakest of the regencies, rarely created problems. The major exception came in 1674 when a new ruler in Tripoli took offence that Charles II had not written to confirm the peace between the two states. Corsairs seized two English merchantmen—one said to be worth £30,000—to signal his displeasure, and the Levant Company called for action. Narbrough was instructed to demand satisfaction, if possible without triggering an open breach. That proved impossible, whereupon war broke out. Narbrough's force was modest, but a raid led by Lieutenant Cloudesley Shovell destroyed four ships in Tripoli's harbour, and several others were sunk at sea. The crown's primary concern was to dissuade Tripoli, and still more Algiers and Tunis, from assuming they could launch unprovoked attacks with impunity whenever they chose. Charles also wanted a peace that would be on 'much cheaper terms to the king' than Spragge's recent

[74] *Articles of Peace and Commerce . . . between James II . . . and Algiers* [on 5 April 1686] (1687); *Calendar of Treasury Books, 1685–9*, 964–5. William Bowtell organized both the ransoms and supplies.
[75] *Calendar of Treasury Books, 1685–9*, 1290–1; *CSPD 1686–7*, 142, 184, 204, 326; *CSPD 1687–9*, 5, 198.
[76] Wolf, *Barbary Coast*, chap. 12; Chapter 7.

treaty with Algiers.[77] He was delighted with the treaty signed in March 1676, in which Tripoli admitted responsibility for the war, agreed to free all British captives without the payment of ransoms, and promised to pay reparations of £18,000 in money, goods, and European slaves. These terms sent a powerful message, and the crown won prestige by liberating other European slaves. As icing on the cake, the humiliated dey fled, leaving his successor to confirm the terms on 1 May.[78] It was an easy triumph over a far weaker adversary.

Morocco and Moulay Ismail

Morocco presented a far greater challenge. Its major cities could not be bombarded from the sea, and its rulers commanded huge armies. Despite the damage they wreaked, Salé's corsairs played a relatively small role in Morocco's politics and economy. Salé itself was also secure from attack, with large warships unable to cross the sandbar at the mouth of its river. In its dealings with Morocco, the crown therefore had to rely primarily on diplomacy. After the Restoration, merchants such as Thomas Warren initially handled negotiations.[79] Warren was also attached to the embassy of Lord Henry Howard, appointed special ambassador to Sultan Mulay Rachid in 1669 to negotiate a comprehensive treaty. The mission proved abortive. The sultan refused to negotiate near Tangier, a British garrison, insisting that Howard come to Fez and travel by sea through Salé. He refused, fearing to be held hostage, and dismissed the sultan as an 'uncultivated tyrannical beast' and 'raving mad'.[80] Warren had been sent ahead to Fez, and over several months he painstakingly negotiated the redemption of forty-five slaves held at Salé, and more later. Howard commented that only Warren appeared able to deal with Mulay Rachid, adding that he had imbibed some of the sultan's own 'frenzy'. It was reported that Warren survived on three hours' sleep a night, and to 'drive off melancholy drinks and smokes tobacco all day long'. Such a regime took its toll, and he died at Fez in 1670.[81]

Morocco and Salé's corsairs remained a threat for many years. In 1676 Samuel Pepys grumbled that going to war was 'chargeable and fruitless', but peace deals rarely lasted long.[82] A generation later, an army of European slaves were said to be labouring on the sultan's vast building projects at Meknes, with several hundred Britons and North Americans among them. Sultan Moulay Ismail (1672–1727)

---

[77] Pepys, *Catalogue*, iii.17–18, 37–9, 48, 63–4, 121, 130–1; iv.97–8, 188–9, 211, 225, 300.

[78] Pepys, *Catalogue*, iii, pp. xiv–xvi; iv.300; *Articles of Peace and Commerce between Charles II and…Tripoli* (1676); Fisher, *Barbary Legend*, 266–8. Tripoli's similarly rash war with France in 1683–85 also ended in a humiliating peace: Weiss, *Captives and Corsairs*, 78–9.

[79] See Chapter 7.

[80] Rogers, *History*, 48–51; TNA SP 71/14, fos. 9-v, 26, 67–8; HMC 25, *Le Fleming*, 70.

[81] TNA SP 71/14, fos. 63–75; HMC 25, *Le Fleming*, 85; *CSPVen. 1669–70*, 86, 239.

[82] Pepys, *Catalogue*, iii.286, 294.

proved a tough and capricious negotiator, reneging on agreements and raising new demands at the last moment. Mohammed bin Hadou, the ambassador he sent to England in 1681, delivered a letter that was couched in extremely forthright terms. It damned the British occupation of Tangier as a 'scandal to us', and demanded an annual tribute if and when a treaty was agreed and ratified. The ambassador secured the release of Moorish captives held in Tangier in exchange for ransoming 130 English slaves in Meknes, at $200 each. Admiral Herbert had to buy Moorish slaves in Spain to make up the numbers required, only for Moulay Ismail to repudiate the treaty, accusing English merchants of trading with rebels in the south of his country. The corsairs continued their depredations, and the English remained enslaved. About fifty were eventually ransomed after England abandoned Tangier, but more remained, along with the slaves privately owned.[83]

Moulay Ismail regarded himself as equal or superior to any European ruler, and refused to conclude a peace unless a high-ranking envoy travelled to Meknes, with a large train and bearing rich gifts. Until then, he was happy to allow his governors in Salé and Tetuan to negotiate short truces in return for gunpowder and other military supplies. Envoys were frustrated by constantly changing demands, and suspected officials of exploiting the fact that Ismail was illiterate. Diplomatic correspondence was often intercepted and concealed, or misrepresented, with officials allegedly choosing to 'read him what they please' and inventing new demands in his name—in effect, bribes. One envoy resorted to sending messages via contacts in Algiers to circumvent such tricks.[84]

William III, Anne, and George I all struggled to secure a lasting peace and the release of British captives. It was impossible to attack the corsairs' base, and their light, fast men-of-war found it easy to snap up small merchantmen and evade naval warships. As officers and diplomats pointed out, capturing a few men-of-war 'crammed full of men not worth the keeping' would in any case never be decisive.[85] A lasting peace would require money and patient diplomacy as well as naval pressure. Moulay Ismail was willing, in principle, to negotiate, and sent several unofficial agents to take soundings. In 1691 a Jewish envoy contacted William III in the Netherlands over the possible redemption of 350 English slaves, and an English slave serving in Ismail's army was allowed to carry a message and take back the king's reply.[86] Another envoy dragged out talks interminably, and was eventually dismissed as 'little better than a cheat'.[87] Ismail, equally dissatisfied, responded in 1698 by sending a bizarre letter to the exiled James II, urging him to convert to Islam and offering to help him recover his throne.[88]

---

[83] TNA SP 71/14, f.183-4v; *A Letter sent by the Emperor of Morocco and King of Fez to his Majesty of Great Britain, and delivered by his ambassador in January 1681* (1682); Rogers, *History*, 52–64; Milton, *White Gold*, 38–48.

[84] TNA SP 71/16, fos. 106-7v, 143.   [85] TNA SP 71/16, fos. 54-5v.

[86] *CSPD 1689–90*, 469, 498, *CSPD 1690–1*, 427; TNA SP 71/14, fos. 223-v, 234–5, 236v.

[87] HMC 71, *Finch*, iv.33, 42; HMC 78, *Hastings*, ii.341.   [88] Rogers, *History*, 66–7.

Successive commanders in the Mediterranean were instructed to explore the possibility of reaching an accord. The level of ransom demands had risen steeply, with £150 now generally expected for every slave. Moulay Ismail demanded payment in kind, along with 'presents' and the release of Moorish captives. In 1698–99, commanders were urged to capture as many Moors as possible to offer in exchange, to reduce the cost of redemptions.[89] Captain George Delaval, deputed to negotiate with the alcaid of Tetuan, complained that Ismail was demanding a 'present' of $68,000.[90] But in October 1699, Moulay Ismail wrote to William III that terms had finally been agreed: 100 gunlocks and six barrels of gunpowder for each British slave, and with one Moorish captive to be exchanged for every two Britons. No Britons would be released unless these terms were met.[91] Delaval returned to Morocco late in 1700, on a ship packed so full with gunpowder that he feared it could explode at any moment. Further negotiations secured a deal for the release of 276 captives, with 10,000 pieces of eight to be paid in England to buy whatever goods Ismail specified. By November 1701, Delaval had unloaded sufficient powder to secure the release of 110 slaves. Another 500 barrels remained on board, but the alcaid refused to free any more without the exchange of some Moorish slaves, on which the sultan was insisting. Having none in his possession, Delaval had to sail to Cadiz and buy twenty-eight surreptitiously, as many as he could procure. After more wrangling, the alcaid agreed to free another forty slaves, with the thirty-four left in Meknes all that now remained alive.[92] The government was delighted with Delaval's success. The archbishop of Canterbury arranged for the liberated slaves to parade through London, to show that the public's charity had been well employed. The final thirty-four were eventually freed in 1705, on the same terms, by the merchant and envoy Jezreel Jones.[93]

The crown hoped that Delaval's truce might lead to a lasting peace, and perhaps also draw Morocco into its war with France. For his part, Moulay Ismail was hoping for British support against the Spanish enclave at Ceuta.[94] When neither materialized, the truce collapsed after only three years and the corsairs resumed their attacks. Conflict and fruitless diplomacy continued throughout Anne's reign, and beyond. Vice-Admiral George Paddon repeatedly explained that to secure a real peace and free the slaves, whose numbers had swollen once more, he would need to go in person to Meknes. The government feared he would be held there, but eventually consented. In 1714 Paddon wrote home, reporting that he had negotiated a peace far superior to the earlier 'paltry truces', and had secured the release of sixty-nine captives. He escorted them to Tetuan to take ship, only to be told that the sultan had changed his mind, and that a further $14,000 was now

[89] TNA SP 71/14, f.236v; *CSPD 1698*, 384–5; *CSPD 1699–1700*, 316–17.
[90] TNA SP 71/14, fos. 284, 302.   [91] TNA SP 71/14, f.305.
[92] *CSPD 1700–1702*, 57, 196–7, 277, 433–6, 466–7.
[93] Rogers, *History*, 67–72; TNA SP 71/21, fos. 7-v; *CSPD 1705–6*, 161.
[94] *CSPD 1703–4*, 125, 179, 188–9; Rogers, *History*, 71–3.

required before they could leave. Paddon suspected this was a fabrication but promised $10,000 to follow, and they were eventually allowed to embark.[95]

In the event, Paddon's 'lasting peace' collapsed within a year, and the cycle of attacks, enslavement, and interminable negotiations resumed once more. A memorandum in 1717 spelled out that peace would require another embassy to Meknes, sufficiently lavish to satisfy Moulay Ismail's vanity, and taking presents worth $19,000. Of this, $10,000 would be to honour Paddon's promise, with $3,000 as a gift to the sultan, and $6,000 to bribe his ministers. Although expensive, it was argued, this would be far cheaper than continuing war, and if the crown baulked at the cost 'it may be defrayed as usual by a collection by brief'.[96] Instead, the conflict dragged on. Between 1715 and 1721 the corsairs captured another thirty-nine ships and almost 400 men (and one woman), of whom at least seventy-one died in captivity.[97] A small-scale mission to Meknes in 1717 proved disastrous, with the sultan deeply offended by the envoy's arrogant manner.[98] Only in 1720–21 did a far grander embassy finally secure a treaty and free the slaves. Commodore Charles Stewart, patient and adroit, brought rich gifts for the sultan and more than fifty members of his entourage, ranging from leading officials and 'queens' (including his English wife) to his 'chief cut-throat' and umbrella-carrier. Stewart negotiated ransom terms, and when Ismail abruptly raised new demands, persuaded one of the royal wives (probably Balqees) to intercede before hastening away with the 291 British and North American slaves still alive.[99]

Stewart's treaty was not quite the end of Salé's part in the story of Britons enslaved. When the *Inspector*, a privateer, was wrecked in 1746 in Tangier Bay, eighty-seven survivors were enslaved. Some died in captivity, others apostatized, and most of those redeemed did not reach home until 1751.[100] Again, the renewed peace did not hold long. In 1755 an English merchant was seized and executed, and in 1758 the sultan imprisoned the British consul, James Read, and threatened to execute him too. In despair, Read committed suicide. The number of British slaves swelled once more to 350, redeemed two years later for $200,000 when peace was renewed again.[101]

Britain's naval superiority thus proved far less decisive against Morocco than against the regencies. Negotiations were conducted on Moroccan terms, and the British crown proved remarkably conciliatory in the face of repeated affronts. Sir

---

[95] TNA SP 71/16, fos. 109v, 133–6, 143–55; Rogers, *History*, 82–3.

[96] TNA SP 71/16, fos. 270–1.

[97] Nabil I. Matar, 'British Captives in Salé (1721), in Stefan Hanss and Juliane Schiel, eds., *Mediterranean Slavery Revisited (500–1800)*, (Zurich, 2014), 520–37.

[98] Milton, *White Gold*, 115–17; TNA SP 71/16, fos. 291-v, 300–1.

[99] Milton, *White Gold*, 173–97.

[100] Thomas Troughton, *Barbarian Cruelty; or an Accurate and Impartial Narrative* (1751).

[101] Rogers, *History*, 90–103; Linda Colley, *Captives. Britain, Empire and the World, 1600–1850* (2002), 66–72.

Henry Sheeres, writing in 1679, hoped that with Tangier as a naval base, Britain would soon be able to make peace with Morocco 'upon equal terms. For to buy a peace (as hath been the practice hitherto) is so mean and dishonourable, and gives them so much contempt for our friendship, that it is not to be supported'.[102] Geography, however, limited what naval pressure could achieve, while Britain's need for supplies from Morocco continued to make conciliation the only realistic approach. The garrison at Gibraltar depended heavily on Morocco for supplies, a crucial factor that enabled Moulay Ismail and his successors to negotiate from strength. Years later, a commentator looking back on the War of Spanish Succession reflected that 'our armies, and those of our allies, in Spain must infallibly have perished, had they not been supported from Barbary'.[103]

The navy had played a decisive role, nonetheless, in curbing the Barbary corsairs, from Rainborough's success at Salé to the exploits of Spragge, Beach, and Herbert. Armed convoys had also proved effective in protecting commerce. By 1700, naval power had ended the threat from Algiers, Tunis, and Tripoli. Britain was emerging as the dominant maritime power, and with Gibraltar and Minorca, ceded under the Treaty of Utrecht (1713), now possessed bases from which its fleets could patrol the seas. By contrast, the Dutch, now declining as a naval power, discovered that without its leverage they were treated by Algiers with growing contempt, and pushed into what has been labelled a 'tributary relationship' to protect their shipping.[104] The corsairs continued to inflict damage on Spanish, Italian, Portuguese, German, and Scandinavian shipping throughout much of the eighteenth century, further underlining the importance of naval power.[105] If Morocco exposed the limitations of that power, the British (and French) navies proved indispensable and eventually decisive in curbing the corsairs in all three regencies.

---

[102] Sir Henry Sheeres, *A Discourse touching Tanger* (1680), 24–6. For Tangier and its disappointments see Colley, *Captives*, 23–41.

[103] Rogers, *History*, 90–103; Colley, *Captives*, 66–72; *Several Voyages to Barbary* (1736), 135.

[104] Erica Heinsen-Roach, *Consuls and Captives. Dutch North African Diplomacy in the Early Modern Mediterranean* (Woodbridge, 2019), 174 and 159–78 *passim*.

[105] Peter Earle, *Corsairs of Malta and Barbary* (1970), 265–6; Ellen G. Friedman, *Spanish Captives in North Africa in the Early Modern Age* (Madison, WI, 1983), 29–31, 126; Wolf, *Barbary Coast*, chaps. 14–15; Jamieson, *Lords of the Sea*, 178–9. On Germany and Scandinavia see the essays by Magnus Ressel and Joachim Östlund in *Historical Social Research*, 35 (2010).

Conclusion

Robinson Crusoe, the eponymous hero of Defoe's novel, had spent two wretched years as a slave in Salé before his more familiar trials as a castaway. When he was eventually rescued and carried to Brazil, he decided to embark on a new career—as a slave-trader.[1] Defoe packed his novel with moralizing advice, and today's readers might wonder why Crusoe's experience at Salé did not open his eyes to the evils of slavery itself. He was far from alone. Real people who had endured slavery, and in some cases had told their stories in print, also failed to condemn slavery and the slave trade.

Almost no-one saw the sufferings of European slaves in Barbary as an argument against the African slave trade, despite some contemporaries being familiar with both. Thomas Phelps, for example, informed readers that his sufferings in Morocco had prompted 'a reflection on captivity and slavery'. Contrasting his former miseries with the joys of freedom regained, he insisted that 'slavery is so strange a condition to England, that to touch its soil is ipso facto manumission'. Phelps had also witnessed slavery in the Americas, but his reflections did not go beyond rejoicing in the liberty that Englishmen enjoyed. Similarly, the minister Richard Mayo could denounce slave-drivers in the American plantations as 'more savage than the negroes themselves', without questioning the institution itself.[2]

A few individuals did speak out. Charles Gildon published a stinging attack on Defoe's novel, marvelling that Crusoe had suffered enslavement and 'yet he neither then nor afterwards found any check of conscience in that infamous trade of buying and selling of men for slaves'.[3] A century earlier, John Harrison, envoy to Morocco, had been a rare early critic of the enslavement of Moors, Britons, and other Europeans alike. Denouncing a secret plan to ship Moorish captives to Italy, to be sold into slavery, he declared that to safeguard the honour of the English crown and nation it was imperative 'not to make slaves, nor buy or sell slaves. Condemned by the Law of God, Exod. 21.' During the war with Spain in the late 1620s, Harrison favoured an alliance with Morocco, but he recoiled from a plan that would have seen a Spanish garrison overrun and enslaved by the Moors. Whether his principled rejection of slavery extended to black Africans is

---

[1] Daniel Defoe, *The Life and Strange Surprizing Adventures of Robinson Crusoe* (1719), 19–36, 51.

[2] *Phelps*, 'Preface to the Reader', 8–9; Richard Mayo, *A Present for Servants . . . especially in country parishes* (1693), 60–1.

[3] Charles Gildon, *The Life and Strange Surprizing Adventures of Mr D—de F—, of London, Hosier* (1719), 14.

British Slaves and Barbary Corsairs, 1580–1750. Bernard Capp, Oxford University Press. © Bernard Capp 2022.
DOI: 10.1093/oso/9780192857378.003.0010

less clear.[4] A few years later the slave William Okeley, who shared Harrison's strong puritan faith, declared that 'Man is too noble a creature to be made subject to a deed of bargain and sale'. Yet this enlightened position comes in the context of his own internal debate on whether it would be 'downright theft' for him to escape from his owner. Early modern attitudes were full of contradictions.[5]

Very few contemporaries saw slavery as intrinsically evil. It had existed around the globe and throughout history. Educated Europeans turned to the Bible and classical Greece and Rome for their moral compass, and found slavery endemic in each. The fact that slavery had existed for centuries throughout the Mediterranean world also helped normalize the rapidly growing Atlantic slave trade. Moreover, paralleling that trade, an estimated 7,000 sub-Saharan slaves were being sold annually in the seventeenth century to Arab and other Muslim lands.[6] The British, like other nations and their rulers, felt strongly about the plight of their compatriots but cared little about slaves from other lands.

The British crown had little interest in acquiring Moorish slaves, for galleys had proved unsuitable in northern seas. But Charles II was happy for commanders to sell their captives into slavery in Spain or Italy, and when the crown acquired two galleys to operate from Tangier, in the 1670s, it had no qualms about using Moorish slaves as oarsmen. During the short war with Tripoli in 1675–76, it even enslaved some Greek seamen captured on a Tripolitanian vessel. By accepting that employment, it argued, they had shown themselves only 'pretended Christians'.[7] Consuls and merchants in Barbary needed to build working relationships with its rulers, officials, and leading *reis*, and accepted slavery as an integral part of that world. How far some came to internalize its values is evident when we find Robert Cole declaring that it was 'foul' for British ships to help slaves escape— a view shared by Charles II and his government. Helping runaways could jeopardize commerce, a far higher priority. The crown was always anxious to avoid damaging relations with the Ottoman Empire and the lucrative Levant trade. Morocco's profitable trade and large army inspired a similar response, and the ambassadors it sent to England in 1589, 1600, 1637, and 1681–82 were treated with great respect.[8]

The expansion of English trade into the Mediterranean in the later sixteenth century had made relations with Barbary a pressing issue. The corsairs soon posed

---

[4] Castries et al., eds., *Sources inédites*, iii.36, 44–5. See my 'John Harrison, envoy to Morocco', forthcoming.

[5] *Okeley*, 46–7.

[6] David Eltis and Stanley L. Engerman, eds., *The Cambridge World History of Slavery. 3: 1420–1804* (Cambridge, 2011). An estimated 11.75 million sub-Saharan slaves were exported to Muslim lands between 670 and 1900: ibid., 51–2; Linda Colley, *Captives. Britain, Empire and the World, 1600–1850* (2002), 64.

[7] Pepys, *Catalogue*, iii.114, 161, 288, 314, 348; iv.187, 218–19; G. E. Aylmer, 'Slavery under Charles II: The Mediterranean and Tangier', *English Historical Review*, 114 (April 1999), 378–88.

[8] Jerry Brotton, *This Orient Isle. Elizabethan England and the Islamic World* (2016); Jamil Abun-Nasr, *A History of the Maghrib in the Islamic Period* (Cambridge, 1987), 231.

a significant threat to English commerce, and one that grew dramatically in the early seventeenth century, with British and Dutch renegades joining the corsairs' ranks and preying on their own countrymen. Large numbers of British mariners were captured and sold into slavery, while many others chose to join the adventurers seeking their fortunes there. A significant minority of both groups subsequently abjured their faith and accepted Islam. Some were enticed by promises of material gain, while many demoralized captives, resigned to their fate, were merely hoping to alleviate their miserable situation. 'Turning Turk', whatever the (often mixed) motives, represented an act of social and cultural accommodation or, from a different perspective, of betrayal. By raising questions of faith, identity, and allegiance, it made the plight of slaves in Barbary a far more sensitive issue than the fate of captives in Flemish, French, or Spanish gaols. For some, apostasy remained an empty performance, while for others it could develop into a firm commitment to a new identity. In many cases, as we have seen, identities proved hybrid, multilayered, and malleable in the light of changing circumstances.

Barbary and its corsairs, renegades, and captives soon came to figure prominently among the concerns of England's politicians and public alike. Jacobean mock-battles and the patriotic accounts of heroic shipmasters offered comforting if illusory messages of reassurance. London's theatres reflected broader concerns over identity in plays that brought Moors, renegades, and captives onto the stage. The plays of Shakespeare and his contemporaries generally depicted Moors in stereotypical terms as innately cruel and treacherous.[9] In *A Christian turn'd Turke* (1612), Robert Daborne addressed issues of religious and political allegiance through a graphic if massively inaccurate account of Captain Ward and his life in Tunis. Philip Massinger's *The Renegado* (*c*.1625), which focused on elite Venetian captives and an Italian renegade, included among its *dramatis personae* an enslaved English eunuch in the seraglio at Tunis. It ends with both eunuch and renegade repudiating their adopted Moorish identities and escaping back to Christendom. Barbary possessed considerable appeal for footloose seamen and adventurers in the early seventeenth century, but playwrights reflected and reinforced popular attitudes that were more fearful and suspicious. A popular ballad on Captain Ward, 'the famous pirate', depicted its hero, or antihero, as a brave but wicked man.[10] Seafaring communities, in London and elsewhere, cared primarily about the plight of the captives and their families, and the dangers that all mariners now faced. Letters and petitions from Barbary always focused on the wretched conditions of the slaves.

---

[9] Nabil Matar, *Britain and Barbary, 1589–1689* (Gainesville, FL, 2005), 12–37; Daniel J. Vitkus, *Turning Turk. English Theater and the Multicultural Mediterranean, 1570–1630* (Basingstoke 2003); Brotton, *This Orient Isle*, 191–7, 200–5, 277–97.

[10] *The Seamans Song of Captain Ward the famous Pyrate* (n.d., 1658–64).

The plight of the slaves in Barbary eventually brought the issue of slavery itself into public discourse. After the civil war, images of Barbary surfaced in debates on England's own society and government. At the Putney debates between army grandees and agitators in 1647, John Wildman declared, 'Our case is to be considered thus, that we have been under slavery. That's acknowledged by all.' Colonel Thomas Rainborough agreed, claiming that for centuries most Englishmen had suffered under the yoke of oppressive landowners. Without sweeping changes, he argued, the soldier would have fought merely 'to enslave himself' in perpetuity.[11] Rainborough had encountered slavery in its literal sense too, for ten years earlier he had accompanied his father on the Salé expedition. Radicals who employed images of slavery were generally thinking primarily of the 'Norman Yoke', supposedly imposed by William the Conqueror, but many also referenced Barbary. In *A Remonstrance of Many Thousand Citizens* (1646), the Leveller Richard Overton contrasted Parliament's zeal to free slaves in Algiers ('at the charge of others', he added drily) with its indifference towards poor 'captives' languishing in debtors' prisons in England. He claimed too that the plight of men pressed into the army differed little from that of a 'galley-slave in Turkey or Argiers'.[12] Gerrard Winstanley, the Digger, mocked hypocritical 'Gospel-professing lords of manors' by likening them to 'Turkish bashaws' tyrannizing over their 'poor enforced slaves'.[13]

Similar images surfaced again in political discourse a generation later, in the fevered atmosphere of the Popish Plot and succession crisis. A lengthy series of fictitious letters 'revealed' the unfolding story of a conspiracy by 'Mahometans' (Catholics) in league with 'Algerines' (the French) to capture a ship at Leghorn (Livorno), kill its captain, install the renegade lieutenant in his place, seize the cargo, and enslave the crew. The elaborate unfolding story was not hard to decode. The captain represented Charles II, the renegade lieutenant his Catholic brother, the duke of York. A grasping Algerian enchantress stood for the king's French mistress, the duchess of Portsmouth, the corrupt purser was the king's minister Danby, and so on. The ship's crew were the English people. Clothing popery in the frightening garb of Barbary slavery gave readers a sense of the horrors they might soon be facing at home.[14]

While these political squibs would have been seen mainly by Londoners, images of Barbary resonated more widely. In 1693 the Presbyterian minister Richard Mayo deployed them in his *Present for Servants . . . especially in country parishes*. They should be content with their lot, he told them, for they were fortunate indeed compared to the poor slaves in Algiers, beaten for the slightest fault and surviving

---

[11] C. H. Firth, ed., *The Clarke Papers*, Camden Society, New Series (1892–1901), i.318, 320, 325.

[12] Richard Overton, *A Remonstrance of Many Thousand Citizens* (1646), 15–16.

[13] Gerrard Winstanley, *A New-Yeers Gift* (1650), 17.

[14] *From aboard the Van-herring. A Letter from Legorn* (1679). The series ran to sixteen items, 1679–81.

on mouldy bread and the 'broth of camels, worn out with work, like themselves'. Mayo mentioned in passing the sufferings of black slaves in America, but clearly saw Algiers as the more powerful image.[15] Images of Barbary and captivity surfaced too in many other contexts. A misogynist wit claimed, for example, that marriage kept men in shackles, enduring lives worse than those of galley-slaves in Algiers. The preacher Thomas Lye found a very different parallel. In this life, he explained in a funeral sermon, the godly were 'usually the world's galley-slaves: this lower orb is to them, but a larger kind of Tunis or Argier, but they are manumitted there [in heaven]; their death ransoms them.'[16]

The popularity of such images makes it all the more remarkable to find several commentators advocating enslavement as a punishment for English criminals. In 1618 Sir Henry Mainwaring recommended that convicted pirates should be enslaved for life. More striking is to find Gerrard Winstanley, who denounced the figurative slavery of the poor, proposing slavery as the appropriate penalty for those transgressing the laws of his communist utopia. Richard Overton was similarly willing to propose 'perpetual servitude' for persistent thieves, who would also be branded in the face and dressed in distinctive clothing.[17] To find even radicals propounding such views underlines the fact that most contemporaries viewed slavery as simply part of the natural order.

Exploring the lives of real slaves in Barbary has been a central concern of this book. Their circumstances have been disputed for centuries, and the debates have occasionally descended into farce. *Several Voyages to Barbary* (1736) included a recent account by the French priest Philémon de La Motte, painting a bleak picture of Moorish brutality and Christian suffering. But the work's anonymous editor and translator provided a running set of footnotes in which he dismissed this picture as false and absurd, and insisted that captives were in fact well treated and lived comfortable lives. It was French Catholics who practised barbaric cruelty, he averred, in their savage repression of Huguenots.[18] The evidence presented throughout this book points to a less simplistic and polarized conclusion. There was no 'typical' experience of enslavement in Barbary, and the evidence reveals enormous diversity. Contemporaries agreed that galley slaves endured miserable lives, and that slaves owned by rulers generally fared worse than those bought by private individuals. Beyond that, as former captives and other writers made clear, a slave's life was shaped by a range of factors such as social and economic status, gender, skills, age, health, and behaviour. The

---

[15] Mayo, *A Present*, 60–2.

[16] *The Batchellors Answer to the Maids Complaint* (1675), 5; Thomas Lye, *The King of Terrors Metamorphosis* (1660), 9.

[17] Keith Thomas, *In Pursuit of Civility* (New Haven, 2018), 240–4; G. E. Manwaring and W. G. Perrin, eds., *The Life and Works of Sir Henry Mainwaring*, Navy Records Society, 54, 56 (1920–22), ii.18–19; Gerrard Winstanley, *The Law of Freedom in a Platform* (1652), 86–7; Richard Overton, *An Appeale from the degenerate Representative Body the Commons of England* (1647), 36–7.

[18] *Several Voyages to Barbary* (1736), 44–8 and *passim*.

slave-owner's own character and circumstances were significant too. The interplay of these variables explains the huge diversity that contemporary accounts reveal.[19]

The Barbary corsairs posed a threat to states as well as to vulnerable mariners. The most basic purpose of government is to provide security for its people, and any state that appeared unable to protect trade, free captives, and prevent raids ashore stood to forfeit credit and legitimacy. No early modern state had the military might to conquer Barbary or the naval strength to crush the corsairs at sea. Yet rulers shrank from the obvious alternatives, ransoming captives or buying off the corsairs. Any state that paid 'pirates' to free or spare its own subjects would inevitably lose honour, while providing the corsairs with a guaranteed flow of ransom or protection money would enable them to expand their operations still further. These were intractable problems with no easy solutions.

The early Stuarts had a poor record in addressing these challenges. The abortive expedition against Algiers in 1620 was politically damaging, while the stream of petitions and appeals from captives, families, merchants, and local magistrates demonstrated the political cost of failing to find an alternative solution. By undermining royal authority, it has been argued, it even helped bring about the civil war.[20] The crown exploited to the full Rainborough's expedition against Salé in 1637, but his success proved insufficient to change the public's verdict. Complaints surfaced as soon as Parliament met in 1640. In November, Edmund Waller, a future royalist, damned the king's Ship Money levies as oppressive and futile, telling the Commons sarcastically that 'it doth evidently appear that to make us slaves at home is not the way to keep us from being made slaves abroad'. A year later the Grand Remonstrance repeated the charge.[21]

The crown accepted its moral obligation to liberate its subjects and curb the corsair threat, and experimented, like its neighbours, with a range of methods to achieve these goals. In the absence of any equivalent to the continental religious orders, it had to devise other ways to raise funds and organize redemptions. In 1624 it facilitated charitable collections throughout England and Wales, using the machinery of the Established Church, and created a new body to disburse the funds, with merchants and consuls acting as intermediaries in Barbary. In this hybrid arrangement the crown was involved only at one remove and without any drain on the Treasury. This new mechanism was at least as good as any on the continent, but Charles I failed to maintain it, leaving individuals to negotiate their own redemptions, if they could, or endure potentially lifelong enslavement. Under the Long Parliament and then Cromwell, the state became far more directly

[19] Joseph Morgan, *A Compleat History of the Piratical States of Barbary* (1750), 363.

[20] Nabil Matar, 'The Barbary Corsairs, King Charles and the Civil War', *The Seventeenth Century*, 16 (2001), 239–58.

[21] John Rushworth, *Historical Collections* (1721), iii, Nov. 1640 (accessed via British History Online); S. R. Gardiner, ed., *Constitutional Documents of the Puritan Revolution, 1625–1660* (Oxford, 1906), 211.

involved. It raised substantial funds for ransoms through the new Algiers duty—a more efficient and reliable mechanism—and used its expanded navy to exert direct pressure on Barbary. The Restoration monarchy abandoned the Algiers duty, reviving instead the Jacobean 'general briefs', but it followed Cromwell in employing the navy against Barbary, both at sea and in ransom negotiations, and with increasing effect.

In many respects, British practices matched a common European pattern. Most rulers expected ransom money to be raised by charitable collections organized by religious orders or local magistrates. England was a more centralized state than most, and the machinery of its Established Church enabled money to be collected speedily and nationwide whenever the crown issued a 'general brief'. That was beyond the capacity of the religious orders. Except in 1662, the Church did not participate in the negotiation of redemptions, generally handled by merchant intermediaries and consuls. If the British record was patchy, so too were continental arrangements. In Spain, the Mercedorians focused on the wealthier captives, whose families were also expected to contribute, and on soldiers, the crown's priority. Many years often elapsed between missions and, overall, more Spanish captives were freed by slave-brokers than by the religious orders. Large numbers of poorer captives were never freed.[22] In the later seventeenth century, the British may well have been more successful than other governments in liberating poorer slaves in the regencies. Like French monarchs, the crown also came to recognize the propaganda value of demonstrating its power and its benevolence, in curbing the corsairs and liberating their captives. The processions to celebrate Rainborough's triumph in 1637 were followed, later in the period, by services in St Paul's. One writer boasted in 1736 that while Britain might not have religious orders dedicated to redemptions, it had something far superior: the intervention and bounty of its powerful kings.[23]

The Barbary corsairs posed a threat to all European trading nations which, in theory, could have combined against them. In practice, co-operation proved impossible, with operations against Barbary scaled down or abandoned whenever war broke out in Europe. Rivalry between the maritime powers ensured, moreover, that British policy on Barbary was always heavily influenced by relations with France, Spain, and the Netherlands, and by Barbary's relations with them. The Stuarts hoped to provoke conflict between Barbary and their enemies, to their own advantage, and European rivals did the same. As they all recognized, Barbary could not afford to have either war or peace with all the major maritime powers at the same time. Their policies owed almost nothing to religious considerations.

---

[22] Daniel Hershenzon *The Captive Sea: Slavery, Communication, and Commerce in Early Modern Spain and the Mediterranean* (Philadelphia, 2019), chap. 2; Ellen G. Friedman, *Spanish Captives in North Africa in the Early Modern Age* (Madison, WI, 1983), chaps. 6–8.
[23] *Several Voyages*, 142.

Elizabeth had fostered friendly ties with Morocco against Spain, their common enemy, and in the late 1620s some again urged a Moroccan alliance. The end of the century saw similar hopes for co-operation against France. Consuls occasionally referred to 'Christendom' and 'the Christian shore', but instead of displaying a sense of Christian solidarity, they did their best to sow discord between Barbary and their European rivals. In 1702 Thomas Baker urged Algiers to break with France and enslave all the Frenchmen it could seize, promising that the British navy could ensure it was not 'insulted' by French attacks. His successor, Robert Cole, urged Algiers to join in humbling the pride of France, the 'common disturber of Europe'.[24] French and Dutch consuls behaved in similar fashion.[25]

Geographical factors, however, made Britain's experience distinctive in some other respects. Distance rendered it impossible for the corsairs to match the scale or frequency of their devastating raids on the coasts of Spain and Italy. Similarly, the huge cost of mounting distant expeditions meant that only from the 1650s did England possess the resources and will to despatch fleets to the Mediterranean on a regular basis. By the later seventeenth century, the naval strength of Venice, Florence, and Malta was in steep decline, while the Dutch were now paying tribute money to safeguard their commerce. By contrast, Britain and France were prepared to deploy their growing naval might, and did so with increasing effect.

In many ways, the circumstances of the slaves themselves saw less change. Capture always remained a traumatic experience, while life in slavery was humiliating, insecure, and often harsh. But the possibility of redemption improved significantly over the period, as the state became increasingly involved in the raising of ransom money and coordinating arrangements. In the early seventeenth century, more slaves died in captivity than returned home; in the later part of the century, most in the regencies were eventually redeemed. By the restoration of Charles II in 1660, Tunisian corsairs no longer posed a threat to British ships and sailors; by his death in 1685, Algiers too had signed a treaty which, unlike its predecessors, proved lasting. Only Morocco remained a running sore for another generation.

The letters that survive from slaves and the petitions organized by their families paint a horrific picture of the misery of captivity in Barbary. That was clearly not the whole story. Several former slaves left more balanced accounts acknowledging they had found kind as well as cruel owners. William Okeley's final owner treated him so well that he fretted it might even be sinful to deprive him of his property by escaping. Yet, he reflected, a slave remained a slave, even when his chains were made of gold. For Okeley, as for most captives, the longing for freedom and home proved irresistible.

---

[24] TNA SP 71/4, fos. 45–6, 58.
[25] Gillian L Weiss, *Captives and Corsairs. France and Slavery in the Early Modern Mediterranean* (Stanford, CA, 2011); Erica Heinsen-Roach, *Consuls and Captives. Dutch North African Diplomacy in the Early Modern Mediterranean* (Woodbridge, 2019).

Bibliography

Manuscript Sources

British Library (BL)
Add. MS 46412
MS Sloane 2755
MS Sloane 3494

The National Archives, Kew (TNA)
SP 16 State Papers, Domestic Charles I
SP 18 State Papers, Domestic, Interregnum
SP 29 State Papers, Domestic, Charles II
SP 71/1–4 State Papers, Algiers
SP 71/12, 14, 16, 21 State Papers, Morocco
SP 71/26 State Papers, Tunis

Primary Printed Sources

Abbott, W. C., ed., *The Writings and Speeches of Oliver Cromwell* (Oxford, 1937–47).
Acts of the Privy Council, 1578–1631.
An Account of what captives hath been freed since the 14th of December Anno Dom. 1647 (1647).
Addison, Lancelot, *The Present State of the Jews (more particularly relating to those in Barbary)* (1675).
Anderson, Gilbert, *All Praise and Glory be given to God alone* (1680).
Anderson, R. C., ed., *The Journal of Edward Mountagu, First Earl of Sandwich*, Navy Records Society, 64 (1929).
Anderson, R. C., ed., *The Journals of Sir Thomas Allin 1660–1678*, Navy Records Society, 79–80 (1939–40).
Apostacy punish'd: or, a new poem on the deserved death of Jonas Rowland, the renegado (1682).
The Arrival and Intertainements of the Embassador, Alkaid Jaurar Ben Abdella (1637).
Articles of Peace between his Sacred Majesty, Charles the II, and ... Algiers (1664).
Articles of Peace ... between Charles II and Algiers (1672).
Articles of Peace & Commerce between ... Charles II ... and Algiers (1682).
Articles of Peace and Commerce between Charles II and ... Tripoli (1676).
Articles of Peace and Commerce ... between James II ... and Algiers [on 5 April 1686] (1687).
Auchterlonie, Paul, ed., *Encountering Islam. Joseph Pitts: an English Slave in 17th –Century Algiers and Mecca* (2012).
Bacon, Francis, *Certaine Miscellany Works of the Right Honourable Francis Lo. Verulam* (1629).
Baltharpe, John, *The Straights Voyage or, St Davids Poem* (1671).
Barker, Andrew, *A True and Certaine Report of the Beginning, Proceedings, and Overthrowes ... of Captains Ward and Danseker* (1609).

The Batchellors Answer to the Maids Complaint (1675).

Bates Harbin, E. H., ed., *Quarter Sessions Records for the County of Somerset, 1646–1660*, Somerset Record Society, 28 (1912).

Bent, J. Theodore, ed., *Early Voyages and Travels in the Levant. The Diary of Master Thomas Dallam, 1599–1600*, Hakluyt Society, 87 (1893; reprinted 2016).

Berriman, William, *The great Blessing of Redemption from Captivity* (1722).

Bion, John, *An Account of the Torments the French Protestants Endure aboard Galleys* (1708).

Birch, T., ed., *A Collection of the State Papers of John Thurloe* (1742).

Blount, Henry, *A Voyage into the Levant* (1636).

Boothhouse, Samuel, *A Brief Remonstrance of Several National Injuries and Indignities* (1653).

Boreman, Robert, *A Mirrour of Christianity . . . or . . . the Life and Death of . . . Lady Alice, Duchess Duddeley* (1669).

Botelho, L. A., ed., *Churchwardens' Accounts of Cratfield 1640–1660*, Suffolk Records Society, 42 (1999).

Bradford, William, *Of Plymouth Plantation, 1620–1647*, ed. S. E. Morison (New York, 1952).

Braithwaite, John, *The History of the Revolutions in the Empire of Morocco* (1729).

Brooks, Francis, *Barbarian Cruelty* (1693).

Bruce, J. ed., *Journal of a Voyage into the Mediterranean by Sir Kenelm Digby, AD 1628*, Camden Society, Old Series, 96 (1868).

(Button, John), *Algiers Voyage [in a Iournall or Briefe Reportary of all occurents]* (1621).

Calendar of State Papers Colonial, America and West Indies.

Calendar of State Papers, Colonial, East Indies.

Calendar of State Papers, Domestic.

Calendar of State Papers, Foreign.

Calendar of State Papers, Ireland.

Calendar of Documents relating to Scotland, 1509–85.

Calendar of State Papers, Venice.

Calendar of Treasury Books, 1660–1714.

Calendar of Treasury Papers, 1556/7–1707.

Carleill, Christopher, *A breef and sommarie discourse vpon the Entended Voyage* (1583).

Cartwright, Francis *The Life, Confession, and Heartie Repentance of Francis Cartwright, Gentleman* (1621).

The Case of many Hundreds of Poor English Captives in Algier (1680).

Cason, Edmund, *A Relation of the whole proceedings concerning the Redemption of the Captives in Argier and Tunis* (1647).

Castries, Henri de, et al., eds., *Les Sources Inédites de l'Histoire du Maroc . . . archives et bibliothèques d'Angleterre* (Paris, 1918–36).

Cervantes, *Don Quixote* (Ware, 1993).

Chalmers, George, *A Collection of Treaties* (1790).

Chamberlain, John, *The Letters of John Chamberlain*, ed. Norman Egbert McClure (Philadelphia, 1939).

Charles I, *By the King. A Licence for a collection throughout England and Wales, towards the redeeming of . . . captives under Muley Abdalwally King of Morocco* (1631).

Charles II, *By the King. A Proclamation relating to the articles concluded between his Majesty, and the government of Algiers* (1675).

Coxere, Edward, *Adventures by Sea*, ed. E. H. W. Meyerstein (Oxford, 1945).

Craven, Alex, ed., *Churchwardens' Accounts of St Mary's Devizes, 1633–1689*, Wiltshire Record Society, 69 (2016).

Crisp, Mrs. (Elizabeth Marsh), *The Female Captive* (1769).

Daborne, Robert, *A Christian turn'd Turke* (1612), in Daniel J. Vitkus, ed., *Three Turk Plays from Early Modern England* (New York, 2000).

Dan, Pierre, *Histoire de Barbarie et de ses Corsairs* (Paris, 1649).

D'Aranda, Emanuel, *The History of Algiers and it's Slavery* (1666).

D'Arvieux, Laurent, *The Chevalier D'Arvieux's Travels in Arabia the Desart* (1718).

D'Arvieux, Laurent, *Memoires du Chevalier D'Arvieux* (Paris, 1735).

Davies, William, *A Trve Relation of the Travailes... of William Davies* (1614).

Davis, Cecil T., ed., *Wandsworth Churchwardens' Accounts from 1631 to 1639*, Surrey Archaeological Collections, 24 (1911).

de Beer, E. S., ed., *The Diary of John Evelyn* (6 vols., Oxford, 1955).

Defoe, Daniel, *The Life and Strange Surprizing Adventures of Robinson Crusoe* (1719).

De la Motte, Philémon, 'A Voyage to Barbary for the Redemption of Captives', in *Several Voyages to Barbary* (1736).

The Demands of his gracious Majesty... sent by the Lord General Montagu (1661).

A Description of the Nature of Slavery among the Moors (1721).

Dunton, John, *A Trve Iournall of the Sally Fleet* (1637).

Elliot, Adam, *A Modest Vindication of Titus Oates* (1682).

Empey, Mark, ed., 'The Diary of Sir James Ware, 1623–66', *Analecta Hibernica*, 45 (2014).

An Exact Journal of the Siege of Tangier (1680).

The Fierce and cruel Battaile fought by the three Kings in Barbarie (1607).

A Fight at Sea, Famously fought by the Dolphin of London (1617).

Firth, C. H. and R. S. Rait, eds., *Acts and Ordinances of the Interregnum, 1642–1660* (1911–14).

FitzGeffrey, Charles, *Compassion towards Captives* (Oxford, 1637).

Foster, Sir William, ed., *The Travels of John Sanderson in the Levant, 1584–1602*, Hakluyt Society, Second Series, 67 (1931).

Fox, George, *To the Great Turk, and his King in Algiers* (1680).

Franklin, William, *A Letter from Tangier concerning the Death of Jonas Rowland, the Renegade* (1682).

From aboard the Van-herring. A Letter from Legorn (1679).

Gardiner, S. R., ed., *Constitutional Documents of the Puritan Revolution, 1625–1660* (Oxford, 1906).

Gee, Joshua, *Narrative of Joshua Gee of Boston, Mass., when he was captive in Algeria of the Barbary pirates, 1680–1687*, ed. Albert C. Bates (Hartford, CT, 1943).

Gildon, Charles, *The Life and Strange Surprizing Adventures of Mr D—de F—, of London, Hosier* (1719).

Gouge, William, *A Recovery from Apostacy* (1639).

Gough, Richard, *The History of Myddle*, ed. David Hey (Harmondsworth, 1982),

Hacke, W., *A Collection of Original Voyages* (1699).

Hakluyt, Richard, *The Principal Navigations* (1599–1600).

Hanham, Alison, ed., *Churchwardens' Accounts of Ashburton, 1479–1580*, Devon and Cornwall Record Society, New Series, 15 (1970).

Hardy, W. J., ed., *Middlesex County Records. Calendar of the Sessions Books 1689 to 1709* (1905).

Harris, G. G., ed., *Trinity House of Deptford Transactions, 1609–35*, London Record Society, 19 (1983).

Harrison, John, *The Tragicall Life and Death of Mvley Abdala Melek the last King of Barbarie* (Delft, 1633).

Hasleton, Richard, *Strange and Wonderfvll Things. Happened to Richard Hasleton... in his ten yeares travailes in many forraine countries* (1595).

Head, Richard, *The English Rogue* (1665).
Historical Manuscripts Commission. Series:
9 *Salisbury*
12 *Bath and Wells*
13 *Westmorland and others*
24 *Rutland*
25 *Le Fleming*
29 *Portland*
32 *Fitzherbert*
45 *Buccleuch*
55 *Various Collections*
63 *Egmont*
71 *Finch*
75 *Downshire*
78 *Hastings*
79 *Lindsey*
James I, *Whereas we have beene informed, aswell by a lamentable petition* (1624).
Journals of the House of Commons
Journals of the House of Lords
Kellet, Edward, and Henry Byam, *A Returne from Argier* (1628).
Knight, Francis, *A Relation of Seaven Yeares Slaverie* (1640).
Lane, Bartholomew, *A Modest Vindication of the Hermit of the Sounding Island* (1683).
Larkin, James F. and Paul L. Hughes, eds., *Stuart Royal Proclamations 1603-1625* (Oxford, 1973–83).
A Letter from the King of Morocco to his Majesty the King of England, Charles I, for the Reducing of Sally, Argiers, &c (1680, 1682).
A Letter sent by the Emperor of Morocco and King of Fez to his Majesty of Great Britain, and delivered by his embassador in Januarv 1681 (1682).
A List of the English Captives taken by the Pyrates of Argier (1670).
A List of the English redeemed out of slavery by the taking of the Golden Horn (1681).
A List of Ships taken since July 1677 from his Majesties subjects, by the corsairs of Algiers (1682).
Lithgow, William, *The Totall Discourse, Of the rare Aduentures* (1640).
The Lives, Apprehensions, Arraignments, and Executions of the 19. late Pyrates (1609).
Loftis, John, ed., *The Memoirs of Anne, Lady Halkett and Ann, Lady Fanshawe* (Oxford, 1979).
Londons Love to the Royal Prince Henrie, Meeting him on the River Thames (1610).
Lurting, Thomas, *The Fighting Sailor turn'd Peaceable Christian* (1710).
Lye, Thomas, *The King of Terrors Metamorphosis* (1660).
Maclean, John, ed., *Letters of George Lord Carew to Sir Thomas Roe, 1615-1617*, Camden Society, Old Series, 76 (1860).
Manwaring, G. E., ed., *The Diary of Henry Teonge, 1675, 1678-9* (1927).
Manwaring, G. E. and W. G. Perrin, eds., *The Life and Works of Sir Henry Mainwaring*, Navy Records Society, 54, 56 (1920–2).
Marsh, Henry, *A New Survey of the Turkish Empire and Government* (1663–4).
Masters, Betty R., ed., *London Chamber Accounts, 1585-6*, London Record Society, 20 (1984).
Mayo, Richard, *A Present for Servants … especially in country parishes* (1693).
McGrath, J. R., ed., *The Flemings in Oxford*, Oxford Historical Society, 44, 52, 79 (1904–24).
Mercurius Publicus (1661–3).

A Message sent from His Highness the Lord Protector, to the Great Turk (1654).

Molloy, Charles, *De Jure Maritimo et Navali* (1690).

Morgan, Joseph, *A Compleat History of the Piratical States of Barbary* (1750).

Mortimer, Russell, ed., *Minute Book of the Men's Meeting of the Society of Friends in Bristol, 1667–1686*, Bristol Record Society, 26 (1971).

Murphy, Martin, ed., 'William Atkins, A Relation of the Journey from St Omers to Seville, 1622', in *Camden Miscellany*, 32 (1994).

A Narrative of the Adventures of Lewis Marott, pilot royal of the galleys of France (1677).

Negotiations of Sir Thomas Roe (1740).

Newes from Sally (1642).

Newes from Sea of two notorious Pyrats Ward the Englishman and Danseker the Dutchman (1609).

Nickalls, John L., ed., *The Journal of George Fox* (Cambridge, 1952).

Ockley, Simon, *An Account of South-West Barbary* (1713).

Okeley, William, *Eben-ezer: or, a small Monument of Great Mercy* (1675).

Okeley, William, *Eben-ezer . . . with a Further Narrative of James Deane and others* (1684).

Olearius, Adam, *The Voyages and Travells of the Ambassadors sent by Frederick, Duke of Holstein, to the Great Duke of Muscovy and the King of Persia* [in 1633–9] (1669).

Overton, Richard, *An Appeale from the degenerate Representative Body the Commons of England* (1647).

Parkinson, Richard, ed., *The Autobiography of Henry Newcome*, Chetham Society, Old Series, 26–7 (1852).

Pellow, Thomas, *The History of the Long Captivity and Adventures of Thomas Pellow* (1751; first published 1740).

Pennell, C. R., ed., *Piracy and Diplomacy in Seventeenth-Century North Africa. The Journal of Thomas Baker, English Consul in Tripoli 1677–1685* (Cranbury, NJ, 1989).

Penrose, Boris, ed., *The Barbary Voyage of 1638* (Philadelphia, 1929).

Pepys: Samuel, *The Diary*, ed. R. C. Latham and W. C. Mathews (1971–83).

Pepys, Samuel, *A Descriptive Catalogue of the Naval MSS in the Pepysian Library*, ed. J. R. Tanner, Navy Records Society, 26, 28, 36, 57 (1903–23).

Phelps, Thomas, *A true account of the captivity of Thomas Phelps, at Machaness in Barbary* (1685).

Philips, George, *The Present State of Tangier . . . to which is added the Present State of Algiers* (1676).

Pitts, Joseph, *A Faithful Account of the Religion and Manners of the Mohametans* (3rd edition, 1731; first published 1704).

Pocock, Thomas, *The Relief of Captives, Especially of our own Countreymen* (1720).

Powell, J. R., ed., 'The Journal of John Weale 1654–1656', *The Naval Miscellany*, 4, Navy Records Society, 92 (1952).

Powell, J. R., ed., *The Letters of Robert Blake*, Navy Records Society, 76 (1937).

Poynter, F. N. L., ed., *The Journal of James Yonge [1647–1721]* (1963).

The Present State of Algiers (1682).

Rawlins, John, *The Famovs and Wonderfvll Recoverie of a Ship of Bristoll, called the Exchange, from the Turkish Pirates of Argier* (1622).

A Relation of the royall magnificent, and sumptuous entertainement giuen to . . . Queene Anne, at . . . Bristoll (1613).

A Relation Strange and true, of a ship of Bristol named the Jacob (1622).

Riley, Stephen T., ed., 'Abraham Browne's Captivity by the Barbary Pirates, 1655', *Colonial Society of Massachusetts*, 52 (1979).

R. H. [Henry Robarts], *Newes from the Levaune Seas. Discribing the many perrilous events of Edward Glenham, Esquire* (1594).

Robarts, Henry, *A True Relation of a most notable and worthy Fight* (1616).

Robinson, Henry, *Libertas, or Reliefe to the English Captives in Algier* (1642).

Ross, E. Dennis, ed., 'Discourse of the Turks by Sr Thomas Shirley', *Camden Miscellany*, Third Series, 16 (1936).

Rycaut, Paul, *The Present State of the Ottoman Empire* (1668).

S. T., *The Adventures of (Mr. T. S.) an English Merchant, taken Prisoner by the Turks* (1670).

Saunders, Thomas, *A true Discription and breefe Discourse, Of a most lamentable Voiage* (1587).

The Seamans Song of Captain Ward the famous Pyrate (n.d., 1658–64).

Several Voyages to Barbary (1736).

Sherlock, William, *An Exhortation to Redeemed Slaves* (1702).

Smith, John, *The True Travels, Adventures, and Observations of Captaine Iohn Smith* (1630).

Spratt, T., ed., *Autobiography of the Rev. Devereux Spratt* (1886).

Statutes of the Realm, v, 1628–80, ed. J. Raithby (1819).

Sweet, Thomas, *Deare Friends: it is now about sixe yeares* (1647).

Tanner, Thomas, *Wisdome and Prudence Exhibited* (1677).

Taylor, John, *A Brave Memorable and Dangerovs Sea-fight* (1636).

Taylor, John, *The Dolphins Danger: and Deliuerance* (1617).

Taylor, John, *Heavens blessing, and earths ioy* (1613).

Taylor, John, *A Valorous and Perillous Sea-fight. Fought with three Turkish Ships* (1640).

To the Right Honourable the Commons of England in Parliament assembled. The humble petition of disconsolate fathers and wives (1681).

The Travels of the Sieur Mouette in the Kingdoms of Fez and Morocco (1710).

Troughton, Thomas, *Barbarian Cruelty; or an Accurate and Impartial Narrative* (1751).

A True and Perfect Relation of the Happy Successe . . . at Bugia (1674).

Veryard, Ellis, *An Account of Divers Choice Remarks, as well Geographical as Historical* (1701).

Violet, Thomas, *Proposals humbly presented to his Highness Oliver, Lord Protector* (1656).

Vitkus, Daniel J., ed., *Piracy, Slavery, and Redemption* (New York, 2001).

Wadsworth, James, *The English Spanish Pilgrime* (1629).

(Walker, Henry), *The Spirituall Experiences of Sundry Beleevers* (1652).

Waller, Edmund, *Poems* (1645).

Webbe, Edward, *The Rare and most wonderfull things which Edw. Webbe an Englishman borne, hath seene* (1590).

Whitehead, George, *Truth and Innocency Vindicated* (1699).

Wilkins, George, *Three Miseries of Barbary: Plague. Famine. Ciuill warre* (1607).

William Whiteway of Dorchester. His Diary 1618 to 1635, Dorset Record Society, 12 (1991).

Windus, John, *A Journey to Mequinez* (Dublin, 1725).

Winstanley, Gerrard, *The Law of Freedom in a Platform* (1652).

Worth, R. N., ed., *Calendar of the Plymouth Municipal Records* (Plymouth, 1893).

Secondary Sources

Abun-Nasr, Jamil, *A History of the Maghrib in the Islamic Period* (Cambridge, 1987).

Andrews, Kenneth R., *Ships, Money and Politics. Seafaring and Naval Enterprise in the Reign of Charles I* (Cambridge, 1991).

Appleby, John C., 'The Problem of Piracy in Ireland, 1570–1630', in Claire Jowitt, ed., *Pirates? The Politics of Plunder, 1550–1650* (2007).

Appleby, John C., *Women and English Piracy, 1540–1720* (2013).

Aylmer, G. E., 'Slavery under Charles II: The Mediterranean and Tangier', *EHR*, 114, April 1999).

Bak, Greg, *Barbary Pirate. The Life and Crimes of John Ward* (Stroud, 2006).

Bennassar, Bartolomé and Lucile Bennassar, *Les Chrétiens d'Allah* (Paris, 2006).

Bewes, Wyndham Anstis, *Church Briefs or Royal Warrants for Collections for Charitable Objects* (1896).

Birchwood, Matthew and Matthew Dimmock, eds., *Cultural Encounters between East and West, 1453–1699* (Newcastle, 2005).

Braithwaite, William C., *The Second Period of Quakerism* (1921).

Braudel, Fernard, *The Mediterranean and the Mediterranean World in the Age of Philip II* (1973).

Bromley, J. S., 'A Letter-Book of Robert Cole, British Consul-General at Algiers, 1694–1712' in Bromley, *Corsairs and Navies, 1660–1760* (1987).

Brotton, Jerry, *The Sultan and the Queen* (New York, 2016).

Brotton, Jerry, *This Orient Isle. Elizabethan England and the Islamic World* (2016) (a variant of the above, with significant differences).

Burton, Jonathan, 'English Anxiety and the Muslim Power of Conversion: Five Perspectives on "Turning Turk" in Early Modern Texts', *Journal for Early Modern Cultural Studies*, 2 (2002).

Carroll, Kenneth C., 'Quaker Slaves in Algiers, 1679–1688', *Journal of the Friends' Historical Society*, 54 (1982).

Chew, Samuel C., *The Crescent and the Rose* (New York, 1965).

Clissold, Stephen, *The Barbary Slaves* (1977).

Colley, Linda, *Captives. Britain, Empire and the World, 1600–1850* (2002).

Colley, Linda, *The Ordeal of Elizabeth Marsh* (2007).

Cory, Stephen, 'Sharifan Rule in Morocco (tenth–twelfth/sixteenth–eighteenth centuries)', in M. Fierro, ed., *The New Cambridge History of Islam, ii* (Cambridge, 2011).

Dávid, Géza and Pál Fodor, eds., *Ransom Slavery along the Ottoman Borders* (Leiden, 2007).

Davis, Robert C., 'Christian Slavery during the Early Alaouite Dynasty', in Stefan Hanss and Juliane Schiel, eds., *Mediterranean Slavery Revisited (500–1800)* (Zurich, 2014).

Davis, Robert C., *Christian Slaves, Muslim Masters* (Basingstoke, 2003).

Dursteler, Eric R., 'Slavery and Sexual Peril in the Early Modern Mediterranean', in Hanss and Schiel, eds., *Mediterranean Slavery Revisited* (2014).

Dursteler, Eric R., *Venetians and Constantinople. Nation, Identity and Coexistnece in the Early Modern Mediterranean* (Baltimore, 2006).

Earle, Peter, *Corsairs of Malta and Barbary* (1970).

Eken, Des, *The Stolen Village. Baltimore and the Barbary Pirates* (Dublin, 2006).

Eltis, David and Stanley L. Engerman, eds., *The Cambridge World History of Slavery. 3: 1420–1804* (Cambridge, 2011).

Epstein, Steven A., *Speaking of Slavery. Colour, Ethnicity, and Human Bondage in Italy* (Ithaca, 2001).

Fierro, M., ed., *The New Cambridge History of Islam*, ii (Cambridge, 2011).

Fisher, Sir Godfrey, *Barbary Legend. War, Trade and Piracy in North Africa 1415–1830* (Oxford, 1957).

Friedman, Ellen G., *Spanish Captives in North Africa in the Early Modern Age* (Madison, WI, 1983).

Fuchs, Barbara, 'Faithless Empires: Pirates, Renegadoes, and the English Nation', *English Literary History*, 67 (2000).

Garcia-Arenal, Mercedes, 'The Moriscos in Morocco. From Granadan Emigration to the Hornacheros of Salé', in M. Garcia-Arenal and G. Wiegers, eds., *The Expulsion of the Moriscos from Spain* (Leiden, 2014).

Graf, Tobias P., *The Sultan's Renegades. Christian-European Converts to Islam and the Making of the Ottoman Elite. 1575–1610* (Oxford, 2017).

Hanss, Stefan and Juliane Schiel, eds., *Mediterranean Slavery Revisited (500–1800)* (Zurich, 2014).

Hebb, David Delison, *Piracy and the English Government 1616–1642* (Aldershot, 1994).

Heinsen-Roach, Erica, *Consuls and Captives. Dutch North African Diplomacy in the Early Modern Mediterranean* (Woodbridge, 2019).

Hershenzon, Daniel, *The Captive Sea: Slavery, Communication, and Commerce in Early Modern Spain and the Mediterranean* (Philadelphia, 2019).

Hershenzon, Daniel, 'The Political Economy of Ransom in the Early Modern Mediterranean', *Past and Present*, 231 (May 2016).

Hershenzon, Daniel, 'Towards a connected history of bondage in the Mediterranean: recent trends in the field', *History Compass*, 15.8 (August 2017).

Heywood, Colin, 'The English in the Mediterranean, 1600–1630: A Post-Braudelian Perspective on the "Northern Invasion", in Maria Fusaro, Colin Heywood and Mohammed-Salah Omri, eds., *Trade and Cultural Exchange in the Early Modern Mediterranean* (2010).

Hornstein, Sari R., *The Restoration Navy and English Foreign Trade, 1674–1688* (Aldershot, 1991).

Jamieson, Alan G., *Lords of the Sea. A History of the Barbary Corsairs* (2012).

Jowitt, Claire, ed., *Pirates? The Politics of Plunder, 1550–1650* (2007).

Klarer, Mario and Daniel J. Vitkus, 'Unkind Dealings', in M. Klarer, ed., *Piracy and Captivity in the Mediterranean 1550–1810* (2018).

Loualich, Fatiha, 'Emancipated Female Slaves in Algiers; marriage, property and social advancement in the seventeenth and eighteenth centuries', in Stephanie Cronin, ed., *Subalterns and Social Protest: History from Below in the Middle East and North Africa* (2008).

MacLean, Gerald M., *Looking East. English Writing and the Ottoman Empire before 1800* (Basingstoke, 2007).

MacLean, Gerald M., *The Rise of Oriental Travel* (Basingstoke, 2004).

Malcolm, Noel, 'Positive Views of Islam and of Ottoman Rule in the Sixteenth Century: the Case of Jean Bodin', in Anna Contadini and Claire Norton, eds., *The Renaissance and the Ottoman World* (Farnham, 2013).

Masters, Betty R., *Tales of the Unexpected: the Corporation and Captives in Barbary*, Guildhall Historical Association (2005).

Matar, Nabil, 'The Barbary Corsairs, King Charles and the Civil War', *The Seventeenth Century*, 16 (2001).

Matar, Nabil, *Britain and Barbary, 1589–1689* (Gainesville, FL, 2005).

Matar, Nabil, *British Captives from the Mediterranean to the Atlantic, 1563–1760* (Leiden, 2014).

Matar, Nabil, 'British Captives in Salé (1721), in Stefan Hanss and Juliane Schiel, eds., *Mediterranean Slavery Revisited (500–1800)* (Zurich, 2014).

Matar, Nabil, 'English Accounts of Captivity in North Africa and the Middle East: 1577–1624', *Renaissance Quarterly*, 56 (2001).

Matar, Nabil, *Islam in Britain* (Cambridge, 1998).

Matar, Nabil, 'Introduction', in Daniel J. Vitkus, ed., *Piracy, Slavery, and Redemption* (New York, 2001).

Matar, Nabil, 'Piracy and Captivity in the Early Modern Mediterranean: the Perspective from Barbary', in Claire Jowitt, ed., *Pirates? The Politics of Plunder, 1550–1650* (2007).

Matar, Nabil, *Turks, Moors and Englishmen in the Age of Discovery* (New York, 1999).

Maziane, Leila, *Salé et ses Corsaires (1666–1727). Un port de course marocain au xviie siècle* (Caen, 2007).

Milton, Giles, *White Gold* (2005).

Nadalo, Stephanie, 'Negotiating Slavery in a Tolerant Frontier: Livorno's Turkish *Bagno* (1547–1747), *Mediaevalia*, 32 (2011).

Östlund, Joachim, 'Swedes and Barbary Captivity: the Political Culture of Human Security, *circa* 1660–1760', *Historical Social Research*, 35/4 (2019), 148–63.

Parker, Ken, 'Reading "Barbary" in Early Modern England, 1550–1685', in Birchwood and Dimmock, *Cultural Encounters* (2005).

Playfair, Robert Lambert, *The Scourge of Christendom* (1884).

Ressel, Magnus, 'The North European Way of Ransoming: Explorations into an Unknown Dimension of the Early Modern Welfare State', *Historical Social Research*, 35/4 (2019), 125–46.

Rogers, P. G., *A History of Anglo-Moroccan Relations to 1900* (1977).

Scott Thomson, Gladys, *Life in a Noble Household* (1950).

Senior, C. M, *A Nation of Pirates. English Piracy in its Heyday* (Newton Abbot, 1976).

Snader, Joe, *Caught between Worlds. British Captivity Narratives in Fact and Fiction* (Lexington, Kentucky, 2000).

Snader, Joe, 'The Oriental Captivity Narrative and Early English Fiction', *Eighteenth-Century Fiction*, 9/3 (1997), 267–98.

Spindler, Robert, 'Identity Crises of Homecomers from the Barbary Coast', in Mario Klarer, ed., *Piracy and Captivity in the Mediterranean, 1550–1810* (Abingdon, 2018).

Starr, G. A., 'Escape from Barbary: A Seventeenth-Century Genre', *Huntington Library Quarterly*, 29/1 (1965).

Thomas, Keith, *In Pursuit of Civility* (New Haven, 2018).

Tinniswood, Adrian, *The Rainborowes* (2014).

Touati, Houari, 'Ottoman Maghrib, and Stephen Cory, 'Sharifan Rule in Morocco (tenth/-twelfth–sixteenth/eighteenth centuries)', in M. Fierro, ed., *The New Cambridge History of Islam*, ii, chaps. 16, 18 (Cambridge, 2011).

Verney, Frances Parthenope, and Margaret M. Verney, *The Memoirs of the Verney Family* (1970).

Vitkus, Daniel J., *Turning Turk. English Theater and the Multicultural Mediterranean, 1570–1630* (Basingstoke, 2003).

Walsham, Alexandra, *Providence in Early Modern England* (Oxford, 1999).

Weiss, Gillian L., *Captives and Corsairs. France and Slavery in the Early Modern Mediterranean* (Stanford, CA, 2011).

Wolf, John B., *The Barbary Coast. Algeria under the Turks, 1500 to 1830* (New York, 1979).

Wood, A. C., *A History of the Levant Company* (1964).

Online Resources

British History Online (<https://www.british-history.ac.uk>)

Dictionary of North Carolina Biography (<https://www.ncpedia.org/biography/sothel-or-sothell>)

'John Bargrave' (<https://www.canterbury-cathedral.org/bargrave>)

Oxford Dictionary of National Biography (Oxford, 2004; <https://www.oxforddnb.com>)

Proceedings of the Old Bailey (<https://www.oldbaileyonline.org>)

'Wirksworth Church Wardens' Accounts, 1658–1727' (<http://www.wirksworth.org.uk/CWA.htm>)

Index

For the benefit of digital users, indexed terms that span two pages (e.g., 52–53) may, on occasion, appear on only one of those pages.